Creating a
Low-Allergen Garden

Creating a Low-Allergen Garden

Lucy Huntington

MITCHELL BEAZLEY

To my husband and partner in everything, Francis

First published in 1998 by Mitchell Beazley,
an imprint of Octopus Publishing Group Ltd,
2-4 Heron Quays, London E14 4JP
New edition 2002

A CIP catalogue copy of this book is available
from the British Library

ISBN 1 84000 567 X

Jacket photo acknowledgments
Front and back jacket: © Flowers & Foliage
Front jacket inset: © Andrew Lawson
Back jacket inset: © Octopus Publishing Group/
Martine Collings

Printed and bound in China by
Toppan Printing Company Limited

Contents

6 Acknowledgements

7 Foreword

8 **Introduction**
Addressing the problem of allergy; The spread of low-allergen gardening; What is an allergy?; Allergic responses; Creating a low-allergen garden; An evolving story

12 **ALLERGIC REACTIONS TO PLANTS**

14 **Breathing Allergies**
Asthma; Hay fever; Pollen and pollination; Fungal spores; Ferns; Scented plants; Other problem plants

22 **Skin Allergies**
Eczema; Urticaria; Contact dermatitis; Irritant contact dermatitis; Photodermatitis; Dealing with skin allergies; Prickles and thorns; Insect bites and stings; Poisonous plants

28 **Gardening with Allergies**
Minimizing allergic reactions; When to garden; Working in the garden; Low-allergen gardening indoors

36 **DESIGNING A LOW-ALLERGEN GARDEN**

38 **Planning your Garden**
How to create a low-allergen garden; Basic decisions; Assessing potential and problems; Functional planning; Choosing features and plants; Designing your low-allergen garden

42 **A Town Garden Plan**
Tranquility

44 **A Family Garden Plan**

46 **A City Oasis**

48 **Horizontal Surfaces**
Design of horizontal spaces; Choosing paving materials; Combining materials; Grass areas; Play areas

52 **Vertical Features**
Containment and enclosure; Use of climbing plants; Hedges

56 **Water in the Garden**
Water features; Pools and ponds; Fountains and waterfalls; Keeping water clear; Planting a water garden; Child safety

60 **PLANTING A LOW-ALLERGEN GARDEN**

62 **Planning and Planting**
Selecting plants; Maintenance; Planting plans

66 **Border for a Sunny Site**
Colour schemes

68 **A Shady Site**
Fences; Trees and hedges

70 **A Low-Maintenance Border**
Ground cover plants

72 **A Bog Garden**
Moisture levels

74 **A Rose Garden**
Bedding roses

76 **Banks and Rock Gardens**
Banks; Steps; Rock gardens

78 **Container Gardening**
Planting a container

80 **Trees and Shrubs**
Selecting and using low-allergen shrubs; Harmful shrubs; Selecting and planting trees; Planning permission; Trees in neighbouring gardens; Problems with conifers

84 **Vegetables and Fruit**
Health benefits; Selecting and planting vegetables; Growing vegetables; Selecting and planting fruit

86 **Herbs**
Herbs in the low-allergen garden; Growing herbs; Herb gardens; Problems with herbs

88 **A–Z PLANTS TO USE**

112 **Plants to Avoid**

124 **Plant Hardiness**

124 **Further Reading**

124 **Useful Addresses**

125 **Index**

128 **Photographic Acknowledgements**

Acknowledgements

I owe the greatest debt to my sister, Selina Thistleton-Smith, without whom there would have been no low-allergen gardens and no book. After we both decided that the low-allergen garden was an idea worth pursuing, it was only her determination that the project should succeed and her perseverance in seeking support and funding that made it happen. This support carried right through the three gardens at the Chelsea Flower Show to the opening of the garden at Capel Manor, and continues in her support of low-allergen gardens throughout the world.

Secondly, to the late John Donaldson, a trustee of the National Asthma Campaign (NAC), who promoted and supported the project from its inception, specifically, by collecting all available information on plants causing allergenic reactions. He then encouraged us in the development of ideas for actual gardens and in the drafting of the original garden leaflets, which formed the basis of this book. Tragically he died from an asthma attack in 1995, but left a legacy which enabled the building of the third low-allergen garden at the Chelsea Flower Show.

Thanks are also due to medical experts who gave much needed support and advice from the start. Dr Bill Frankland, who assisted so much on the actual gardens and has always been ready with help, advice and information whenever asked. He kindly read, and corrected, the manuscript of the first part of the book and checked the illustrations for accuracy. At the Royal Brompton Hospital, London, Dr Stephen Durham and Dr Duncan Geddes also checked the manuscript and have always been ready with essential medical advice when requested.

The NAC and its very professional staff supported the idea of the low-allergen garden and have been instrumental in bringing the subject to the notice of the press and media, which ultimately resulted in the request for a book on the subject. Among the army of volunteers within the NAC were several people who gave their time to help directly with the gardens, particularly Beryl and Brian Schirn whose stalwart encouragement kept us going, and David Thistleton-Smith who has always been ready to give practical assistance whenever needed.

The many unnamed asthma, hay fever and skin allergy sufferers who answered questionnaires and came forward with ideas for the garden – without them there would have been no gardens and no book.

At a personal level, writing the book has absorbed much of my time in the past year and without the help of our invaluable 'home team', Ian, Annette and Jenny, in keeping the rest of the business going it would have been impossible.

To the staff at Mitchell Beazley who took on an unknown author and helped to educate her in the ramifications of the world of publishing, particularly Guy Croton and Ruth Hope who promoted the idea and Selina Mumford who apart from editing the text, kept me going to complete the book.

Finally for my long-suffering husband, Francis, who endlessly read and re-read the manuscript and gave continuous encouragement and advice.

Lucy Huntington

Foreword

I'm frequently asked what I think are the biggest changes to have taken place in gardening over the last ten or twenty years. And I have no doubt that among the most important is the way that we now take account of the needs of gardeners who have some form of disability. When I've given this response in the past, however, I've usually had in mind the rather obvious features of physical disability.

But few of us are totally without some form of disablement, even though it may be one, called allergy, that is less obvious to others. We might suffer from the almost universal reaction to the effects of *Urtica dioica*, the stinging nettle, or perhaps from one of the legion of separate pollen allergies that plague the summer, or maybe from some individual and rather rare but, nonetheless, highly inconvinient and painful reaction to contact with one particular type of plant.

The importance of allergy has been underlined by the increasing frequency with which I am asked another question: 'Can you suggest some garden plants for hay fever sufferers?' I've always tried to give helpful if rather conventional answers, like avoiding grasses and growing double flowers that produce no pollen. But how my responses pale against the quite remarkable study that Lucy Huntington has now made of the subject. How rarely is it possible to say with such genuine admiration 'here is the definitive work'. Yet having had the pleasure of knowing Lucy as a garden designer and teacher for many years, her thoroughness comes as no surprise. She has identified a need and met it. All gardeners will derive some novel and unexpected benefit from this book; and it certainly must be put in the hands of every garden designer and general practitioner in the land.

Professor Stefan Buczacki

Introduction

All my life I have loved gardens and gardening and I have been very fortunate in having suffered only the odd itch, sneeze or sniffle as a result. However, there are millions of gardeners who cannot go out into their gardens without sneezing, wheezing or scratching, or without their eyes streaming and nose running, and this book is written for all of them, and their families and friends.

The idea of low-allergen gardening started in 1992, when I was discussing the possibility of designing a garden for the National Asthma Campaign (NAC), to be shown at London's Chelsea Flower Show in 1993. My sister, whose daughter Marylou has suffered from asthma all her life, was interested in raising public awareness for the work of the NAC and Chelsea seemed an ideal venue as it is a prestigious horticultural event which attracts extensive media coverage.

As far as we knew, nobody had ever designed a garden specifically to eliminate, or at least reduce, the risk of causing an asthma or hay fever attack, so it seemed a worthwhile concept to develop. From the beginning I felt that it was vital to get the support of the medical profession, in order to give the garden real credibility. Asthma is potentially a very serious illness and it was inevitable that a number of doctors would scoff at the idea of a low-allergen garden as being unrealistic and of little real benefit. Thankfully, many others, particularly those specializing in the treatment of asthma and related illnesses, were very supportive from the outset, and gave much useful information and advice, and continue to do so.

BELOW: *The vegetable area in the National Asthma Campaign's Low-Allergen Garden at the Chelsea Flower Show in 1994.*

Although the garden was specifically aimed at asthma and hay fever sufferers, once we had coined the title 'low-allergen garden' I felt sure that it should also exclude any plant known to cause an allergic reaction in any part of the body, not just the nose and chest. There had been a great deal of research done on plants known to cause skin allergies and this information was studied and suspect plants excluded from the garden.

Addressing the problem of allergy

The garden I designed for the 1993 Chelsea Flower Show stimulated a tremendous amount of interest, not only in the press but, more importantly, among sufferers from asthma, hay fever and skin allergies and those close to them. The overwhelming response was relief that at last someone was addressing the problem of the keen gardener who found their enjoyment of their garden seriously restricted by the presence of allergens. In addition, parents of asthmatic children were all eager to discover any way in which they could reduce the risk of attacks in their children and allow them the freedom to play in the garden. Many of the visitors to the flower show offered suggestions and ideas which were then incorporated into subsequent low-allergen gardens.

ABOVE: *Hostas and rodgersias are useful and attractive plants for the low-allergen garden.*

Allergy sufferers wanted more information and also wanted to share their experiences. For instance, in the first garden we had included ceanothus, lupins and wisteria, but, given the number of visitors who told us that these triggered their own asthma or hay fever attacks, it was obvious that they should be added to the list of plants to be excluded. Another exciting response to the low-allergen garden was from members of the medical profession who, at first sceptical about the idea, later found that there were ideas there that they could pass on to help their patients enjoy their gardens.

The following year we built and planted a second garden at the Chelsea Flower Show, this time including a vegetable garden and play space. As in the previous year the garden received an excellent response, including a positive feedback from people who had seen the first garden and tried out the ideas at home and could give us further suggestions based on their own experience. At the end of the week-long show the garden was taken down, transported and rebuilt in a permanent location around the first low-allergen house, built for the Futureworld Exhibition at Milton Keynes, Buckinghamshire, south England.

The spread of low-allergen gardening

By this time interest in low-allergen gardening was beginning to spread around the world, with the Asthma Foundation of New South Wales, in Australia, taking up the challenge by designing gardens for horticultural shows and producing an informative booklet which includes the allergenic properties of their native plants, as well as introduced garden plants. This has led to the setting up of an allergen trail within the Royal Botanic Gardens in Sydney, and the proposal to use low-allergen plants around the village being built for the Olympic Games in 2000. This is a major step forward as athletes suffering from asthma and hay fever are restricted in their use of drugs and the Games take place in late spring, at the height of the pollen season, when the risk of allergic attacks due to pollen is very high. The restriction of the use of plants, particularly grasses and trees, to low-pollen varieties should help athletes who suffer from these conditions to take part in the Games on equal terms with other competitors.

The Spread of Asthma, Hay Fever and Skin Allergies

• In Britain some 10 million people suffer from hay fever and three million from asthma

• The number of asthma sufferers is increasing each year, and 10 percent of children are now reckoned to be asthmatic. Worldwide the figures are similar, with an even greater incidence of asthma in Australia and New Zealand, where it affects 20 percent of children and 10 percent of adults

• Skin allergies, including eczema, contact dermatitis and urticaria, are also common and are showing an increase. Indeed, most people have suffered from an allergic skin reaction at some time in their life even if it is only a mild rash that rapidly disappears

• In short, allergic reactions of one kind or another affect most people at some time in their life

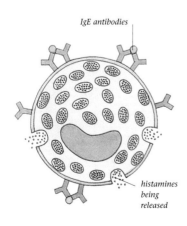

IgE antibodies

histamines being released

ABOVE: *The binding of IgE antibodies to a mast cell, which triggers the release of various substances including histamines.*

In New Zealand the Auckland Asthma Society has designed and displayed a low-allergen garden with an accompanying booklet and a list of the country's plants both allergenic and non-allergenic. The Lung Foundation of North America has exhibited low-allergen gardens at various flower shows and produced information on the subject.

In 1996 we built a third garden at Chelsea, this time a green 'oasis' for an enclosed city garden, and once again it stimulated a lot of interest among the media, the medical profession, visitors to the show and, in particular, allergy sufferers and their families. Afterwards the garden was moved to a permanent site at the National Garden Centre at Capel Manor in Hertfordshire, south England. In the same year I was asked to design a garden for another permanent site in the demonstration gardens at Probus in Cornwall, south-west England.

After four years and six gardens, it seemed appropriate to put down all the accumulated knowledge on low-allergen gardening in a book so that it is accessible to everyone who needs it. Hopefully, it will enable gardeners who suffer from asthma, hay fever and skin allergies to work in their gardens without having to worry about these conditions spoiling their pleasure.

What is an allergy?

The word 'allergy' derives from the Greek 'allos', meaning 'other', and 'ergon', meaning 'work', and describes an abnormal reaction of the body, or part of it, to substances which are normally harmless. 'Allergen' is the term that is used for any substance that induces an allergic reaction. The range and intensity of allergic reactions varies greatly between individuals. Some people suffer only a mild rash after eating prawns, muscles or any other type of shellfish, or a painful lump when stung by a bee, whereas eating shellfish or getting stung by a bee sting can prove fatal to someone who is extremely allergic to either of these allergens.

Allergic responses

The tendency to develop allergic responses, known as atopy, runs in families, although repeated contact with potential allergens by a family member is required before the person develops an allergy. An affected individual develops a particular type of antibody, known as the IgE, after exposure to an allergen. The IgE is taken up on the surface of cells, particularly those known as mast cells, which are present in large numbers in the lining of the nose, bronchial tubes, gut and skin, where allergic reactions occur.

After the specific binding of the allergen to IgE on mast cells, these cells release their granular contents, with the result that various substances, including histamine, are produced. It is these that give rise to symptoms such as coughing and wheezing, a runny nose and itching eyes, and skin rashes. The body's immune system creates a specific IgE to fight each allergen, so the first time the allergen is encountered there will be few or no antibodies present and there may be no reaction. As a result of the first encounter with an allergen the immune system of an allergic person produces more IgE antibodies and, on subsequent encounters, more IgE-sensitized mast cells until enough are present to provoke a reaction. This is why allergies can get worse the more frequently an allergen is encountered, although immune tolerance may develop so that symptoms do not appear.

An enormous variety of substances act as allergens, from specific foods to domestic dust mites and animal dander. In the garden respiratory allergies result from pollen grains and mould spores, and skin allergies from contact with plant sap and hairs. The majority of these garden allergens cause seasonal allergies – that is, the allergic reaction happens only at those times of the year when plants are pollinating or leaves are present. Hay fever (not an appropriate name since it is neither caused by hay nor produces a fever) frequently results from exposure to pollen and in such cases is more correctly labelled 'seasonal allergic rhinitis', which means inflammation of the nose and eyes owing to an allergic reaction at one season of the year.

Creating a low-allergen garden

The aim of this book is to show you how to design and plant your own garden to prevent, or at least limit, the chances of your encountering the outdoor allergens. The first part outlines the range of allergies and their causes and then looks at ways of minimizing or preventing allergic reactions when in the garden or while gardening. The second part outlines the process of designing a low-allergen garden. It explains which features to include and exclude, and suggests specific ideas for different types of gardens.

The third section deals with plants and planting and includes planting plans for a range of different situations. All the plans use plants which are least likely to cause an allergic reaction in even the most sensitive of gardeners.

The final section gives details of some of the best and most useful garden plants, all of which should be safe to use. These are the plants that are least likely to cause an allergic reaction in susceptible people. The plants are listed under the usual categories used in catalogues or garden centres – for example, Annuals and Biennials, Herbs and Shrubs. Also included are lists of the additional plants that are safe to use. This is followed by details of all the plants you should exclude from a low-allergen garden and suggests low-allergen alternatives.

An evolving story

It is important to realize that this book marks just the start of the low-allergen garden story. Intended simply as a summary of the knowledge to date, it is by no means the last word on the subject. Individual readers may well disagree with the inclusion of some plants in the 'safe' category, while others may have found they have no problem with plants in the 'dangerous' group. As we have already seen, allergies are very personal and there may even be someone somewhere who is allergic to every plant in existence. What I have done is to take the known facts and added anecdotal evidence in an attempt to demonstrate how a garden, which is unlikely to create problems for the many sufferers from outdoor allergies can be planned and planted.

Allergic Reactions

ANAPHYLAXIS
affects the cardiovascular system

ASTHMA
affects the lungs

CONJUNCTIVITIS
affects the eyes

ECZEMA, URTICARIA, CONTACT DERMATITIS AND PHOTODERMATITIS
affect the skin

GASTRITIS
affects the stomach and intestines

HAY FEVER
affects the eyes and nose

OTITIS
affects the ears

BELOW: *The round pink flowers of* Thalictrum aquilegiifolium *and* Allium hollandicum *make a soft corner of colour in the low-allergen garden at the Chelsea Flower Show in 1994.*

ALLERGIC
REACTIONS TO PLANTS

Breathing Allergies

Asthma

Asthma is characterized by coughing, difficulty in breathing, tightness of the chest and wheezing. It can start at any time between early childhood and old age, and may appear in childhood but disappear later, or may be a lifelong problem. It can be mild or severe, intermittent or chronic, but even the mildest intermittent asthma can be upsetting for sufferers and their families.

How we breathe

(See diagram opposite.) Air is inhaled into the lungs first through large airways, known as bronchi, then into the smaller airways, the bronchioles, and finally into the alveoli. All these airways are lined with a smooth moist lining, the mucosa, and are controlled by muscles that draw air in and out as we breathe. The muscles are controlled by the brain and their movement is largely involuntary, which means that we are not in control of our breathing and most of the time are unaware of it happening. Asthmatics can be taught special breathing exercises so that they can use their diaphragm correctly to help control their breathing.

During an asthma attack (see diagram) the muscle contraction, the swelling of the lining and the 'clogging' effect of the mucus combine to narrow the airways and cause difficulty in breathing in or out. The result is coughing brought on by the mucus, wheezing as the lungs try to draw sufficient air in and out through the restricted airway, and a tightness of the chest caused by the muscle spasm.

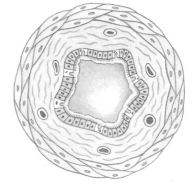

ABOVE: *Cross-section through healthy bronchiole showing the airway open and clear.*

Causes of asthma

There are several reasons why people develop asthma. These include an inherited tendency towards allergy and exposure in early childhood to excessive dust and the associated dust mite. Asthma may also be the result of an infection such as a cold or flu. Once an individual develops a tendency to asthma, attacks can be set off by 'triggers' in the form of allergens, pollution, emotional upset, over-exertion or infection.

Asthma is not curable but it can be controlled by medication. Sufferers should seek medical advice to get the most appropriate medication to prevent an attack and to treat symptoms when an attack does occur. Preventative medication must be taken regularly to work effectively. Medication to treat the symptoms of asthma often takes the form of bronchodilators, which are taken only when necessary. Bronchodilators are usually prescribed in the form of 'puffer' sprays and in severe cases as 'nebulizers'; asthmatics should carry their 'puffer' sprays with them at all times. An alternative to complete reliance on medicine is to try to avoid exposure to the triggers that cause attacks, and this is where the low-allergen garden, by eliminating plants known to be allergenic, can prove very helpful.

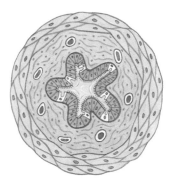

ABOVE: *Cross-section of a bronchiole during an attack of asthma. Asthma causes the muscles surrounding the bronchioles to become irritated and start contracting and going into spasm. At the same time the lining of the airway becomes inflamed and swollen and produces excess mucus.*

Airborne particles

Two of the major outdoor allergens known to cause asthma are pollen grains and fungal spores, both of which are tiny airborne particles. Pollen grains can be as small as 20 microns (one micron equals one thousandth of a millimetre), while mould spores are even smaller: *Aspergillus* and *Penicillium* measure only 2.4 microns. Both are readily inhaled as we breathe in. The smallest of them travel through the bronchi to the bronchioles, and in susceptible people can set up an allergic reaction which leads to inflammation and an asthma attack.

Hay fever

An allergy affecting both the eyes and the nose, hay fever is much more common than asthma. It affects people of all ages, from babies to the elderly, but is most prevalent among children and young adults. While it is not life-threatening, hay fever can make the sufferer feel very miserable and can limit his or her outdoor activities, including gardening, during the warmest months of the year.

Symptoms of hay fever

When an allergen such as pollen enters the nasal passages of a hay fever sufferer it causes the lining to become inflamed and produce excess mucus, and this gives rise to the typical symptoms of a runny nose, sniffing and sneezing. When the eyes are affected they may become puffy, red or very itchy. Other common symptoms include catarrh, a blocked nose and an itchy mouth and throat. In addition there may be a sore throat, headache and general lethargy, but not, despite the condition's name, a raised temperature or fever. The symptoms usually start in spring and continue through the summer months. However, where the allergen is encountered all year round, as in the case of dust mites in bedding, the symptoms are continuous. The family cat is a common cause of perennial symptoms, and these often lessen when the sufferer is away from home and the cat.

BELOW: *A cross section showing the respiratory system. An average respiratory rate is 16 breaths each minute.*

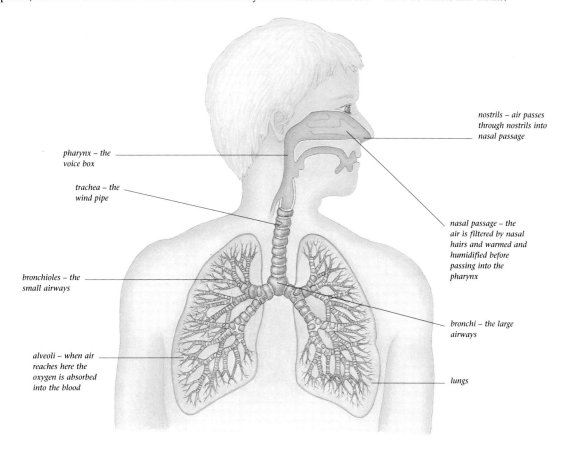

pharynx – the voice box

trachea – the wind pipe

bronchioles – the small airways

alveoli – when air reaches here the oxygen is absorbed into the blood

nostrils – air passes through nostrils into nasal passage

nasal passage – the air is filtered by nasal hairs and warmed and humidified before passing into the pharynx

bronchi – the large airways

lungs

Hay fever caused by pollen

The most common allergen in the garden is grass pollen, which is produced by grasses in summer. Almost as bad are tree pollens, abundant in spring and the early summer months. However, where hay fever is worse in autumn, weed pollens or mould spores are the most likely cause.

When hay fever is known to be caused by pollen, simple precautions may be taken to prevent or reduce contact with the allergens. These include planting low-allergen plants and, in the months when the pollen count is at its highest, either staying indoors or not going outside without a protective face mask. In addition, various medicines are available, including topical nasal sprays and antihistamines. However, if the sufferer avoids contact with allergenic plants, it may be possible to restrict the reliance on medication to times when the allergen cannot be avoided or when the reaction is prolonged or interferes with normal activity.

Pollen and pollination

Although pollen has been shown to be a major cause of an allergic reaction, many people are not sure what it is. They know that it is small and dangerous, but where does it come from? It comes from the flowering part of the plant, and is the means whereby the male gamete, or sperm cell, from one flower is transferred to fertilize the female gamete or egg cell of another.

All plants produce pollen at some point during their life cycle to ensure the continuation of the species. Plants consist of roots, stems, leaves and flowers. The flower is the reproductive part of the plant and is designed to ensure that pollination and fertilization take place as efficiently as possible. After fertilization seeds are formed and the female part of the flower becomes the fruit. A typical flower is made up of four sets of modified leaves arranged in circles around the flower stalk. The outer ring consists of sepals, usually green, which protect the flower when in bud. Inside the sepals is a circle of petals; these are frequently brightly coloured to attract insects to pollinate the flower. Within the circle of petals is a ring of stamens, the male part of the flower, and on each stamen are anthers, which produce the pollen. In the middle of the flower are the carpels, the female part, consisting of ovaries containing ovules, and above the ovaries are

BELOW: *A cross-section showing an insect-pollinated flower. The large colourful petals attract insects to the short stamens, which stay within the confines of the petals.*

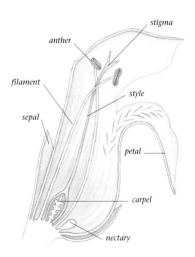

the style and the stigma on which pollen lands to fertilize the ovule. Plants depend on a variety of agents to ensure that pollination takes place, the most important of which are insects and the wind.

Insect pollination

Some plants are pollinated by insects, including bees, wasps, butterflies and moths. The insect will visit a plant to feed on nectar, a sugary liquid produced inside it, and in foraging for this will unintentionally collect pollen, which adheres to its body. Having extracted nectar from one plant, it moves to another nearby, when some of the pollen on its body will fall, or be rubbed off, on to the stigma. If the two plants are of the same species and are both ready, fertilization will take place. Most insect-pollinated plants require the attention of specific types of insect, and the flower size, colour and type of nectar are designed to attract these.

Wind pollination

The wind is far less efficient than insects as a method of pollination as there is no guarantee that the pollen of one plant will land on the stigma of another plant of the same species. However, plants that depend on the wind for pollination have become adapted to take maximum advantage of this freely available agent.

Since plant species which are pollinated by the wind have no need to attract insects, their petals and stamens are reduced to inconspicuous, dull-coloured bracts that protect the developing stamens and carpels. The style and stigmas are adapted and exposed to catch every pollen grain that is blown in their direction. The catkins, seen on hazel bushes in early spring, are typical of the flowers of wind-pollinated plants. There are virtually no petals or sepals to be seen – just masses of pollen, creating a yellow cloud around the plant whenever the wind blows. Inevitably, such an unpredictable method of pollination leads to the wastage of a large amount of pollen, so each plant produces huge quantities of pollen grains. These are dry, powdery and much lighter and more buoyant than those produced by insect-pollinated plants. They can float on air currents for several miles in order to maximize the chances of a proportion being blown on to the stigmas of the same species of plant.

Wind-pollinated trees and shrubs in temperate climates produce flowers in the spring before the leaves appear, possibly to ensure that all the flowers are exposed to the wind without the surrounding leaves' interference. Another group of wind-pollinated flowers are grasses. Incidentally, it is because farmers make hay from grass that the term 'hay fever' came to be used to describe the allergic rhinitis suffered by many people as soon as haymaking begins. It is the vast numbers of airborne pollen grains which cause problems for hay fever and asthma sufferers.

Not all pollen grains cause asthma and hay fever; they will do so only if they are abundant, buoyant, small and strongly allergenic. They must be abundant in order to be inhaled, buoyant so that they float in the air we breathe, small enough to enter the bronchioles and strongly allergenic in order to

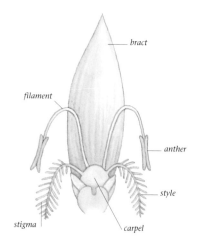

bract

filament

anther

style

stigma

carpel

ABOVE: *The stamens of wind-pollinated plants are larger and more numerous than those of insect-pollinated plants and they have extra-long filaments that hold the pollen-bearing anthers out of the flower, until the pollen is blown away by the wind.*

BELOW: *A false-colour scanning electron micrograph showing the pollen exploding from the catkins of this wild hazel (Corylus) into the atmosphere. Magnification x 100.*

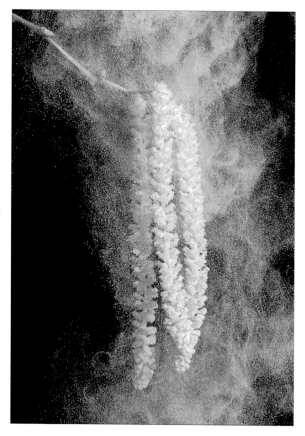

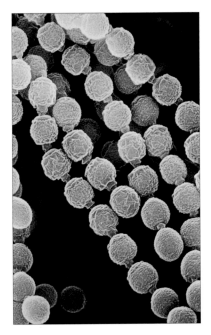

ABOVE: *A close-up photograph of the fungus* Penicillium chrysogenum *showing spore chains. Magnification x 850.*

provoke production of IgE (see pp.10–11) in susceptible people, and thus cause an allergic reaction when they reach the nose or lungs. Only wind-pollinated plants produce large enough quantities of buoyant pollen grains, and of these grains only some are both sufficiently small and allergenic to cause allergic reactions. Strongly allergenic pollen is found in specific groups of related plants called families, and sufferers are usually allergic to the members of a particular plant family.

Fungal spores

Another major group of allergens that cause asthma and hay fever are the spores of fungi. Fungal spores, also called mould spores, grow on dead and decaying material such as diseased plant material, decomposed vegetation in a compost heap and rotting wood in wood piles. They are very light and float in the air, settling on flat surfaces such as lawns and flowerbeds and drifting into hedges.

Fungi are a specialized group of organisms that can survive only by living on plants or animals. Some are beneficial to their host and form what is known as a symbiotic relationship, but others damage the host, causing diseases such as powdery mildew and rose rust.

Fungal spore production

The growing part of a fungus is called the mycelium and consists of strands of simple cells, frequently white in colour. If you lift the bark from a decaying tree stump you can often see the white tracery of fungal mycelium. Fungi reproduce by spores, which are the equivalent of the seed of a plant, and these are produced in large numbers and then dispersed by wind, or very occasionally water or insects. Fungal spores may result from the division of specialized strands of the mycelium, as found in the particularly nasty allergen *Alternaria*. This is a very common fungus found on straw, grass clippings, rotten fruit and other plant remains, and develops its dark, tadpole-shaped spores with great speed and efficiency. These spores are very light and buoyant and can travel thousands of miles as an invisible cloud.

In what are known as the higher fungi, for example the mushrooms and toadstools, the fruiting body can be quite complex and rises out of the ground from the mycelium, which grows on plant and animal debris in the soil. The mushroom which we pick in autumn to eat is the fruiting body of the *Agaricus campestris*, or field mushroom. If you look under its 'cap' you will see the spores as a brown powder attached to the creamy 'gills'. In allergy the main culprits are the spores of the simpler fungi, but if you suffer from asthma or hay fever it is probably a bad idea to start growing mushrooms in your cellar!

Many fungi release their spores in late summer and the autumn, and this is when they are likely to cause a problem for allergy sufferers. Three of the known offenders are *Cladosporium*, which causes leaf rot, *Alternaria* and *Aspergillus*. The last is particularly nasty and can cause an allergic asthmatic condition called aspergillosis which can lead to a chronic inflammation of the bronchial tubes with destruction of the larger airways, as well as to a more severe chronic asthma. Another condition caused by mould spores is 'farmer's lung', which can result from the inhalation of mould spores of *Actinomycetes*, a fungus that grows on hay which has been baled while still damp. Asthma sufferers can be tested to see if they are allergic to these particular species of fungi. However, there are thousands of other fungal species which may be found to cause allergies.

Limiting fungal spores

It is possible to reduce the concentration of fungal spores within the garden by eliminating areas where fungi are found and by keeping your plants healthy so that they do not succumb to fungal disease. Removing hedges and lawns which trap the airborne spores blown into your garden from other areas will also help. High fungal concentrations in the atmosphere occur in late summer and autumn, particularly during thunderstorms and after heavy rainfall. When the atmosphere is full of clouds of fungal spores the best advice if you are allergic to fungi is to stay indoors with the windows closed. If you must go out, try wearing a protective mask. Wearing a mask may be restricting, but it is preferable to an attack of asthma or hay fever. In addition to the regular pollen counts given by the media during the pollen season, some countries now provide seasonal counts of some of the fungal spores, including *Alternaria* and *Cladosporium*.

Ferns

Like fungi, ferns are a group of plants which reproduce by spores rather than by seeds. Their spores are produced in fruiting bodies called sori (see below), which appear as brown lines, circles and patterns on the underside of the leaves and are one of the means by which the different ferns can be identified.

Botanically, fern spores are different from pollen grains and fungal spores but they may still be implicated in causing allergies. Work on the connection between fern spores and asthma and hay fever is being undertaken in various parts of the world and some allergists insist that allergy sufferers should avoid these spores.

LEFT: *The underside of a frond of the fern* Polypodium vulgare *showing the regular arrangement of sori, which contain the spores.* **INSET:** *A scanning micrograph of a fern sorus in which the spores are formed and mature.*

The fragrant flowers of the honeysuckle Lonicera periclymenum *'Belgica' can trigger attacks of asthma.*

At present there is disagreement on whether ferns should be featured in the low-allergen garden. Many make very useful garden plants, particularly for shady gardens, and I would love to include some in most gardens. But until the spores of all fern species have been investigated thoroughly, all ferns must be treated with suspicion by allergy sufferers. Nevertheless, if you can find sterile cultivars of ferns which will produce few if any spores, it should be safe to plant these.

Scented plants

One of the great pleasures of having flowers in your garden is the wonderful variety of aromas that they produce: from the heady scent of carnations to the fresh apple fragrance of the climbing rose 'Albertine'. Unfortunately, some people are sensitive to the smell of scented plants and this can act as an irritant, giving rise to an attack of asthma or hay fever. The process is not clearly understood, but many asthmatics complain that heavily-scented plants are a problem, and sometimes it is a single plant such as honeysuckle that is the cause, although for some sufferers the culprits appear to be all scented plants.

There are two types of fragrance found in plants: the scent found in flowers, and the aromatic fragrance found in all, or most, parts of aromatic plants. In scented flowers the scent is located in nectaries on the petals, and is given off when the flowers are ready for pollinating and when the insects which are attracted by it are flying around. Night-scented stock and evening primrose are pollinated by moths and therefore give off their scent in the evening. Plants that are pollinated by bees tend to give off more scent during the middle of the day and when the sun is shining.

The aromatic plants contain aromatic or 'essential' oils within their cells and these are released only when the cell walls are broken by being rubbed, crushed or heated. Many of these plants are herbs: plants used for the beneficial effects of their essential oils. It is not clear whether these plants have the same effect on asthmatics as the scented plants. Lavender is an aromatic plant that is known to cause asthma, but it is not clear whether this is due to its essential oil or its leaf hairs. As a group, the herbs are very useful plants, both in the garden and in the house, and unless you are sure that they are implicated in your own allergies I would suggest that you give them a chance.

BELOW: *A cross-section through the flower of a foxglove,* Digitalis, *showing nectary guides leading a visiting bee to the nectary.*

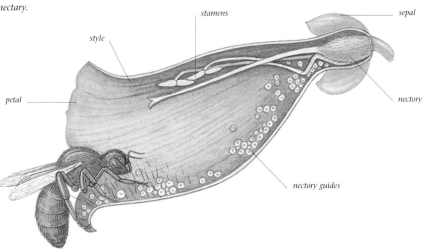

stamens

style

sepal

petal

nectory

nectory guides

One group of heavily scented plants are the various species of *Dianthus*. This includes carnations, sweet williams and pinks, many of which have a strong spicy scent which is known to act as a trigger in some cases of hay fever and asthma. Other heavily scented plants include lilies, particularly *Lilium regale* whose fragrance on a warm summer's day can pervade a whole garden. All the strongly scented plants are best excluded from the low-allergen garden. There are some scented plants like the daylily, such as *Hemerocallis* 'Whichford', whose delicate fragrance can only be enjoyed when close to the flower and should only present a problem when planted beside a garden seat, or if cut and brought into the house.

Other problem plants

We have seen that scented plants, fern and fungal spores, and wind-pollinated plants are all potential hazards for hay fever and asthma sufferers. For this reason they should be excluded from the low-allergen garden.

There is a further group of plants which are not wind-pollinated and not necessarily scented but which may cause problems. These include many of the plants within the daisy family, the Asteraceae, some of which produce pollen that is allergenically toxic. The family includes asters, chrysanthemums, marigolds and zinnias, and all its members have flowers that look like a daisy or a chrysanthemum. If you are allergic to any of the above plants it is probably sensible to eliminate all the plants within this family from your garden. There are parts of the world, particularly North America, where ragweed, *Ambrosia* spp., is the major cause of seasonal hay fever. Ragweed is present in Eastern Europe, but not in the UK, although it has spread into parts of France. It is a member of the Asteraceae and is a very profuse producer of small allergenic pollen.

Many different parts of the world have indigenous species of trees, shrubs, herbaceous plants and weeds that are strongly allergenic. Advice on local plant pollens should be sought from allergists, chest physicians and dermatologists. Throughout the world, wherever grasses grow grass pollen is the most common allergen. Check the pollen count, if this information is available, as this is a useful indicator of the start and finish of the grass pollen season. On days when the count is high, it is sensible to avoid gardening.

ABOVE: Leucanthemum x superbum, *with its daisy-like flowers typical of all plants in the family Asteraceae.*

Skin Allergies

ABOVE: *The flowers of ivy,* Hedera helix, *which can cause contact dermatitis.*

A wide range of allergic reactions affect the skin, from mild rashes that last a few hours to eczema, which can persist for a lifetime. Although not dangerous or contagious, they are unsightly and can be extremely uncomfortable. The first three forms of skin diseases outlined below result from an individual's being allergic to a particular substance. However, there are types of dermatitis that result from contact with substances which are in themselves toxic, rather than from the body's allergic reaction to them. Some garden plants cause skin problems in anyone who comes into contact with them, whether they have an allergic tendency or not.

Eczema

A form of dermatitis, eczema appears as an itchy rash. It usually occurs first in early childhood and may disappear at any age, but in about 25 percent of cases it persists well into adult life. The precise cause is not known, but eczema is thought to be the result of an allergy to the same allergens that cause asthma and hay fever. Many children who suffer from childhood eczema develop hay fever or asthma as they get older. The condition also tends to occur in atopic families – those which are prone to allergies and whose members have asthma, hay fever or eczema.

Urticaria

Urticaria consists of small red, itchy areas with a raised, round, whitish centre like a mosquito bite. The rash, or welts, may be restricted to a small area or be scattered all over the body. This condition develops only after previous exposure to the allergen and although it can develop quickly, sometimes it needs prolonged contact with the substance. In a few cases of urticaria the face or other parts of the body become swollen and distorted. Where only a small amount of welts appear they can be distinguished from insect bites by checking for a tiny hole in the centre of the welt. If there is a hole, the swellings are insect bites.

Pollen, moulds, specific plants or even just sitting on grass can cause urticaria in susceptible people. A child who is allergic to grass pollen may get itchy legs from playing on grass with bare legs, because minor abrasions can allow the pollen present on the surface of the grass to enter the skin.

Contact dermatitis

Plants cause dermatitis in a variety of ways. In some the plant sap is the problem, in others it is hairs on the leaves and stem, while in other plants merely touching the foliage may cause an adverse reaction. In the case of hyacinths and tulips the bulb itself is the cause, so once this is in the ground there is usually no problem.

Contact dermatitis is a skin inflammation caused by contact with a substance to which the skin is sensitive. Typically, it is a red rash with tiny blisters, but unlike eczema this does not usually occur in the bends of the arms and legs but on the site which has been exposed to the contact. There are several plants that produce the condition in those with sensitive skin, and preventing contact by removing such plants or wearing gloves when gardening will eliminate the problem. Among the plants implicated in contact dermatitis are the leaves and sap of the common

Skin Allergies

CONTACT DERMATITIS
causes itchy rash, like tiny blisters, which occur at the site of contact with allergen, frequently the fingers and hands or face

ECZEMA
causes dry itchy rash to arms and legs, particularly in creases, and on the face and neck

PHOTODERMATITIS
itchy rash and blisters which reappear in hot sunlight and occur at the site of contact with allergen, frequently arms and hands

URTICARIA
(also known as nettle rash or hives) *causes itchy welts, like red raised lumps which can occur anywhere on the body*

marigold, *Calendula officinalis*, and the leaves and stem of ivy, *Hedera helix*. These two plants are very common in gardens and are both attractive to children, so if a child who is known to suffer from contact dermatitis is likely to touch them it is advisable to remove both species. *Primula obconica*, a popular houseplant, is a strong sensitizer and, once sensitive to these plants, the sufferer may become sensitive to the other members of the Primulaceae family, which includes all the primroses and polyanthus. Chrysanthemums can cause contact dermatitis, as can several bulbs. Tulip bulbs cause 'tulip fingers', a rash that causes the skin of the fingers to crack and itch.

Irritant contact dermatitis

Anyone can be affected by this type of dermatitis if a toxic substance that causes it occurs in sufficient quantities. A prickly red rash may appear on the area of contact, or the skin may just feel prickly and sore. Usually the discomfort disappears quite quickly and may be considered just part of the gardener's lot, along with an aching back and sore knees. One frequent culprit is the lovely yellow-flowered wall shrub *Fremontodendron*, which is covered with minute hairs that can cause the condition in its unsuspecting owner.

ABOVE: *The plant hairs of* Fremontodendron *'California Glory', with its lovely yellow flowers, can cause irritant dermatitis.*

Photodermatitis

A more serious condition is photodermatitis, in which simultaneous exposure of the skin to a specific plant and bright sunlight results in redness, itching and blistering that in many cases last for several weeks. When the rash clears the skin may be left discoloured and subsequent exposure of the same area of skin to bright sunlight may bring the rash back. Plants such as rue, *Ruta graveolens*, which are known to cause photodermatitis should always be pruned wearing gloves and must be eliminated from gardens where there are children.

There is now a list of plants which catalogues those that are most likely to cause contact dermatitis and photodermatitis, and in the UK most nurseries and garden centres adhere to a recommended code of practice and label these plants before they are put on sale. The Horticultural Trade Association (HTA) list on page 24 gives the plants that have been well documented as causing dermatitis in a substantial number of cases. However, many plants remain unlisted which are known to cause dermatitis in susceptible people. The HTA list includes only cultivated plants grown for sale to the general public, so few of our wild plants are included and some of these are potentially dangerous.

Extract from Horticultural Trades Association (HTA) Members' Code of Practice

This is a code of recommended retail practice drawn up by the horticultural authorities and relates to the labelling of potentially harmful plants. Plants are listed in one of three categories A, B or C depending on how harmful the plant is considered to be, category A is the most harmful and category C is the least.

Category A
The sale of these plants to the public should be discouraged. The three plants listed are rarely seen in Britain and should be excluded from all gardens

Rhus radicans	poison ivy
Rhus succedanea	wax tree
Rhus verniciflua	varnish tree

These plants are poisonous if eaten and skin contact commonly causes severe blistering dermatitis.

Category B
These plants require a warning on the plant label and on the bed label when on sale to the public. This list includes many poisonous plants and those causing severe skin allergies. All should be excluded from the low-allergen garden particularly where there are children.

The following should be labelled **CAUTION toxic if eaten**

Aconitum	monkshood
Atropa	includes deadly nightshade
Colchicum	includes meadow saffron
Convallaria majalis	lily of the valley
Daphne	
Datura	thorn apple
Digitalis	foxglove
Gaultheria	(section Pernettya only)
Gloriosa superba	glory lily
Hyoscyanus	henbane
Laburnum	
Lantana	
Nerium oleander	oleander
Phytolacca	pokeweed
Ricinus communis	castor-oil plant
Solanum dulcamara	woody nightshade
Taxus	yew
Veratrum	false helleborine

The following also cause skin allergies and require to be labelled as shown:

Arum	CAUTION toxic if eaten/skin + eye irritant
Daphne laureola	CAUTION toxic if eaten/may cause skin allergy
Daphne mezereum	CAUTION toxic if eaten/may cause skin allergy
Dictamnus albus	CAUTION skin irritant in sunlight
Dieffenbachia	CAUTION toxic if eaten/skin + eye irritant
Primula obconica	CAUTION may cause skin allergy
Ruta	CAUTION severely toxic to skin in sunlight

Category C
These plants require a warning on the plant label, they include less toxic poisonous plants and plants that may cause skin irritation or allergy. Those listed that can affect the skin have been eliminated from the low-allergen garden but the less toxic plants are included as human poisonings by these plants are uncommon.

The following should be labelled **Harmful if eaten**

Aesculus	horse chestnuts and buckeyes
Agrostemma githago	corncockle
Aquilegia	columbine
Brugmansia	angels trumpet
Caltha	marsh marigold
Catharanthus roseus	Madagascar periwinkle
Delphinium	
Euonymus	
Gaultheria	
Helleborus	
Hypericum perforatum	
Ipomoea	morning glory
Iris	
Juniperus sabina	
Kalmia	calico bush
Ligustrum	privet
Lupinus	lupin
Ornithogalum	star of Bethlehem
Polygonatum	Solomon's seal
Prunus laurocerasus	cherry laurel
Rhamnus	buckthorn
Scilla	
Thuja	
Wisteria	

The following may cause skin allergies or irritations and should be labelled as shown:

Alstroemeria	May cause skin allergy
x *Cupressocyparis leylandii*	May cause skin allergy
Dendranthema (excluding pot mums)	May cause skin allergy
Echium	Skin irritant
Euphorbia	Harmful if eaten/skin + eye irritant
Ficus carica	Skin irritant in sunlight
Fremontodendron	Skin + eye irritant
Hedera	Harmful if eaten/may cause skin allergy
Hyacinthus	Skin irritant
Lobelia tupa	Harmful if eaten/skin + eye irritant
Narcissus	Harmful if eaten/skin irritant
Schefflera	May cause skin allergy
Tulipa	Skin irritant

Dealing with skin allergies

It should be easier to avoid skin allergies while gardening than with asthma and hay fever, in that simply avoiding contact with allergenic and irritant plants prevents the problem. However, most of us touch our plants when we are dead-heading or pruning, or brush against them when weeding. The best approach is to exclude all plants you know to be a major problem for you and members of your family, and then to take care when handling any plant on the HTA list (see p.24). When gardening it is a sensible precaution to wear gauntlets or gloves which cover your wrists and, if you have very sensitive skin, to wear long sleeves and trousers or thick stockings or tights. If this feels too uncomfortable or restrictive you should eliminate any plant that may cause dermatitis. If, despite your precautions, sap from an allergenic or irritant plant touches your skin, wash the area immediately with soap and water.

One plant to handle with extreme care is euphorbia, whose milky sap can cause a nasty problem if it gets near the eyes; even if you are wearing gloves when handling this plant, remember to avoid rubbing your eyes until you have washed your hands.

Prickles and thorns

Many plants have prickles and thorns which dissuade grazing animals from eating them. In some of these a minute amount of an irritant substance is released if the tip of the thorn is broken. If this happens when you are working with the plant the substance may penetrate the skin and cause a reaction. For example, the common holly contains illicin, which can cause irritant contact dermatitis when you are pruning a holly hedge and can't avoid being pricked. A liberal application of antiseptic cream to the affected area of skin will usually ease the discomfort quite quickly. If you suffer from eczema or another skin allergy ask someone to prune prickly plants for you.

Precautions to Avoid Skin Allergies

Remove all plants known to be skin allergens or irritants, or if you want to grow these plants carry out the following:

● plant problem plants at the back of the border and away from paths to avoid possible contact

● avoid any contact with plants causing photodermatitis, for example rue; on hot sunny days one brief contact is enough to cause severe blistering

● always wear tough long gardening gloves or gauntlets when gardening and handling plants, and when planting bulbs

● wear a long-sleeved shirt or blouse to protect your arms in summer

● wear trousers rather than a skirt or shorts particularly when strimming to protect your legs from flying sap

● wear goggles or sunglasses to protect your eyes and avoid touching your eyes with your gloves

● wear a hat to protect ears, forehead and scalp

● never garden barefoot and preferably wear shoes and socks rather than sandals

● always wash your hands and any exposed skin immediately after gardening

If a plant does irritate your skin

● wash the area well with plenty of cool water and avoid exposing the skin to the sun

● try not to rub or scratch the skin

● if the irritation worsens then seek medical advice

LEFT: *One of the attractive variegated hollies, Ilex aquifolium 'Handsworth New Silver', showing the prickles on the edge of the leaves, which can cause contact dermatitis.*

RIGHT: *A close-up view of a honey bee in the process of stinging a finger; the sting is embedded in the skin.*

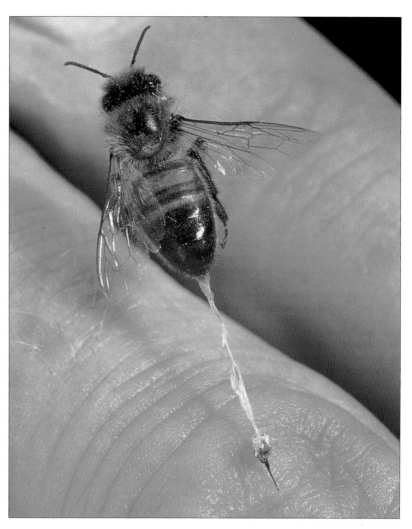

List of Bee Plants

Bees visit plants to collect pollen and nectar. The following low-allergen garden plants are frequently visited by bees.

Alcea rosea	Lythrum salicaria
Armeria	Malus spp.
maritima	Melissa
Astrantia major	officinalis
Aubrieta	Myosotis spp.
deltoidea	Nepeta
Centranthus	x faassenii
ruber	Origanum
Cotoneaster	vulgare
horizontalis	Papaver orientale
Crataegus spp.	Perovskia
Cytisus spp.	atriplicifolia
Echinops ritro	Polemonium
Filipendula	caeruleum
ulmaria	Prunus avium
Foeniculum	Rosmarinus
vulgare	officinalis
Geranium (most	Salvia officinalis
species and	Satureja
varieties)	montana
Hyssopus	Scrophularia
officinalis	auriculata
Limnanthes	Thymus spp.
douglasii	Ulex europaeus
Linaria purpurea	Veronica spicata

Insect bites and stings

For some gardeners insects, rather than plants or pollen, are the main cause of allergic reactions. Although insects can be kept out of the house by the use of screens on windows and doors, there is no such remedy in the garden. Allergic reactions to insect bites and stings are at the very least painful or itchy, but in very sensitive people they can be fatal. Bees, wasps and hornets are among the most common stinging insects and many people have an allergy to their stings, particularly those of bees. If you suffer from an allergy to any of these insects, the first time you are stung the result may be inflammation with very marked local swelling which may take two or three days to subside. Subsequent stings may cause more generalized inflammation, difficulty in breathing and anaphylactic shock. Anyone who experiences an abnormal reaction to a sting should seek specialist medical advice and will probably be advised to always carry antihistamine drugs and adrenalin for an emergency. The specialist should also be consulted about whether or not desensitization treatment is required.

If a member of the family shows a severe allergic reaction to stings, all plants which attract bees or wasps should be removed from the garden, or at least from those beds and borders close to the house and sitting areas. Similarly avoid growing fruit if allergic to wasps, as they are attracted to ripe and decaying fruit.

Other insects whose bite can cause an allergic reaction are those which, in biting their victim, inject saliva into the wound. An adverse reaction to mosquito bites is quite common, and may include abnormal swelling in the area of the bite and possibly associated weakness, headache and an upset stomach. The symptoms are eased by taking antihistamine tablets and applying an anti-irritant cream to the affected part. Measures that you can take to reduce the risk of mosquito bites include checking the garden for areas where these insects are likely to breed – for example, ponds and streams. Mosquitoes tend to be most active in the evening and if the water feature is in a distant part of the garden, simply avoiding that part of the garden on a summer evening may be sufficient. However, a pool close to the house presents more of a problem. Try using insect-repellent creams or sprays, and wearing long-sleeved tops and trousers or thick stockings. I suffer from this allergy myself and spend summer evenings trying to protect myself from mosquitoes in the garden. In warm weather when they are breeding, and in gardens where they are abundant, I avoid going into the garden after sunset.

Red spider mites are a pest to many garden plants, particularly those grown in greenhouses and conservatories, and can cause urticaria, sneezing and asthma in susceptible people.

Poisonous plants

Although poisonous plants are not a specific concern of the low-allergen gardener, if we intend to make any garden into a safer place we must be able to recognize which plants are poisonous and to distinguish those which are toxic from those which are simply harmful. Toxic plants are those which, if eaten, can have serious consequences, including death, although this is an infrequent occurrence. Harmful plants may cause vomiting and gastro-intestinal discomfort when eaten, but do not usually have more serious effects. The HTA list on page 24 classifies poisonous plants under these two categories.

In the low-allergen garden I have always excluded toxic plants because of the seriousness of the risk they present. On the other hand, some of the harmful plants are so useful and decorative that, unless they cause skin allergies, I usually plant them in the beds and borders. This group includes aquilegia, delphiniums and irises, all of which I value highly as garden plants.

Poisonous plants create a problem only if they are eaten. Adults are unlikely to do this unless they mistake them for another similar edible plant, which is indeed how most cases of poisoning in adults occur. However, young children will eat brightly coloured berries simply because they look attractive. When my son was two years old he came in with his mouth bright red from eating the berries of wild arum. As a result I removed all potentially harmful plants from my garden until he was old enough to understand the dangers. It makes sense to remove all poisonous plants which could prove irresistible to children.

BELOW: *The Laburnum Arch at Barnsley House, Gloucestershire, south-west England. Unfortunately all parts of laburnum are poisonous and the seeds pose a particular risk, as they are readily eaten by children.*

Gardening with Allergies

Minimizing allergic reactions

I'm not a doctor, but I am convinced that the best way to cope with an allergy, including allergens in children, is to find out everything there is to know about how and why it occurs. This means discovering to which substances the sufferer is personally allergic and this is best done with the help of a doctor, who may refer you to a consultant allergist. Keeping a diary of when symptoms occur and what they are like, including their severity, will help the doctor or allergist help you. For example, if you find that your symptoms are always much worse as soon as summer comes, and are particularly bad when you are outside, you are almost certainly allergic to grass pollen.

Once you know some of the causes try to avoid them as much as possible, prevention being better than cure. Where particular plants are known to be a problem for you, check your garden for specimens and remove them if possible. If fungal spores are causing trouble, look for areas and features that may encourage their growth (see p.18) or may trap them. Taking out hedges, covering the compost heap or removing piles of rotting grass will all help to reduce fungi populations. While you are trying to eliminate allergens you must be sure to keep on taking any medication that has been prescribed for you, and only reduce or change it on the advice of your doctor or allergist.

Protective clothing

There are a number of other precautions you can take, and these are determined by the type of allergy. First, consider what you wear when gardening. For skin allergy sufferers gardening clothes should cover as much of the bare skin as possible. Where eyes are affected it is a good idea to wear sunglasses or goggles. If

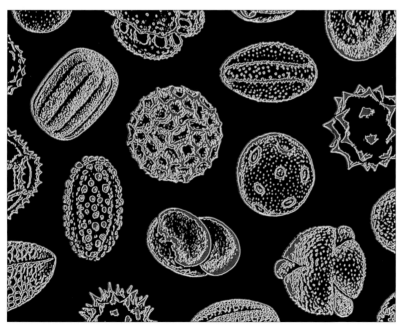

BELOW: *A scanning electron micrograph of a range of pollen grains. The size, shape and surface texture of a particular pollen grain is unique to each species.*

pollen or fungal spores are a problem, always wear a hat to catch these airborne allergens, but remember to take off the hat before returning indoors. To increase your chances of keeping pollen and spores out of the house, have a pair of trousers and jacket to wear in the garden and put these and the hat on when you go outside and remove them before going back indoors.

Whenever pollen levels are high, be sure to wash your hair after gardening to remove pollen. Where the allergy is moderately severe it may help to wear a mask over your nose and mouth to prevent pollen or fungal spores from reaching your nose and lungs as discussed on page 16. This may feel restrictive, but if it allows you to work

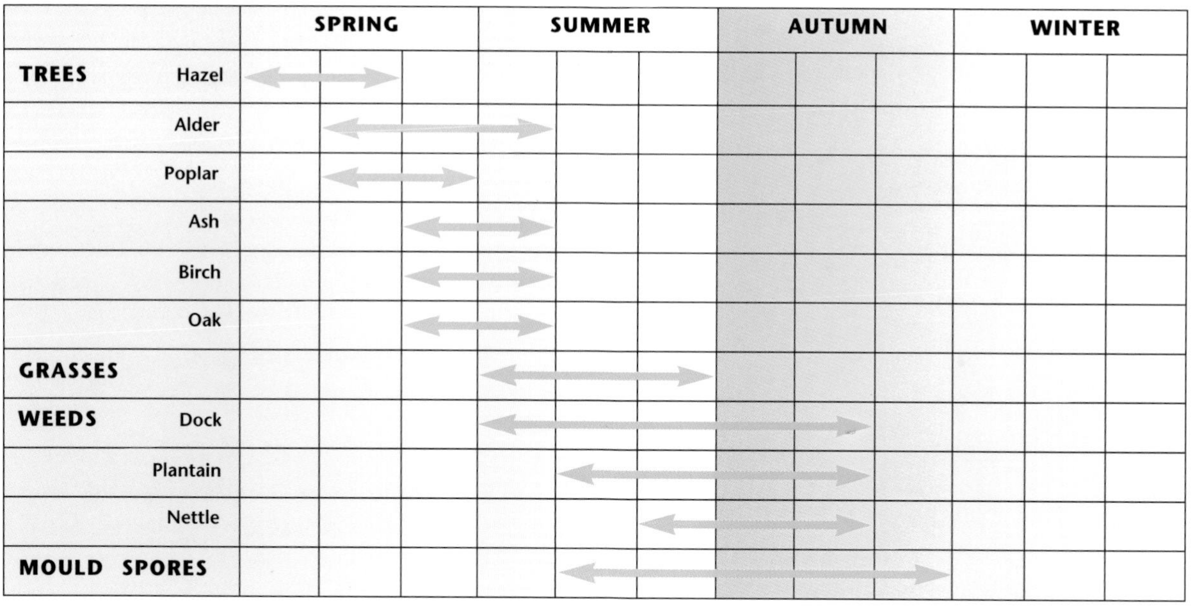

		SPRING			SUMMER			AUTUMN			WINTER		
TREES	Hazel	←→											
	Alder		←→										
	Poplar		←→										
	Ash			←→									
	Birch			←→									
	Oak			←→									
GRASSES					←→								
WEEDS	Dock				←→			→					
	Plantain					←→		→					
	Nettle						←→	→					
MOULD SPORES					←→				→				

ABOVE: *This chart shows when the pollens and mould spores, which cause asthma and hay fever, are released.*

in the garden without sneezing or wheezing it must be worth considering. Having taken all this trouble to keep pollens and fungal spores out of the house, be sure not to hang your washing in the garden in summer. It may smell wonderful if you do, but as you savour that freshness you will also be breathing in all the pollen, spores and dust which it gathered while outside.

When to garden

I enjoy gardening at any time of year, provided it is neither raining nor blowing a gale. And while I prefer the temperature to be above freezing I don't like it to be uncomfortably hot. Anywhere between 8°C (40°F) and 27°C (80°F) suits me, and I suspect that this is true of most gardeners accustomed to a similar climate. However, for those who suffer from allergies the time of year, the weather and the time of day may each affect the risk of a reaction and also influence the severity of the symptoms. These factors may make it necessary for them to change the timing of their gardening activities.

Seasonal variations

Sunny but cold days in winter are ideal for pruning and for having a tidy-up in the garden, and in such conditions there will be very few airborne allergens. A word of caution is needed, however. Some asthmatics find that cold weather exacerbates their asthma and, in particular, inhaling cold air brings on an attack. If this is the case for you, wrap up well and stay indoors when the temperature falls.

Spring can be a bad time for asthma and hay fever sufferers as this is when many of the wind-pollinated tree species release their pollen into the atmosphere. The first tree to produce pollen is hazel, followed by alder, poplar and sycamore, then ash, plane, birch and oak in late spring.

In summer grass pollens are released in their millions and then several of the common garden and roadside weeds, including docks, nettles and plantains, produce masses of allergenic pollen, which is known to bring on attacks of asthma and hay fever.

Harvest time is the signal for the release from the cornfields of millions of fungal spores which drift in air currents for many miles. Fortunately, these seem to be more prevalent at night, when few people will be out in their garden. But during the day asthma and hay fever sufferers should avoid getting anywhere near a combine harvester.

For some sufferers from these conditions, going into the garden can be a real problem for almost nine months of the year, and it is during this time that replanning it as a low-allergen garden should pay dividends.

As for skin allergies, any time of the year can be a problem if the plant, or part of the plant, which causes the allergy is present; however, hot sunny days are the worst times for contact with plants causing photodermatitis (see pp.23 and 25) and warm weather tends to make any rash more troublesome. Additionally, most clothing worn in the summer months exposes more bare flesh so the risk of contact with problem plants is higher.

Bees and other pollinating insects are only present in the garden when the plants they pollinate are in flower and when the weather is warm and the air still, so you are unlikely to encounter them on a cold winter day. Incidentally, remember that at the start and end of summer bees may be less active but there is more chance of putting your hand down on a 'sleepy' one or treading on it.

The weather

There is much confusion as to which types of weather create problems for allergy sufferers. Warm, damp conditions favour the growth of many species of fungi, which subsequently release a superabundance of spores into the atmosphere, creating a problem for anyone who is allergic to them. Windy days allow dust, pollen and fungal spores to be blown around and to travel much further than on calmer days. Calm, sunny days bring out insects such as bees to visit flowers for nectar and this weather also causes pollen sacs to open and release pollen. In summer a sunny, dry day with a brisk wind creates the worst conditions for asthma or hay fever suferers who are allergic to grass pollen. On such days it is advisable to either stay indoors or venture out in a car with closed windows and the air-conditioning on, and then only if the air-conditioning system has a pollen filter.

After a period of high temperatures and low humidity the air becomes dry. This can reduce the moisture of the linings of the nose and lungs, triggering an attack of sneezing or wheezing. A further problem can arise in urban areas after a period of still, calm weather, when, without wind to blow away the airborne pollutants from industry,

BELOW: *It is inadvisable for asthma and hay fever sufferers to go outside before, during and after a storm.*

buildings and traffic, these pollutants reach sufficient density to trigger asthma attacks. Records are kept of air quality which are broadcast daily. A warning of 'poor' air quality indicates a day when it is advisable to stay indoors with the windows shut; when the air quality is given as 'good' you should be safe to garden.

However, even during a time of good air quality the weather must be suitable. On several occasions thunderstorms have been implicated in epidemics of asthma, an abnormally large number of people reporting a sudden onset of symptoms directly before, during, and just after a storm. Research is being undertaken in several parts of the world into what happens during such storms. In some instances there was a marked increase in the number of airborne fungal spores; in another case it appears that the rain and the electrically charged atmosphere caused the pollen grains of rye grass to split, and release large numbers of allergenic starch particles into the air. These starch particles were then inhaled into the lungs and caused asthma attacks in susceptible people. Until the research is complete we won't know the full answer, but in the meantime it is a wise precaution for all asthma sufferers to stay inside, with the windows closed, from the point at which the first rumble of thunder is heard until well after the storm is over.

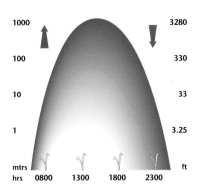

ABOVE: *This chart shows wind-blown pollen rising into the atmosphere during the morning and then descending back to ground level in the early evening. This happens on still, warm, dry days when the best time to enjoy your garden will be from the middle of the day until late afternoon, when the pollen is high up in the sky out of harm's way.*

Time of day

Another factor that determines the best times for the allergy sufferer to work in the garden is the time of day. As the temperature increases during the hours of daylight all surfaces trap the sun's heat and become warmer, and this trapped warmth heats the surrounding air. The warm air rises as a convection current into the upper atmosphere, where it gradually cools and falls back to earth to be reheated. In warm, calm conditions pollen and fungal spores released during the day are carried up by the convection current out of harm's way. However, in the early evening they begin to fall to earth with the cooled air and can then be troublesome. So, on calm, sunny days those allergic to pollen and fungal spores will find that the best time of day to garden will be from late morning to late afternoon.

To discover when is the best time for you personally to be out in the garden, you should first find out what triggers your allergy and then keep a daily diary listing your symptoms and their severity, along with the weather conditions each day. Eventually a pattern should emerge that will help you decide when, and in what kinds of weather, you can work safely in the garden.

BELOW: *In this garden gravel and paving have been used instead of grass and the beds are full of low-allergen ground cover plants, including* Alchemilla mollis, *geraniums and* Stachys byzantina.

Working in the garden

There are some garden features which may harbour allergens, and a number of gardening activities which may exacerbate allergic conditions. Examine whether any features or activities may be a problem and if they are, decide what is the best way of dealing with them. Where a specific activity, such as digging, is unwise because of asthma, the answer may be to find a member of the family, or an enthusiastic gardening friend, to help with this.

Lawns and lawn-mowing

Lawns are a major problem for many allergy sufferers. The grass, unless kept immaculately, will produce pollen but, more importantly, pollen from other plants, fungal spores and dust collects in the spaces between the blades of grass. When the grass is cut the action of the mower disturbs whatever has settled there, and this potent mixture of allergens rises up in a cloud around the gardener and

is almost certain to bring on an attack of asthma or hay fever in anyone who is susceptible. Coumarin, a chemical released by the grass when it is being cut, is another allergen which affects some people. In cases where asthma is brought on by exertion, the effort of lawn-mowing itself may trigger an attack. Grass is also known to cause eczema in a number of people and many of the common weeds found in poorly maintained lawns can also cause skin allergies (see pp.22–5). Mowing grass and, even more so, strimming it, is also fraught with problems for people who suffer from a skin allergy caused by grass or any of the common lawn weeds, as a fine spray of allergic material is flung up around the limbs and may come into direct contact with bare skin.

In short, it is best to eliminate the lawn from the low-allergen garden, as this will remove all the above problems. Paving stones or gravel can replace the lawn in areas to be walked on, and ground cover plants can be introduced where a green cover is wanted.

Digging and weeding

Two unavoidable garden activities, digging and weeding, can lead to overexertion and the onset of an attack of asthma, and neither should be undertaken by an asthma sufferer who is feeling unwell or is physically unfit. Digging will also disturb the fungi and fungal spores within the soil and bring them up to the surface ready to be blown by the wind straight into the nose and down into the lungs. Note also that deep digging can damage the structure of sandy soil. An alternative is to use low-allergen mulches (see pp.33–4) and ground cover plants (see pp.96–9), or to get a kind volunteer to do the digging and weeding.

Hedges

A variety of allergic problems are caused by hedges, depending on the species planted and how the hedge is maintained. Some plants used for hedges – for example, Leyland cypress – are known to cause dermatitis, while others, such as privet, produce pollen which is known to cause asthma and hay fever. The regular clipping of hedges creates very close branching which harbours dust, pollen and fungal spores – all ready to be released when the hedge is pruned. As with lawn-mowing, digging or weeding, the exertion of pruning hedges may also bring on an attack of asthma. All in all, hedges are not recommended for the low-allergen garden and alternatives, as well as safer hedges, are looked at in detail on page 52 to 55.

Bonfires

Burning garden rubbish on a bonfire is not a good idea in the low-allergen garden and in any case there are many local authorities that have bylaws prohibiting it. Smoke is an irritant to asthma sufferers, and if you are allowed

BELOW: *A well-maintained close-clipped hedge provides a trap for pollen and spores, as well as needing a lot of maintenance. Inside the garden is a large specimen of lilac* Syringa vulgaris, *which has scented flowers that can act as a trigger to an attack of asthma or hay fever.*

to light a bonfire and if it really is essential to burn your rubbish then an allergy-free member of the family should take over the task. Light a bonfire only when there is no wind, or when the wind is light and blowing away from the house, and ensure that any family members prone to asthma are inside the building with the windows closed.

Compost-making

Making compost poses a dilemma for the keen gardener who is an asthma or hay fever sufferer. A compost heap provides an excellent, free source of organic matter for the garden soil, but it harbours a high concentration of fungi and fungal spores. A plentiful supply of organic matter is essential to build up the humus in the soil and provide the perfect growing medium for healthy plants. Moreover, waste garden material needs to be put somewhere and a compost heap offers an easy and accessible solution.

The answer lies in how you go about making the compost. One option is to use a closed system rather than an open heap, or at the very least, to cover the compost heap with a mould-inhibiting barrier such as a thick plastic sheet. There are two types of closed systems; one is similar to the conventional heap but uses a bin or barrel with a lid, while the other makes use of worms which are kept in a closed wormery.

Once the compost is ready to use, get an allergy-free household member or a friend to spread the compost on the areas where it is needed. The compost should be forked into the soil and allowed to rot down still further. Any member of the family who is known to be allergic to fungal spores should not undertake any gardening in areas of the garden where compost has been recently spread.

ABOVE: *Wooden compost bins with a fold-back lid which might prove a possible solution for the low-allergen garden, because it will stop fungi and their spores being released in to the atmosphere.*

Mulches

There are two reasons why mulches have become popular: firstly, they restrict weed growth and, secondly, they add organic matter to the soil. A wide range of materials can be used as mulch, depending on which of these two functions is more important. However, many of these cause problems for allergy sufferers, especially the various forms of bark and peat. The bark of some trees, particularly conifers, can give rise to dermatitis (see pp.22–3), and all bark mulches contain fungi and fungal spores, although the less composted the bark the lower the concentration of fungi is likely to be. All organic mulches contain some fungi, but the mulches of nutshells are almost free of them, although, of course, you may be allergic to nuts. Spent mushroom compost is full of fungi and fungal spores and should be kept out of the low-allergen garden.

Black mulching polythene is a good alternative to organic mulches and is an excellent weed suppressant but it does nothing for your soil quality and looks rather unattractive. Gravel is not quite as good for suppressing weeds, but it looks attractive and will not harbour mould. Use a coarse gravel of at least 10mm (½in) size – it is available in standard sizes – and make sure that it is free of fine particles. Mulching polythene covered with gravel will eliminate all weeds beneath it, but this combination is not suitable for all garden areas, as it will eventually compress the soil it covers.

If you are starting a garden from scratch and creating new beds and borders it is worth considering the use of 'green' manure. To do this, begin by sowing the area to be cultivated with a leguminous plant, such as clover, for the season before you start planting. At the end of the season dig the crop into the soil before you plant the border. All leguminous plants trap nitrogen from the air in their tissues, and as the remains of the plants break down this trapped nitrogen is released into the soil, ready to feed the plants that follow. As with all plants decaying in the soil, the crop will break down as compost and finally as humus.

Garden chemicals

It is senseless to plan and plant a low-allergen garden and then spoil your efforts by using a cocktail of garden chemicals to control weeds, pests and diseases. Many chemicals are poisonous and dangerous to handle, and the best policy is to banish as many as you can from the garden. The use of ground cover plants and safe mulches, combined with a little gentle weeding when necessary, should remove the need for weedkillers. Good husbandry, which includes making certain that you choose plants that thrive in the type of soil in your garden and then planting them in their preferred amount of sun and moisture, will usually result in the growth of strong, healthy plants with more resistance to pests and diseases.

Another way to avoid using chemicals is to choose disease-resistant cultivars in plants known to be prone to disease. For example, if you are using bedding roses select those which are resistant to black spot and mildew or use shrub roses, which are particularly resistant to rose pests and diseases. Follow the practice of

BELOW: *A companion planting of climbing roses with alliums. The smell of the alliums acts as a deterrent to many pests and they are also said to help in the control of fungal diseases, particularly black spot.*

organic gardeners and avoid monoculture: mix your decorative plants in beds and borders (doing the same in the kitchen garden) and try using companion planting, which means putting together plants which appear to enhance each other's growth.

There is a selection of organic substances, including pyrethrum, which are sold for the control of common insects pests and diseases and appear to be quite safe and pleasant to use. Fruit trees can suffer from scab and codling moth – no one relishes the thought of finding a caterpillar in an apple – but the choice of scab-resistant varieties and the use of physical controls such as grease bands should help with these problems.

Hostas are suitable plants for the low-allergen garden, but slugs can be a serious problem in that they often completely strip the leaves. Slug pellets are the usual answer but if you want to avoid using these there are some non-chemical methods of controls, including sinking a jar of beer into the ground close to the plant to trap the slugs and surrounding the plants with coarse gravel, which slugs find uncomfortable and so tend to avoid. Some gardeners pour salt on slugs, but I find this a particularly gruesome form of control.

Other extremely common pests that may need controlling are aphids, especially when they smother new shoots. The easiest remedy is to spray them with a weak solution of liquid soap and water, and then wipe them off the plants with your fingers. This book is not long enough to go into all the organic methods of pest and disease control but many excellent sources of advice are available, (see Useful Addresses, p.124).

Low-allergen gardening indoors

If you suffer from an allergy then the problem with plants and outdoor allergens doesn't stop at the garden door but can follow you inside, as houseplants and cut flowers. If a member, or members of the household, have severe allergies to plants then all forms of plants should be firmly kept outside the house. If you do not have a garden, however, and your only chance of gardening may be a windowbox or growing plants indoors, you may want to give it a try.

Houseplants

Great care needs to be taken in choosing houseplants as many are poisonous or allergenic, or both. If you suffer from skin allergies you will need to take especial care in the selection process but, providing you choose the right plants there should be no other plant-related problems. However, for asthma and hay fever sufferers, houseplants pose other problems. The compost in which houseplants are planted can be full of spore-producing fungi and the leaves of the plant can harbour dust. To control the release of fungal spores from the compost cover its surface with gravel and always water from the top of the pot to keep any fungal spores flushed downwards and trapped within the compost in the pot. Regularly wipe the leaves of all houseplants with a damp cloth to keep dust at a minimum.

If you only grow non-flowering foliage plants then there will be no pollen problem, even so it is sensible not to have any houseplants in the bedrooms. Do not grow the weeping fig, *Ficus benjamina*, indoors if you are rubber sensitive. It has no flowers but can cause hay fever and asthma if you suffer from an allergy to latex. Watch your houseplants for any signs of disease which may be due to fungal infection and remove dead and dying leaves at frequent intervals. 'Manky' plants will almost certainly harbour fungi and should be thrown out rather than kept going in the hope that they will improve.

Cut flowers

Cut flowers can cause problems, but a few precautions can remove most of them. In cutting the flowers or foliage you will expose the sap which may be a problem with any plant that causes skin allergies. The arranger can wear gloves for protection, but remember that once in the house, the flowers will be readily accessible to being handled by other members of the family, so avoid using these plants (see Plants to Avoid, pp.112–123). Arranged flowers will be close to nose level so any dust or pollen lying on the petals will be inhaled, including pollens that have been blown onto the plant by their, possibly wind-pollinated, neighbours. Where other members of the family suffer from asthma and hay fever it is a sensible precaution to arrange flowers outside the house. The flowers should be well shaken or rinsed with water to remove all extraneous pollen and dust, and leaves, stems and flowers showing any signs of mould or damaged tissue should be removed. Check the vase to see that it is clean and free from accumulated dust, and then, using fresh water, arrange the flowers before bringing them into the house. A final point, all scented plants must be excluded if they are known to provoke symptoms in an allergic member of the family.

ABOVE: *A group of pot plants inside a conservatory, including abutilons and sedges. The latter plants resemble grass but their pollen is not allergenic.*

DESIGNING
A LOW-ALLERGEN GARDEN

Planning Your Garden

Allergenic Features in the Garden

Any of the following features may be a problem for you or your family's allergies:

close clipped hedges
compost heap
'daisy' flowers
lawn
ornamental grass
piles of grass clippings
scented plants
skin allergen plants
weeds – nettles and plantains
wind pollinated trees

How to create a low-allergen garden

In Part I we looked in detail at the allergies from which gardeners can suffer. Now we need to consider how to design or redesign a garden to avoid or minimize contact with garden allergens and so reduce the risk of an allergic reaction. In fact, designing a low-allergen garden is like designing any other type of garden to the extent that all gardens have certain problems in common. Important among these is the owner's desire for a specific type of garden. The site itself may be problematic, as with a windswept coastal garden, or a downland garden with a very thin topsoil over chalk. The problems involved in creating a low-allergen garden are not necessarily difficult, although if the proposed site also happens to be on the coast and has a thin, chalky topsoil, the answers may take rather longer to find. To make an attractive low-allergen garden you just need to follow a few rules and be particularly careful when selecting plants. But neither of these restrictions should prevent it from being a beautiful and rewarding garden.

Basic decisions

The starting-point is to decide whether you really need a low-allergen garden or if you can solve your problems by simply removing a few particularly allergenic plants. Your decision will depend on the severity of the symptoms affecting you or members of your family, specifically how much they already restrict your use and enjoyment of the garden. As explained in Part 1, begin by finding out as much as you can about what causes allergies in your household and make a list of probable allergens and triggers in your own garden. In addition, it is often just as important to consider potential causes in adjoining gardens, which may require your neighbours' co-operation. The list might include grass pollen, fungal spores and hairy plants, or perhaps all pollens, dust and just chrysanthemums. Naturally, it also helps if you can identify a particular season or type of weather that exacerbates the symptoms.

Make a note of all the plants and features that may be producing the allergens which are causing problems – for example the lawn, the yew hedge, the scented plants by the house, the clump of silver birches in the corner. Next you should decide whether the plant or feature should be removed or whether it can be adapted to be less of a problem – for example, you could cover the compost heap to reduce fungi and their spores. A decision about removing a source of problems should strike a balance between the severity of the symptoms that it provokes and its visual importance to the garden.

BELOW: *This attractive wooden summerhouse would act as an excellent feature in any garden. Here it has been placed next to a large tree, which could easily have acted as a second and competing focal point, but put together they make a complete picture.*

I would find it almost impossible to remove a large oak tree but would have no problems with a scruffy *Lonicera* hedge. If your garden is just an empty patch of soil make your lists of your own or your family members' allergens, but you won't have the worry of removing existing plants or features.

Assessing potential and problems

The next stage in planning a low-allergen garden is the same for any garden. You must inspect the site, and look closely at the soil, to see how well the land drains and establish which areas are in full sun or in partial, or full shade. An analysis of these factors will indicate the types of plants that will grow well in the existing conditions, and which will suffer and possibly die. It is also important to discover from which direction the wind usually blows – that is, which are the prevailing winds, and whether these change with the seasons. For example, the garden might receive westerly winds in spring and summer, and northerly winds in winter. The prevailing winds can be a particularly important consideration in the low-allergen garden as they introduce pollen and fungal spores from the surrounding countryside.

Now look around the garden to see if there are any views extending beyond the boundaries that would be worth retaining or even enhancing by adding a frame of trees or shrubs. At the same time, check for any ugly features, such as a neighbour's satellite dish or an unsightly roofline, that you would like to screen. Try to identify trees in adjoining gardens and decide if they are a potential source of pollen. Note also if your neighbours' compost heaps and bonfire sites are next to your boundary. It may be possible to persuade them to move these further away from your garden.

Functional planning

Next, sit down and decide exactly what you want from your garden. Do you want somewhere to enjoy meals alfresco? Do you need space for entertaining? Would it be good to have room to lie in the sun, or a place for the children to play? You may want an area for growing vegetables or fruit, or even a place to exercise or a tennis court, or just plenty of beds and borders in which to grow your favourite plants. Many combinations of these roles are possible, and indeed every family is different in what it requires of its outside living space. Use the checklist above to decide what you need. If the garden is very small you may have to prioritize your needs by using a points system: say, five points for essential requirements, to one point for something which would be useful but isn't strictly necessary.

Choosing features and plants

Your next task is to make a separate list of the features and plants that you want to include in your new garden. This might include a rose arch, pergola, a water feature or a summerhouse and lots of plants in containers. It is best to compile, or at least discuss, your list with the rest of the family as you all share the garden. If everyone wants a water feature, give it five points; if only one person wants it, give it one point.

It is also worth considering the garden features that none of you want. If, for example, you hate rockeries, or at least the idea of looking after them, omit this from the list of possibilities and agree to remove the rockery if one is already present. It is important to highlight features that need to be excluded as a potential cause of allergies in your family.

Garden Planning Checklist

The following are some of the things which you may want to include in your garden:

FUNCTIONAL AREAS
car parking, compost heap, dustbins, greenhouse, shed, wood/coal store

LEISURE AREAS
barbecue, conservatory, exercise area, play area, room to relax, sandpit, summerhouse, tennis court, terrace

PLANTING AREAS
flower borders, fruit, herb garden, planted pots, raised beds, rose garden, vegetables, wildlife area

FEATURE
arches/pergola, rocks, seats, statues, trellis, water

Designing your low-allergen garden

Next you will need an extending metal rule and a piece of paper no smaller than A3 size so that you can measure your garden and draw up a scale plan of it. It is best to use graph or squared paper as this will enable you to keep your lines straight and make the corners true right angles where necessary. It is relatively easy to measure a simple rectangular garden but for a larger garden, or a more complex site, you may need some help with the surveying. When you draw up your plan, you can use a standard scale – for example, 1:50 – or devise your own scale, perhaps using one square of your graph paper to represent 1m (3ft).

Mark the garden boundaries on the plan and include a plan view of any trees or features that you want to keep, making sure that you draw these to the correct size, particularly the trunk and the canopy of trees. On a corner of the paper outside the boundaries of the garden draw an arrow to show the direction of north; this will help you decide which areas are in sun and which in shade. Mark clearly any good views that you want to retain and how you will frame them, and then any ugly views that you plan to screen. Indicate the position of any items in the neighbouring gardens which may cause allergy problems.

Functional requirements

Once the plan is complete, look for a suitable area for each of the items on your checklist of functional requirements. You will almost certainly want an area for a table and chairs. For convenience this is best sited near a door or French windows leading into the house, and you may need to pave the area to improve access between the two. Any such area should, of course, be placed well away from your or your neighbours' compost heap. Draw a rectangle, square or circle, as appropriate, to represent your garden table and around it place a number of smaller squares to represent chairs. By drawing these to scale you can check that the sitting area is large enough.

Your other needs may well include a children's play area. The position of this will depend on the interests and age of the children. Young children need a relatively small but safe area close to the house with perhaps some paths for tricycles; older children need a large area away from the house, with trees for climbing and perhaps to contain a hideout.

Consider an appropriate space for each of the remaining garden functions, weighing up all the possibilities before you mark the plan. When this task is complete you can start allocating the items on your list of garden features and plants. Flower gardens and formal rose gardens look better close to the straight lines of the house (and terrace or patio, if there is one), whereas wild or woodland gardens belong away from the house and close to the boundary. If you plan to

BELOW: *Plan of an existing garden showing the various elements that may need to be excluded from the proposed low-allergen garden.*

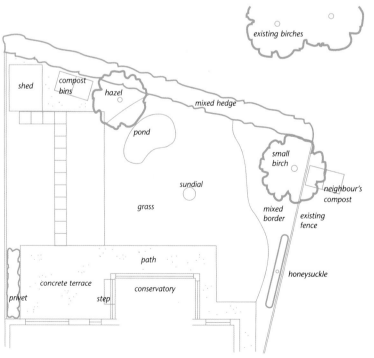

make an artificial pond, it will look most natural if it lies at the lowest point in the garden. A herb garden should be sited near the kitchen door so that you can easily gather herbs for cooking. The next job is to link the different areas with paths. You will now have a functional plan, and what you need to do to complete the picture is to consider the composition of the garden — that is, how the different elements work well individually and together.

Composition

To create a well-designed garden, you need to compose a series of linked 'pictures', each with one of your chosen garden features at the centre. The focal point could be a summerhouse, seat, view, statue or tree. Place each feature carefully so that it can easily be seen across the lawn or paving, or along a path, and keep this view clear of any interruption. If the feature is not bold enough, strengthen the picture by adding extra details – for example, paint the summerhouse or seat white, place the statue on a plinth, or frame the view with a pair of trees. It may be that all you see when you look down your garden is a mass of flowerbeds, shrubs and trees. If so, your problem is a lack of a focal point. Find an attractive seat and place it at the end of the garden in front of shrubs or trees, and see how it brings your garden to life.

Harmony

A harmonious garden is created by a combination of unity and simplicity. Unity is achieved by making the different areas and features of the garden look as if they all belong in the same space, so look for ways to link these elements. For example, try repeating a shape in all areas and details of the garden – circles, squares and rectangles are all comparatively easy to use in this way. For a more informal approach, use generous curves and try to get them to flow around the garden. Using the same paving materials through the garden will also provide a strong visual link. Simplicity means no more than keeping everything simple, and one of the keys to this is repetition. Repeat simple plants, colours, shapes and details.

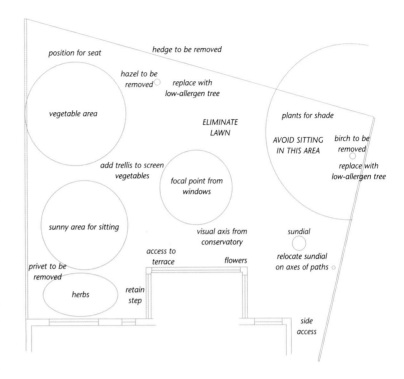

ABOVE: *The functional plan for the garden showing how the different areas might be used.*

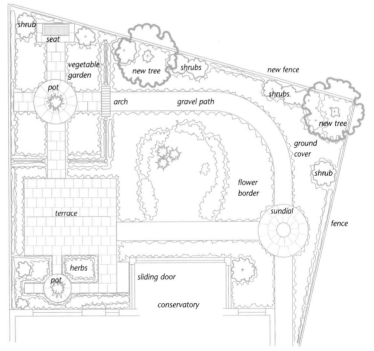

BELOW: *The completed plan for the new low-allergen garden.*

A Town Garden Plan

This plan is for a small town garden for a family with teenage children in which one or more members of the family suffers from allergies. The garden was designed for the National Asthma Campaign and built for the Chelsea Flower Show in 1993, and was the very first low-allergen garden ever created. The colour scheme was bright yellow and deep blue, which was very striking and lent the garden a feeling of warmth and sunshine on even the dullest days. Accordingly, the plants had yellow or green foliage with blue, purple and yellow flowers. The garden features followed the colour scheme, including the paint used for the trellis, gazebo and furniture. The paving, a combination of blue engineering bricks and yellow-buff paving slabs, was chosen to complement the basic choice of colours.

Tranquillity

The space was designed to incorporate a relatively large area of water to provide reflections of the sky and surrounding features in order to give a feeling of tranquillity. The water replaced the traditional lawn as the calm centre of the garden, while the gentle waterfall was added to lend an unintrusive touch of excitement. Generous paved areas allowed room for entertaining, eating outdoors or just relaxing, and an adjacent gazebo provided welcome shade on the hottest days. Painted trellis surrounded the garden, to avoid the use of hedges, and additional trellis within the garden created secret areas just waiting to be explored.

Gravel was used both as a mulch in the planted areas and as part of the surfacing at the rear of the garden, where the pattern of paving slabs and bricks would look too formal. Plants, chosen for their strong shape or elegant habit, were planted in pots and placed on the paved areas to add extra colour and interest. The soil at the top of the pots was covered with gravel to retain moisture and contain any fungal spores.

All the plants selected were low-allergen plants, apart from ceanothus, lupin and wisteria; visitors to the show suggested that these plants caused problems and so they were not used in our subsequent low-allergen gardens. To reduce the need for maintenance, extensive use was made of ground cover plants. These plants often look dull, so care was taken to select cultivars which displayed variegated or coloured leaves and attractive flowers.

BELOW: *The first low-allergen garden designed for the National Asthma Campaign and shown at the Chelsea Flower Show in 1993. The colour scheme of blue and yellow was followed in the paintwork, as well as in the planting.*

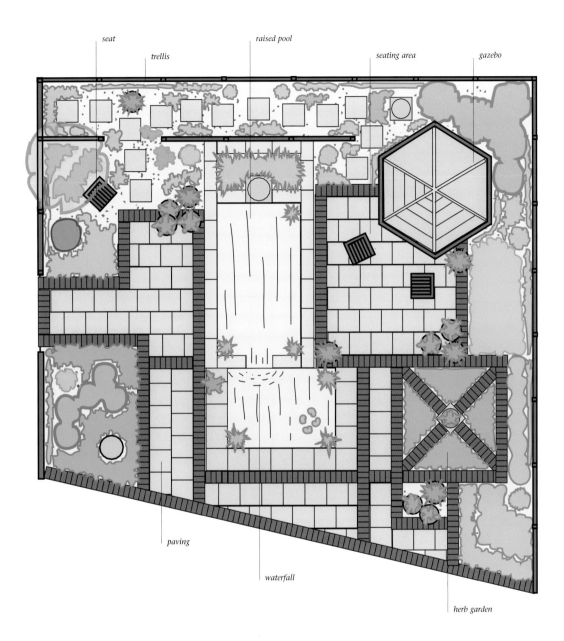

seat

trellis

raised pool

seating area

gazebo

paving

waterfall

herb garden

Adapting the Plan for your Garden

1 The plan is for a garden that measures 9m sq (30ft sq), but it could easily be adapted for a larger space by increasing the size of the planted areas or the secret area at the back, or extending the paving. For a smaller garden you could reduce the size of the paved areas and the pools.

2 The vibrant colour scheme will not suit all tastes and could look out of place against some buildings – for example, a red-brick house. The use of a paler blue, with pink to replace the yellow, would lend a softer look. In the original garden the trellis was backed with painted boards to block out the view of the adjacent gardens, but these could be left unpainted or omitted altogether.

3 The low side trellis with openings was a requirement of the site at Chelsea. This could be readily replaced with taller trellis without openings. The paving to the opening could be removed or left to provide a space for a garden seat.

4 The hexagonal gazebo could be replaced with an enclosed summerhouse or shed, particularly if a lockable store is needed.

5 If you have difficulty in getting electricity into the garden for the water pump, or prefer to have a simpler water feature, keep the top pool but brick in the waterfall lip and put a flowerbed in place of the lower pool.

6 A different choice of plants could be made from among the low-allergen plants on pages 90 to 111.

A Family Garden Plan

This is a functional garden for a family with young children where one or more members, including the children, suffers from allergies. It was designed for the National Asthma Campaign and built for the Chelsea Flower Show of 1994. It incorporated ideas that arose from the first low-allergen garden, and included an exercise area and a fruit and vegetable garden.

The design was based on circles linked with straight lines, the circles forming pools of water and the exercise area. As the site allocated for the garden was on a slope, retaining walls were used to create three level areas that were linked, functionally by steps and visually by waterfalls. The steps' risers were relatively low, at 15cm (6in), to avoid overexertion as the family climb up and down the garden. The colour scheme was based on a combination of muted purples, pinks, plums and grey, which proved to be peaceful and relaxing but could be considered a little dull by some gardeners. The colours were repeated in the paintwork of the fence, shed, walls and seats, and extended to the use of grey paving slabs and plum-coloured paviors.

The exercise area was included in order to provide a safe play space for young children and was just large enough for step or aerobic exercises. Its surface was green rubberized tiles (see Useful Addresses, p.124) similar to those used in public playgrounds. While these make a very comfortable and safe surface, it should be noted that they would not be suitable for a family in which anyone is allergic to rubber.

Space was allocated for a small organic vegetable and fruit garden. This allows the family to grow their own produce while avoiding the risks associated with the use of agricultural chemicals. Herbs were also included, both in pots and in two small areas on the middle level.

The garden was surrounded by a wooden fence to keep out neighbouring dogs and cats, and privacy was ensured by a backing of groups of evergreen shrubs and fruit trees. A gate at the top of the garden led enticingly into the surrounding countryside.

BELOW: *A photograph of part of the low-allergen garden at Chelsea Flower Show in 1994. The shed and fence were painted pale lavender to complement the purple, pink and blue colour scheme.*

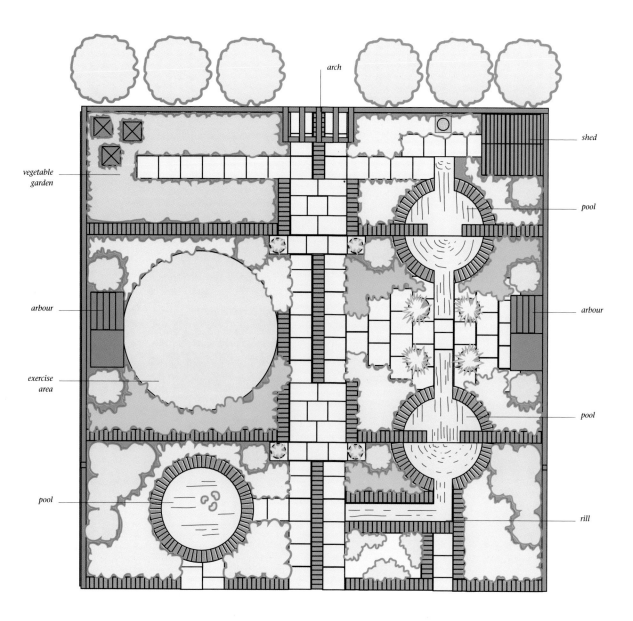

arch

shed

vegetable
garden

pool

arbour

arbour

exercise
area

pool

pool

rill

Adapting the Plan for your Garden

1 The garden measures 10m sq (33ft sq), but it could easily be adapted for a larger space by increasing the width of each level and allowing more room for planting. In a smaller space, omit one of the levels: if you are a keen gardener, leave out the middle level; if you have young children, leave out the lower level.

2 If you have very small children, it would be sensible to omit the water features altogether. Replace the pools with paving slabs on the two lower levels and with a bed of plants on the top level.

3 The plan is for a sloping site but can be readily adapted for a level garden by omitting the steps, walls and waterfalls.

This will be much cheaper and easier to build and maintain, but less exciting.

4 Any colour scheme could be used instead of the muted plums, pinks and purples. You could replace these throughout the garden or you could use a different colour scheme for each level.

5 If the gate at the top of the garden is not a practical feature, an alternative would be to have a seat or statue under the arch.

6 The plants shown can be replaced by those listed on pages 90 to 111. Check your garden's soil, drainage and aspect, and only select the plants that will grow well in the conditions in your garden.

A City Oasis

This plan is for the third and final garden of the trilogy of low-allergen gardens designed for the National Asthma Campaign and built at the Chelsea Flower Show of 1996. The idea was to create an oasis in the centre of a city for a young couple without children, one or both of whom suffers from allergies.

A wall was built around the garden to give a feeling of complete enclosure and protection from the world outside. The wall was rendered and sponge-painted to resemble a yew hedge and to provide an attractive, dark background to the planting. Many city gardens are already enclosed by walls, some of which are very ugly and could well be transformed by rendering and/or painting.

The design was based on a series of curving lines and spirals, which were repeated in the design of the gates, stools and water feature. A simple mosaic with a bubble fountain acted as a focal point, drawing the eye down into the garden and along the one straight line in the garden to the raised platform at the far end. The fountain was made from fourteen stainless-steel tubes of different heights, welded together in a spiral formation. Water was pumped up and out of the top two tubes, to fall gently, filling each of the tubes in turn and creating a feeling of the gentlest of movements and the slightest of sounds. The paving material consisted of a range of cream-coloured concrete paviors, with brick 'slips' for detail which picked up the main flower colours of orange and cream. The steps' risers were rendered and painted dark green to match the walls.

The basic colour scheme was green, orange and cream, which was followed in the walls, paving and mosaic, and in the majority of the planting. Other colours were used, in specific beds, to illustrate colours that can be used with orange. Blue is the complementary colour for orange, and blue flowers were included in one of the borders against the high wall. In another border purple flowers and foliage were used to illustrate the triad of colours – green, orange and purple.

Rosa 'Free As Air' was included as a feature plant as it had been offered to, and named by, the National Asthma Campaign. Several of these roses were planted in the shell-like pots lining the main paths. This variety has a very distinctive colour, with an orange bud which opens to a brown flower and fades to a dusky pink.

BELOW: *The low-allergen garden at the Chelsea Flower Show in 1996.*

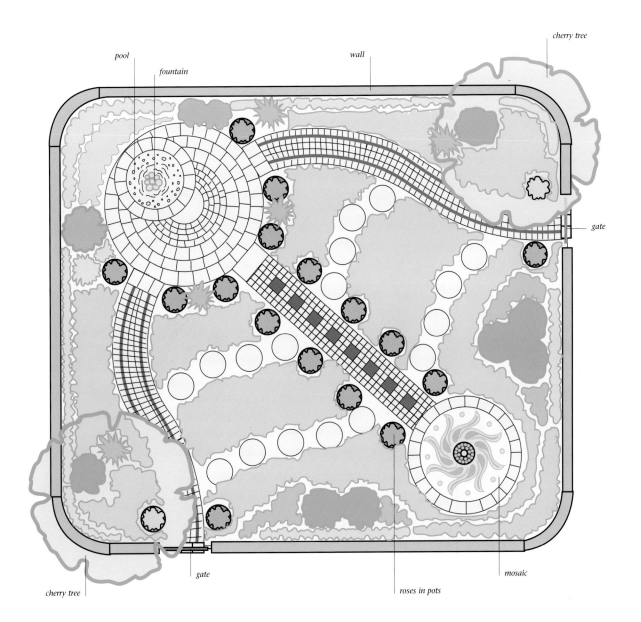

pool
fountain
wall
cherry tree
gate
gate
cherry tree
roses in pots
mosaic

Adapting the Plan for your Garden

1 The garden measures 7.5m (24ft) by 9m (30ft) and can readily be adapted to a variety of different-sized spaces by enlarging the beds and borders. The borders below the high wall and around the platform are rather narrow and would be improved by having more space. It would also be possible to reduce the size of the garden for a smaller plot by decreasing the widths of the paths and the size of the beds.

2 Either of the two gates could be omitted and the side path terminated with a pot or seat. Depending on the position of your house relative to the garden, you could provide access into the garden around the mosaic. Alternatively, the mosaic itself could be replaced by a circle of paving.

3 Although the water spiral is a major feature of the garden, it could be replaced by a statue. Alternatively, if you need room for a table and chairs, you could eliminate the water spiral completely and pave over this area.

4 The paving is quite complicated and a simpler alternative would be to use cream paving slabs for the sitting area and gravel for the paths. Round or square slabs could be incorporated into the gravel, as in the smaller paths.

Horizontal Surfaces

Design of horizontal spaces

When considering the overall layout of the low-allergen garden, the first decision concerns how to cover all the horizontal surfaces. This is important because if you don't cover them nature will – with weeds. These surfaces are the flat areas in which you sit, walk, play and relax. In the majority of gardens the areas for sitting and walking close to the house are usually paved or covered in gravel, and the larger horizontal spaces, away from the house, are grassed. The problem is that, wherever possible, all grass should be eliminated from the low-allergen garden. There may be some horizontal spaces designed to look at rather than walk on, and if so these can be covered with water or low-growing plants instead of grass.

Formal or informal design?

On your functional plan you will have allocated spaces of appropriate size for different activities. The next decision is whether each area should be formal or informal and, if formal, whether planned symmetrically. Formal areas are of regular shapes, and composed of squares, rectangles or circles, whereas informal gardens are usually based on flowing curves. Symmetrically arranged formal areas are laid out with a central line or path and matching shapes arranged on either side of this division. Asymmetry uses the same formal shapes but without the centre line; instead, the squares or circles are arranged haphazardly. Whether you opt for a formal, informal, symmetrical or asymmetrical design is a matter of personal choice, although it is wise to take into account the shape of the garden and any symmetry displayed in the façade of the house. A square-shaped plot in front of a house with a central door and identical windows spaced at regular intervals will be easier to design if you use a formal approach. Conversely, the space connecting an old rambling cottage to a meandering stream will look more natural with flowing curves.

In our first garden at the Chelsea Flower Show we used square shapes, arranged asymmetrically and for the next year's garden there were circles with a central axis and the result was more formal. In a small garden it is better to stick to either symmetrically or asymmetrically formal shapes, whereas in a larger garden you can start with a formal terrace and then lead into informal curves beyond. Remember that you should always start by shaping the horizontal spaces in the garden and not the beds and borders.

BELOW: *A narrow courtyard with a formal pattern of paving slabs and bricks which create strong lines leading the eye to the arched trellis at the end.*

Choosing paving materials

When selecting paving materials you should consider several factors. First, all of the paving you use must be frost-proof and generally durable, and its durability will depend on the amount and type of traffic that will use the area to be paved. The paths around the house will be used heavily whereas a path at the end of the garden may be used only occasionally. In the front garden the paving may have to support a parked car; if so, you should use thick paving slabs or the bricks known as paviors, in each case laying them on a concrete base. Most slabs are frostproof but not all bricks: there are some still available which will shatter in the first cold winter.

The second consideration is that paved areas must be safe to use. When wet, some paving materials become much more slippery than others – indeed some natural stone slabs can be dangerous after rain – and although this may not matter in a distant part of the garden, it can be inconvenient on a regularly used path or terrace. Paving should be laid by a professional craftsman or a competent amateur using the method recommended by the manufacturer of the material. It is important that all paving materials are laid on an appropriate and properly prepared base so that there is no possibility of their becoming uneven and therefore dangerous.

Cost may well be an important factor, but even concrete slabs, which are not expensive, can look attractive if laid correctly and in an interesting pattern. The catalogues produced by paving manufacturers are full of illustrations of how to be creative with paving.

ABOVE: *An old stable yard converted to an attractive enclosed garden, where a range of reclaimed paving materials have been used to create an area in sympathy with the old buildings around.*

BELOW: *A simple brick and gravel detail beneath the pot. The bricks have been individually cut to make each circle.*

Combining materials

In each of the low-allergen gardens designed for Chelsea Flower Show I used a variety of paving materials to create different patterns. For every such garden I select a minimum of two paving materials: a larger type, usually a paving slab, for the main pedestrian areas, and a smaller type, such as a brick or sett, to edge the paved areas or to create a pattern. I then find a loose material, often gravel, to surface less frequently used paths and to fill in odd corners.

When selecting the slab, first check if there are already slabs in the garden; if there are and you like them use more of the same style for any new paved areas. If you want to start afresh, select a slab that complements the style of your house or the external building materials used for it. A neoclassical stone-built mansion will look best with natural stone slabs, a cottage – whether brick, rendered or clapboard – with old bricks, a Victorian red-brick house with a mixture of red bricks and grey-coloured slab, while square concrete slabs laid in a formal pattern are usually the best choice for a modern bungalow. When you have selected your materials for each of your horizontal areas according to their function, you should decide how and in what pattern you are going to lay them.

Grass areas

The use of grass in the form of a mown lawn is extremely widespread in British gardens. Lawn grasses grow superbly well in our soils and in our damp, equable climate and provide us with an ideal flat, green base on which to place the features and plants of our gardens. Grass can be walked on, sat on or played on, and is relatively inexpensive to produce. However, almost all lawn grasses are highly allergenic and if you suffer from asthma or hay fever proximity to a lawn will often make it worse.

In a small garden where one or more family members are allergic to grass it is best to remove the lawn and any other grass areas. Many urban gardens are surrounded by high walls and/or overhanging trees and the grass is frequently too shaded for satisfactory growth, so it may well be no real loss. The green base provided by grass can be replaced with low ground cover plants such as *Vinca minor* and the tranquil effect of a smooth lawn can be replaced by a pool of water. Any areas needed for sitting or for access can be covered with paving or gravel.

The removal of all grass may be quite feasible in a small suburban garden but in a larger, rural one it can be a massive undertaking involving a daunting expenditure. Indeed the lawn plays an essential part in the country garden and, even when a sufferer's allergy to grass is severe, it may be decided that some of the lawn must remain, to preserve a garden's character.

BELOW: *This small area of closely mown grass makes a calm, green centre to the garden. However, in the low-allergen garden the grass should be removed and replaced with paving and low ground cover plants.*

Low-allergen lawns

So what can you do about the lawn in a low-allergen country garden? With a little effort you can allow it to stay. First, look at the reasons why grass is a problem and see if you can minimize these. Bear in mind that although grass produces large quantities of allergenic pollen, it does so only if it is able to flower. Therefore, if the lawn is mown at regular intervals so that no flowers can develop, the problem should be solved. Another difficulty is that the flat surface of a lawn traps masses of fungal spores, as well as the pollen from other plants, and when the grass is cut these are disturbed and released. The only answer is for a non-allergic member of the family to cut the grass, while all allergy sufferers stay indoors. If all family members are allergic to pollen and fungal spores you will have to find someone outside the family to do the job.

A further problem is that the debris trapped at the base of the grass, which will include old grass clippings, provides a host to some of the nastier fungi. The risk of this causing an allergic reaction can be reduced by making sure that you remove all the cut grass from the lawn when mowing and regularly rake the grass to remove any other waste material. Finally, the blades of grass themselves can cause eczema in some people, and if you are susceptible you should avoid sitting on the grass or walking on it barefoot.

Play areas

When we built our first low-allergen garden at the Chelsea Flower Show we used water and paving, instead of grass, to cover the horizontal spaces. As a result, I was confronted by several mothers who asked where their children could play in such a garden.

ABOVE: *The rubberized tiles used in the 1994 Chelsea Flower Show garden form a hard-wearing, safe play surface.*

This prompted me to look for suitable low-allergen, non-grass materials for play areas. In the following year's garden I included an exercise and play area which was covered in rubber tiles similar to those used in children's playgrounds (see Useful Addresses, p.124). This material is not normally seen in the domestic garden, but there is no practical reason why it should not be used, although great care is required when laying the tiles.

There is a wide range of colours from which to choose, and for the Chelsea Flower Show garden I chose tiles in a dull green colour which worked well as a foil to the plants in the surrounding beds. This material can alternatively be laid as a single sheet. The benefit of using a rubberized material in tile or sheet form is that it forms a hard-wearing, safe play surface which is comfortable to walk on and which can be washed easily to remove all traces of dirt, pollen, fungal spores and animal waste. However, there are two drawbacks. The first is that the material is expensive. The other problem is the possibility that an allergic child will prove allergic to rubber too. This 'latex' allergy affects a substantial proportion of the population and you should not use this material until you have had children checked medically for the condition.

Other alternatives to grass for play areas include artificial turf, which is used in 'all-year-round' tennis courts and playing areas. This is particularly appropriate for areas which are to be used for playing games rather than for fixed play equipment such as climbing frames and slides. Where these are used, sand provides an inexpensive low-allergen alternative to grass or rubber tiles. The sand needs to be of the non-staining kind, with fine, rounded grains so that it drains freely, and it must be laid to a depth of 30cm (12in) on a coarse, free-draining gravel. The only problem will be that cats will use the sand as a toilet, and for this reason you may need to fence the play area.

Vertical Features

Containment and enclosure

All gardens need some vertical elements for a sense of scale, to create interest and to define boundaries that divide the garden into separate areas. These elements include arches, fences, hedges, pergolas, pillars, screens, trellis and walls. Trees also provide vertical height and interest, but not usually in such structured form as the other methods of division. On your survey plan (see p.40) you will have marked existing vertical elements, including trees, and added their height and condition. The planning stage is the time to decide which kinds of additional vertical elements you need or want.

Boundaries

The first elements to consider are any structures that define the boundaries of the garden. It is not always obvious whose these are, but it is important to establish your ownership before doing anything to them. If they are your property you need to find out if the structures are in good condition or need replacing. Also check whether they form a barrier that will keep out animals, particularly dogs and cats. In addition to preventing neighbouring pets soiling or damaging your garden, it is important to exclude them if a member of your family is allergic to animal dander. If you have had to get rid of the pet because of an allergy you will not welcome your neighbour's cat or dog shedding hairs all over your children's play equipment or your garden furniture. As for the height of boundary structures, you may need to increase this to give you privacy or to screen ugly views.

In country gardens boundaries are often formed by hedges, and if a hedge poses an allergy problem to one of the family (see pp.54–5) you may decide to replace it with a fence. In the low-allergen garden the most practical boundary structures are fences and walls. Both fences and walls should be capable of keeping out neighbouring animals and keeping in yours, and, of course, young children. They can also be constructed to be rabbit-, fox- and deer-proof, which may be a necessity in some areas of the country.

BELOW: *This open picket fencing with an interesting finial detail, makes a secure boundary but allows views in and out of the garden.*

Dividing a garden

The vertical elements that are used to divide a garden into a number of separate sections can be seen as defining or even emphasizing different areas. Walls of brick or stone create these divisions effectively and durably, and in some cases exist as long-established and mellow features. However, nowadays walls are expensive to build, so wooden fences and trellis, or hedges, are more often used.

Fences come in a range of styles and sizes, from 1.8m (6ft) high panels of closeboard positioned to mark boundaries to simple picket fencing suitable for surrounding a lawn or herb garden. Panel and post fences are usually made of wood and can be treated with a protective agent such as creosote or, if the wood is already treated, stained any colour. Picket fences may be similarly treated and coloured, although when purchased they may be already painted with gloss paint if they are made of planed wood.

A trellis is more ornamental than a fence, although the construction and material usually make it less durable. It is ideal for enclosing the more formal features of the garden, such as part of a terrace or a rose garden. In ready-made form trellis ranges from the simple to the elaborate and expensive, but a basic trellis can be made up quickly and cheaply by the competent amateur. Whatever the design, the whole structure must be supported on strong posts properly set into the ground so that it is completely stable. Trellis can be treated or stained, or painted if the wood is planed, and used to provide an excellent support for climbing plants or wall shrubs.

Use of climbing plants

Climbing plants can be used to clothe and soften walls, fences, trellis, arches and pergolas, any of which may be important visually in gardens where hedges have been removed. These plants provide colour and a contrast in texture when used on a free-standing structure, or when supported by a wall above other plantings. Great care needs to be taken in the selection of climbers as many are either allergens or triggers for allergies. One of our most useful evergreen climbers, ivy, is an allergenic plant which causes dermatitis (see p.116) and may need to be excluded from the low-allergen garden. Sadly, there is a wide range of beautiful climbers, such as wisteria, honeysuckle and jasmine, which are heavily scented and therefore implicated as asthma triggers. Climbing roses are fine unless they are scented or if you are allergic to rose thorns. Other climbers – for example, solanums – have poisonous berries which are very attractive to children.

However, there are some attractive climbers which are unlikely to cause problems, including Virginia Creeper, the climbing hydrangea, *Hydrangea anomala* and *Parthenocissus quinquefolia*. Both of these will spread up a high wall without the need of support by wires or trellis. Unfortunately, both are deciduous, although the hydrangea's leaves emerge very early in spring. Among the recommended evergreen climbers is the self-clinging *Pileostegia viburnoides*, but note that this is very slow growing. Another good choice is the winter-flowering evergreen clematis, *Clematis cirrhosa*, provided you can give it some support and a warm, sunny wall. There are some useful and attractive non-scented honeysuckles, such as *Lonicera sempervirens*, which is evergreen and has bright red flowers with yellow centres in summer. Recommended

ABOVE: *Wattle fencing creates a rustic feel and forms a complete visual barrier.*

BELOW: *The roses 'Handel' and 'Climbing Iceberg' trained over an arched seat. Both roses have little scent so are suitable for the low-allergen garden.*

ABOVE: Clematis montana *adding to the visual pleasure of a trellis screen.*

climbers for the low-allergen garden are given on pages 100 to 101. If it proves difficult to find a suitable climber, another option is to use a wall shrub, such as pyracantha or cotoneaster, and train it against the wall or fence.

Hedges

It is usually best to exclude hedges from the low-allergen garden as their close branching, although good for a visual barrier, provides a perfect harbour for fungal spores and pollen, which collect throughout the year until the hedge is cut, when they float into the air and can enter the nostrils. A similar problem is caused by a strong wind, which will disturb the branches of the hedge and release the accumulated matter. The thicker and denser the hedge the greater the potential hazard for asthma and hay fever sufferers.

As well as harbouring troublesome spores, many of the most popular hedging plants are allergenic. Privet pollen is a major allergen and just the scent of its flowers can trigger an attack of asthma. Holly and Leyland cypress cause skin allergies. Yew is wonderful to look at but contains quantities of dust and its berries are very poisonous. The pollen of beech and hornbeam can cause asthma and hay fever, although there may be less risk with these hedges as they require freqent clipping which prevents the production of flowers and pollen. Finally, since physical effort can trigger an asthma attack in some people, cutting hedges can be a problem.

Dealing with hedges

If you already have hedges in your garden, consider carefully whether they are causing a problem for you or any member of your family. If they are, you may decide that it is best to lose them, although in conservation areas hedges are covered by tree preservation orders (see p.82) and, if they exceed a certain size, you may need planning permission to remove them. Unfortunately, this permission will not be granted on medical grounds. However, if a hedge is in good condition and providing enclosure where it is needed, you may decide to compromise by retaining it and asking a non-allergic member of the family, or a friend, to cut it.

If there are no hedges in the garden think very carefully before planting any, particularly if younger members of the family have severe asthma, hay fever or eczema. If you want to divide the garden with an attractive green line, use a fence or trellis covered in climbers or consider a line of shrubs and leave them unpruned. Shrubs will have the effect of a hedge but will not be as formal, as you will be unable to create the neatness of a clipped hedge by pruning and they will also take up more room.

Where the non-allergic gardener would use box – another problem species as it is poisonous and its scent can trigger asthma attacks – as a low-growing edging plant, try instead a row of hebes or wall germander, *Teucrium chamaedrys*.

Low-Allergen Hedging Plants

The following shrubs can be planted in rows to form hedges which do not need regular clipping, just the occasional tidying up:

LOW HEDGES
height under 45cm (18in)
 Hebe rakaiensis
 Hyssopus officinalis
 Teucrium chamaedrys
 Thymus vulgaris

TALLER HEDGES
height from 90cm (3ft) to
1.5m (5ft)
 Cotoneaster simonsii
 Potentilla fruticosa
 Prunus x cistena
 Pyracantha rogersiana
 Rosa glauca
 Rosmarinus officinalis
  'Miss Jessopp's Upright'
 Symphoricarpos x doorenbosii
  'White Hedge'

LEFT: Alchemilla mollis *used to edge a border instead of box or lavender, which are not suitable for the low-allergen garden.*

Water in the Garden

Water features

Whether it is natural or artificial, a water feature enhances any garden. When flat and still it is a haven of tranquillity and can provide pleasing reflections; when moving, particularly as a fountain or waterfall, it brings vitality, sparkling light and sound. On hot days it gives welcome coolness, whereas in deepest winter it is transformed into an enchanting expanse of ice or hanging icicles. Water also provides the habitat for a wide range of plants which would not grow elsewhere in the garden.

While many consider water an essential ingredient in the design of their garden, others see only the problems associated with it and dismiss the idea. Nevertheless, water in various forms can be a valuable feature in the low-allergen garden for several reasons. It can replace the lawn if necessary, providing a still, calm centre, as in the first low-allergen garden that we designed for the Chelsea Flower Show. In that garden the pool-sides and base were painted black, although with hindsight I feel green might have created a more peaceful effect. Moving water in the form of a waterfall or fountain can provide a focal point for a garden and, more specifically, bring interest to an expanse of lifeless paving. A pond or pool also gives you the opportunity to enjoy fish and other aquatic life, and this may be a good idea if allergy has led to furry animals being banned from the home. It may not be possible to cuddle a goldfish, but keeping fish gives a child the chance to learn about caring for other living creatures.

When we designed the very first low-allergen garden we sought advice on whether any types of water feature might be a problem for allergy sufferers. The only real risk we could discover was that vigorous fountains and waterfalls might create localized air disturbance and cause pollens and fungal spores to move around more vigorously, but even this possibility remains unproven. Nevertheless, it is probably sensible, as well as less costly, to install a relatively simple fountain or waterfall rather than try to imitate Icelandic geysers or create a miniature Niagara Falls.

If you are lucky enough to have a garden with a natural water feature, such as a stream or pond, all you may

BELOW: *A simple circular pool with rill set in a cobbled surround decorated with plants.*

need to do is clear the view, provide access to the water and do some planting along the banks. However, if you have no natural water feature available but would like to introduce one, you must think about which type is most suitable for you and your garden. Start by making a list of why you want water. Is it for movement? To reflect the sky? For sailing model boats? To grow water plants and marginals? For keeping and breeding goldfish or koi carp? You will then be able to decide whether a pool, fountain or waterfall will best meet your needs. It is also sensible at an early stage to make two further decisions: where in the garden do you want to place the water feature and how much are you prepared to spend on it?

Pools and ponds

The terms 'pool' and 'pond' tend to be used rather arbitrarily for any small area of water. I use the first to refer to a constructed water feature which is usually, although not always, formal in shape. Pools can be set flat in the ground or raised above their surroundings and may contain plants and/or fish and other aquatic life, but can still give pleasure without any of

these. Pools may be enhanced by the addition of a fountain or fountains, and two adjacent pools, at different levels, may be linked by a waterfall.

ABOVE: *A circular pool with central feature in the dry garden at RHS Wisley gardens, Surrey, designed by Julie Toll.*

To my mind, a pond is a natural area of water, usually informal in shape, and never raised but rather set down in the lowest part of the garden, preferably in a natural hollow in which drainage water collects. Ponds are almost always planted with a range of water plants, including oxygenating and floating plants such as duckweed. These plants help to control the algae which are a by-product of any pool or pond. When properly maintained, a pond can also provide a habitat for fish and other aquatic life.

Fountains and waterfalls

Movement in the garden is very effectively provided by fountains and waterfalls. Fountains can range from a single jet bubbling out of the surface of a pool to multiple jets swirling many metres into the air. Waterfalls vary in the amount of water that falls and this depends on the width of the lip over which the water drops and the depth of the water on the lip. The amount can be a slow trickle or a torrent, and ranges from a single fall between two ponds to a whole series of falls in the form of a cascade. Provided you have access to a reliable water supply and

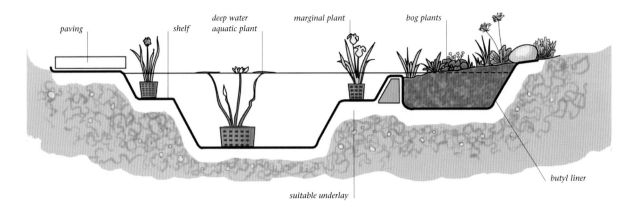

paving

shelf

deep water
aquatic plant

marginal plant

bog plants

butyl liner

suitable underlay

ABOVE: *A cross-section through a butyl-lined pond to show the position of deep water lilies, a shallow shelf for marginal plants and an adjacent bog garden kept moist from the overflow of the pond.*

electricity to provide power for a pumping system, many impressive effects are possible. The rest is a matter of your imagination and, if you choose to construct a fountain or waterfall yourself, plenty of hard work.

Keeping water clear

Water is a wonderful medium for the garden, but it does bring its own problems of a practical rather than allergenic nature. The main problem is that it attracts algae, which arrive in the air currents and drop into the water, where, if the water is warm enough and there is even a small amount of nutrients, they multiply very rapidly. The result is a pea soup of green algae or a cover of blanketweed. Neither of these improves the look of a water feature, although they are not harmful nor, to date, regarded as allergens. Before finally committing yourself to installing any water feature you must consider how you will control the algae. There are various methods, including chemical treatments, filtration, physical removal and competition from other plants and you should seek specialist advice as to which is the best for your water feature.

Planting a water garden

For many gardeners the only reason for having a pond in their garden is to enable them to grow water plants. Some gardeners will be interested in just one or two specific plants such as water lilies or water irises, others will want to grow the full range from deep water aquatics and floating plants to marginals and even bog plants. If you want to grow water lilies, you must first consider their size, as they vary from the tiny *Nymphaea odorata* var. *minor*, which needs a water depth of just 30cm (12in) and can be planted in a small water barrel, to the giant *Nymphaea* 'Gladstoniana', which will grow in water as deep as 2–2.4m (6–8ft) and needs plenty of room to grow. If you want to grow a large range of plants the ponds need to be carefully planned allowing a ledge of 22.5cm (9in) below the water level around at least part of the edge of the pool for placing marginal plants, and an expanse of water of at least 45cm (18in) and preferably 60cm (24in) deep in the centre for water lilies.

A well planned pool may also solve the problem of algae as the plants will compete for the available nutrients and sunlight. For a completely balanced pond you will also need to add some oxygenating plants.

Most water plants are insect-pollinated and can be included in the low-allergen garden. However, there are a few problem plants which need to be checked against you or your family's allergies before planting. These include water plantain, *Alisma plantago-aquatica*, whose tubers can cause irritant dermatitis; the common yellow water iris, *Iris pseudacorus*, whose sap can irritate the skin and which is also mildly poisonous; and the elegant arum lily, *Zantedeschia aethiopica* and the water arum *Calla palustris*, both of which are mildly poisonous. The last two only need to be excluded if there are small children in the family. Some water lily cultivars and the water hawthorn *Aponogeton distachyos* are scented, but this should not be a problem when planted in the middle of the pond away from susceptible nostrils.

Child safety

Whether you are planning to create a water feature in your garden or you have acquired a garden where one is already present, you must consider the question of safety. A number of children drown each year in garden pools and ponds, and a toddler can drown in just several centimetres of water. If your household contains babies or young children it is wisest to eliminate existing water features, and postpone plans for adding them, until they are old enough to look after themselves. However, some water features are safe, even for the youngest child, and these include fountains playing on to pebbles which conceal a sump of water containing the pump. Provided you use pebbles which are too large for a child to swallow, you could incorporate one of these attractive and restful features in your garden.

Where there is an existing water feature which cannot be removed or temporarily filled in, such as a natural stream or pond, fencing it off from young children is often the safest course of action. Alternatively, if a stream is not visually important it can be culverted, while an unwanted pond can be deliberately silted up and turned into a bog garden. These safety measures may seem extreme and may require planning permission – you should inform the local authority or the Environment Agency of your intention – but they are worth considering for your peace of mind.

Low-Allergen Plants for Ponds

DEEP WATER AQUATICS
These plants grow in the deeper water at the centre of the pond:

> *Hottonia palustris*
> *Nymphaea* spp. (all but
>   scented cultivars)
> *Nymphoides peltata*

FLOATING PLANTS
These plants float on the surface of the water:

> *Azolla filiculoides*
> *Hydrocharis morsus-ranae*
> *Stratiotes aloides*
> *Trapa natans*

MARGINAL PLANTS
These plants grow with their roots covered by water at the edge of ponds:

> *Butomus umbellatus*
> *Houttuynia cordata*
> *Mimulus luteus*
> *Myosotis scorpioides*
> *Pontederia cordata*
> *Sagittaria sagittifolia*
> *Veronica beccabunga*

LEFT: *This exciting aerated fountain falling over large flints makes a water feature that is safe for babies and small children.*

PLANTING
A LOW-ALLERGEN
GARDEN

Planning and Planting

Selecting plants

When your overall garden plan is complete you can enjoy planning which plants you are going to use in each planted area, in the beds and borders. Beds can be viewed from all sides, like rose beds in a rose garden. Borders have a backing structure, such as a wall or fence, and are viewed only from the front or sides, like the traditional herbaceous border.

As with horizontal spaces in the garden, beds and borders can be formal or informal in shape, but for the most pleasing effect their shapes must relate to those of the spaces surrounding them. Formal beds and borders can be square, round, rectangular or even L-shaped. Informal beds and borders have gentle curves and may be irregular in outline. The choice of formal or informal planting areas may also depend on the overall style of your garden and house. The plants they will contain should also play a part in determining the shape of the borders and beds. For example, roses, herbs and bedding plants usually look more attractive in formal shapes, while shrubs and mixed planting are better suited to informal borders. But don't worry: there are no hard and fast rules, so if you want to grow herbs and roses in informal drifts there is no practical reason why you shouldn't.

Once you have decided on the shape of your beds and borders, the next step is to check that the soil, aspect and drainage in your garden are suitable for the kinds of plants you wish to grow. Note that this choice is a matter of personal preference and that, even if the conditions are not perfect for the plants you favour, there are a number of ways around such problems. For example, if you want to grow acid-loving plants, such as azaleas and rhododendrons, and your soil is neutral or alkaline, you can plant them in pots of lime-free soil and place them on a terrace in just the right amount of sun or shade. Consider each border or bed in turn and choose the range of plants you want to include, and also decide on a colour scheme and the period of the year when you want these areas to be at their most interesting.

In all the low-allergen gardens I have designed for public display I have had to exclude every plant that might cause an allergic reaction in any susceptible person, so the choice of plants in some areas was extremely restricted. However, in your garden you will need to omit only those plants to which you, or any members of your family, are known to be allergic, and those plants which are known to cause problems to everybody. Rue is a good example of the kind of plant that I would not use in any garden. It can cause the skin allergy, photodermatitis (see p.23) in almost anyone who handles the sap in bright sunlight, whether or not they suffer from other allergies. If a member of your family is extremely sensitive, and this applies particularly to young children, it is prudent to exclude all the plants listed on pages 112 to 123.

Maintenance

Before making final decisions on which plants to use in your garden it is worth considering the amount of time you have available for maintenance of all the proposed planted areas. All beds and borders need looking after, although the

FORMAL BEDS

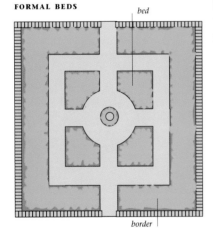

INFORMAL BORDER

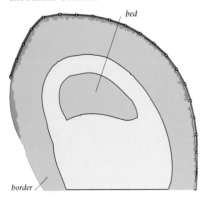

TOP: *A formal arrangement of beds in a square garden;* **ABOVE:** *An irregularly shaped garden with an informally shaped bed and surrounding border.*

amount of work varies widely. The jobs that require doing range from annual weeding for an established area of ground cover plants to a more vigorous weekly hoeing of the herbaceous border, plus tying-in and deadheading if you want a top-quality border.

When you are at the preliminary stages of planning a low-allergen garden it is important to note when the maintenance would need to be done and to plan accordingly. In this way you can avoid having to work outside during periods when the pollen or fungal spore count is high. If you can include planted areas which require the most attention in the early spring, before the first tree pollens start to fly but after the coldest weather, you should be able to enjoy your gardening without problems at this time of year. Fruit trees and roses need pruning in the winter months, so it is worth considering planting these, along with ground cover plants that require an annual clean around the same time. Bear in mind that roses also need feeding in early spring and spraying in summer, and that the latter task could be handed over to a less allergic member of the household. Keeping a careful diary of your symptoms, as suggested earlier, will allow you to see which time of year will be the best for you to garden, and will help you to plan your planted areas accordingly.

ABOVE: Penstemon 'Garnet' is a lovely plant for the low-allergen garden.

Finally, one good thing about maintenance is that looking after plants which are your special favourites can be considered part of your leisure time, whereas having to tend to plants or garden features which don't bring you much pleasure feels like a chore. So, if you dislike rockeries, roses or vegetables, get rid of them and keep only the plants and features you really enjoy.

Planting plans

The best way to work out the planting scheme for each area is to put plants together which enjoy the same conditions and then to plant them in large enough groups of one plant for the clump to make a strong visual impact. Start by making a list of possible plants, checking carefully against the list on pages 112 to 123 that these are low-allergen as far as the problems affecting you and your family members are concerned. Choose plants for the colour scheme and period of year already selected. It is also a good idea to add the heights of the plants and a note of leaf, as well as flower colour to your list.

Scale plans

To draw a scale plan of the border I always use a scale of 1:50, but you can use any scale, provided it is large enough to allow you to label all the plants clearly. Using a pencil, so that you can erase mistakes, draw circles to represent individual plants, filling the bed with circles and leaving no spaces. The size of the circle denotes the space needed for that particular plant. Regardless of their ultimate spread I aways draw circles with a diameter of 45cm (18in) for most ground cover and medium-sized herbaceous plants; 60cm (2ft) for larger herbaceous plants, very vigorous ground cover, bedding roses and small shrubs; and 1m (3ft) for medium shrubs and shrub roses. I plant large shrubs 1.5m (5ft) apart. Put a cross or dot in the centre of each circle to indicate the planting position for each plant.

When you have filled the bed or border with circles, decide how large each group of plants will be. I always use at least five plants together of the 45cm (18in) size or three plants of 60cm (2ft) and one plant of 1m (3ft). This '5:3:1' rule ensures that each plant has equal impact within the planted area. It is a good method for ornamental planting, but if you are planning ground cover planting, consider placing at least 10 plants in each group and, if you want to make your task even easier, try using much bigger groups or drifts of a single species. Once you have decided on the size of group you are going to use then start outlining groups of circles as shown in the plan on page 67. You can have clumps or lines or drifts, it is entirely up to you, but divide up the whole bed or border into groups before you begin deciding where each plant on your list is going to go.

BELOW: *Recently planted heathers with plenty of space between them to allow for growth.*

You will need to check the heights of your chosen plants with the width of your bed or border. This is because another widely accepted rule states that the height of any plant, when in flower, should not exceed the width of a border or half the width of a bed. Therefore, if your border is, say, 1.5m (5ft) wide, the tallest plant should not be higher than this when in full bloom. The only exception is climbers trained against the wall; these can be as tall as you wish.

Filling borders and beds

Now take your list of selected plants and place them in the border, writing a plant name in pencil in each group of circles. I always start with the front row of plants, using the lowest-growing plants from my list. These are the most important plants visually as they are visible throughout the year. By contrast, plants in the middle or at the back of a border tend to be partly covered by the plants in front of them. Select plants with dense foliage for the front row so that the planting will look attractive before and after the flowers have had their period of glory. This also prevents weeds appearing and so reduces the amount of maintenance needed. Work along the border, alternating colours within your colour scheme. If you are planning a border in front of a wall on which you plan to grow climbers, these are the next plants to be placed. Less vigorous climbers should be spaced 2m (6½ft) apart and stronger varieties 3m (10ft) apart.

The next job is to place the plants in the middle and back rows. Plants selected for the middle rows should be taller than those in the front row and should be selected for maximum visual impact. This means colour impact in most ornamental borders, but it might be bold foliage in a bed of shrubs or ground cover. I use plants with large flowers, such as peonies, roses and phlox, or plants with brightly coloured foliage, such as the golden-leaved cornus. This is also the position in which to place roses in a mixed border. Plants in the back row should be the tallest and one approach is to select them for the attractive shape of their flowers, which will be seen standing up above the rest of the planting. Here the blue spikes of delphinium are very useful. Alternatively, back-row plants can be chosen as a foil to the rest of the planting in the border. A good example is the cloudy effect produced by gypsophila or macleaya.

To plan a bed, you follow almost the same process you use for the borders. The difference is that low plants should go all round the edges of the bed, with the medium plants forming a rough circle inside the low plants, and the tallest plants should fill the centre.

When you have filled up your bed or border with plant names, use coloured pencils to colour in each group with the approximate colour of the flowers. This will show you whether the colours are balanced and you can then move plants around until the colours look right. Coloured pencil is not easy to erase, so if you want to experiment with different colour schemes you can rub out the plant names on the plan, write in their replacements and then lay a sheet of tracing paper, appropriately coloured in, over the plan. It is much easier to move names and colours around on paper than plants around in the garden.

If the purpose of the planted area is to provide low ground cover, choose plants with attractive foliage, and select some cultivars with variegated or coloured leaves to add interest, rather than selecting plants for their flowers. Use large groups of each plant and alternate green and variegated plants through the bed. You will get the best effect by either using plants of the same height for all of the planting or increasing the height slightly in the middle.

Planting schemes

In the next section I look at a range of planting schemes for use in different parts of the garden depending on whether the area is in sun or shade, and whether the soil is dry, moist or permanently damp. In each bed or border I have used a different and distinctive colour scheme. Many of these ideas have been tried out in the low-allergen gardens that I designed for the Chelsea Flower Show and in the garden at Capel Manor, Hertfordshire, south England. You should be able to use these plans in your own garden by adjusting the dimensions to fit your beds and borders, and perhaps adding some of your own favourite plants. All the planting shown is based on the spacing of plants described above and follows the rules I have given.

Planting Checklist

For each bed or border in your garden decide the type of plant to use, which season of interest you require and a colour scheme.

TYPE OF PLANT

alpines	mixed border
bog plants	roses
ground cover	shade lovers
herbaceous border	shrub border

SEASON OF INTEREST

spring – bulbs	autumn colour
spring – bedding	winter flowers
summer – bedding	winter evergreens
summer – mixed border	

COLOUR SCHEME

pink and blue	yellow and orange
pink and purple	yellow and purple
blue and cream	yellow and green
green and white	bright reds

Border for a Sunny Site

ABOVE: *Full sun and fertile, well-drained soil provide ideal conditions for the golden-yellow* Kerria japonica. *This graceful shrub is best positioned at the back of the border.*

In most gardens there is at least one area on which the sun shines throughout the day, and where this site is backed by a wall or fence there is the opportunity to create a sunny border. When soil is exposed to the sun it will rapidly heat up and the surface will become dry. Luckily, there are many attractive plants that thrive in dry, sunny positions, so planning borders for such sites is not difficult. In gardens protected from cold winds, a border set against a wall warmed by direct sun should allow you to grow plants that are usually considered too tender for the rest of the surrounding area.

Colour schemes

You should start by deciding on a colour scheme, and with a sunny site there are many possibilities from which to choose. One of my favourite combinations is yellow intermingled with purple and blue, which was the colour scheme used throughout the low-allergen garden at the Chelsea Flower Show of 1993. You can use these colours in several ways. For a gentle, soft effect use grey foliage and pale yellow, blue and lilac flowers, a mixture that is particularly effective in a herb garden. For greater impact use bright yellow with deep blue and purple flowers, and add golden foliage. Leave out the purple and add more blue flowers and you can achieve a border similar to the one illustrated opposite.

For strong colour impact use gold and bronze foliage and bright yellow, orange and red flowers; this will really 'sizzle' on a hot sunny day. Or you can go for a traditional border using pink and pale blue flowers and lots of grey foliage. Plants with grey foliage naturally grow in dry, sunny places. This greyness is often due to the presence on the leaves of white hairs which protect the surface from losing excessive moisture during hot weather. A word of warning: these hairs may irritate the skin of sensitive individuals, so before deciding to include grey-leaved plants check whether you may be allergic to their hairs.

There are many plants that would prefer not to be planted in dry, sunny places and these include most plants with large, glossy leaves. Plants of this description usually like moist soils and partial shade and should be omitted from the sunny border.

To copy the plan illustrated on the opposite page, use the plants shown or substitute plants from Plants to Use, see pp.88–111. Plan the layout of your border as explained in the last chapter, taking care to balance colours, numbers of plants and heights.

BELOW: *Bringing together harmonious colours of purple, pink and white creates a restful feel in this sunny border.*

A YELLOW AND BLUE SUNNY BORDER

Here is a plan for a sunny border mainly consisting of plants with yellow and blue flowers. The plants chosen will thrive in a well-drained neutral to alkaline soil, but can also survive in a wide range of conditions. The flowers appear from late spring through to late summer, and the rose will go on flowering into the autumn.

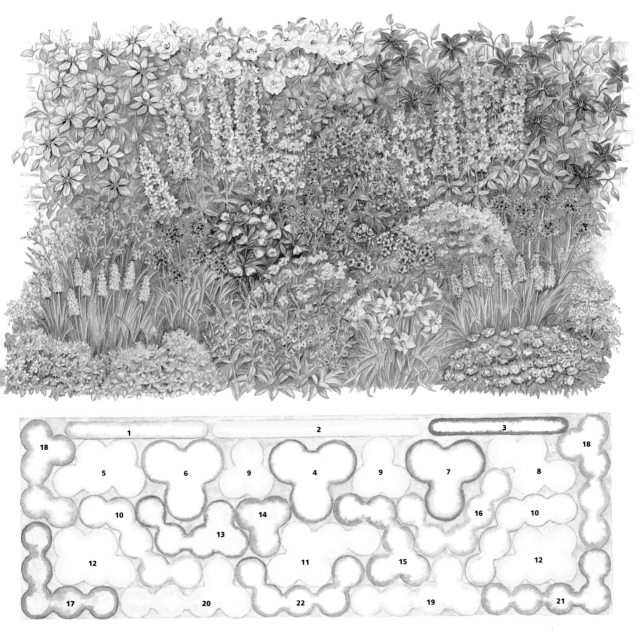

1 *Clematis* 'Perle d'Azur' x 1
2 *Rosa* 'Golden Showers' x 1
3 *Clematis* 'William Kennett' x 1
4 *Campanula lactiflora* x 3
5 *Crocosmia* 'Jenny Bloom' x 5
6 *Delphinium* 'Blue Bird' x 3
7 *Delphinium* 'Blue Jay' x 3

8 *Hemerocallis* 'Hyperion' x 4
9 *Verbascum chaixii* 'Gainsborough' x 3
10 *Agapanthus* 'Headbourne Hybrids' x 5
11 *Geum* 'Lady Stratheden' x 5
12 *Kniphofia* 'Candlelight' x 5

13 *Oenothera* 'Fireworks' x 5
14 *Platycodon grandiflorus mariesii* x 3
15 *Polemonium foliosissimum* x 5
16 *Potentilla recta* x 5
17 *Geranium wallichianum* 'Buxton's Variety' x 5

18 *Alchemilla mollis* x 5
19 *Hemerocallis* 'Stella de Oro' x 5
20 *Origanum vulgare* 'Aureum' x 5
21 *Scabiosa* 'Butterfly Blue' x 5
22 *Veronica gentianoides* x 5

A Shady Site

ABOVE: Epimedium perralderianum *makes an excellent low-allergen plant for shady parts of the garden.*

Shady beds and borders present several problems when it comes to choosing plants. Taking account of the degree of shade is the key to getting the planting right, but it is often difficult to decide exactly how much shade is cast over the area to be planted. The amount of shade depends on what is causing the area to be blocked from the sun: a wall, a fence, a large bush or one or more trees. A wall running north-south across a garden creates a sunless spot on one side of the wall and, depending on the height of the wall, this area may be in full shade throughout the day in both summer and winter, while the other side will be in continual sunshine. Any plants selected for such a site must be able to thrive in full shade. An east-west wall creates less of a problem as the areas either side of it will have direct sunlight in either the morning or the evening, and the plants will need to tolerate only partial shade. House walls can produce wide areas of total shade, particularly if the house has several storeys, and plants for borders affected in this way must be selected for the precise amount of shade the house creates.

Fences

Solid fences produce the same degree of shade as walls but are usually a maximum of 1.8m (6ft) high, so that the area of total shade is quite restricted. Picket fences will allow some light to penetrate and will create what is known as dappled light. Both walls and fences will cast a longer shadow in winter, when the sun is low, than in the middle of summer, when it is almost overhead. This is important to remember if you want to use evergreen plants in the shade of walls or fences.

Trees and hedges

The degree of shade produced by trees is different from that produced by walls and fences, mainly because it is unusual for a tree canopy to be solid enough to prevent any sunlight penetrating it. As a result, most trees cast a dappled light in summer and, if the tree (or trees) in question is deciduous, very little shade at all in the winter. Evergreen trees tend to cast a greater degree of shade, but, as they do not shed their leaves in winter, this remains much the same all year. The main problem with areas beneath trees is that the tree roots will be extracting food and moisture from the soil, leaving it dry and impoverished – not ideal conditions for any plants sited there.

BELOW: *The leaves and flowers of* Geranium macrorrhizum *form dense ground cover under the shade of a tree.*

Hedges also create shade areas on the sides away from the sun, and, like trees, take most of the available moisture and food from the soil around their roots. The answer is to leave a path 60cm (2ft) wide along both sides of each hedge. This is doubly useful in that it avoids the problems associated with planting border plants on the roots of a hedge and it allows access for cutting the hedge when necessary.

The shady bed illustrated is full of low-allergen plants which are happy in partial and, in most cases, full shade, so you could copy this planting in any sunless area.

PLAN FOR A SHADY BED

This is a bed planted beneath the shade of two trees which will restrict the amount of sunlight reaching the plants below. The plants chosen will be happy in almost complete shade so will continue to thrive as the trees increase in size over the years ahead.

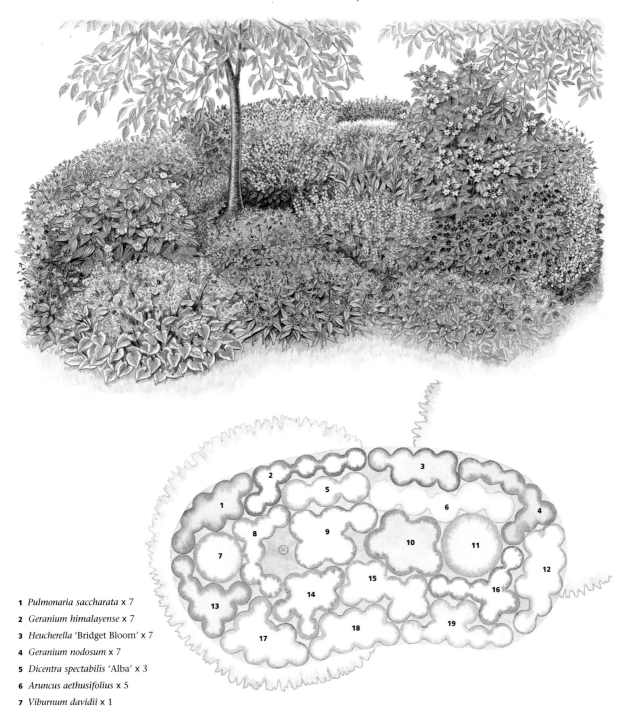

1 *Pulmonaria saccharata* x 7

2 *Geranium himalayense* x 7

3 *Heucherella* 'Bridget Bloom' x 7

4 *Geranium nodosum* x 7

5 *Dicentra spectabilis* 'Alba' x 3

6 *Aruncus aethusifolius* x 5

7 *Viburnum davidii* x 1

8 *Omphalodes verna* x 6

9 *Tellima grandiflora*
   'Purpurea' x 5

10 *Symphytum uplandicum* x 5

11 *Viburnum sargentii*
   'Onondaga' x 1

12 *Tiarella cordifolia* x 8

13 *Epimedium rubrum* x 7

14 *Geranium macrorrhizum* x 7

15 *Heuchera cylindrica*
   'Greenfinch' x 8

16 *Geranium phaeum* x 7

17 *Brunnera macrophylla*
   'Hadspen Cream' x 8

18 *Pulmonaria angustifolia* x 7

19 *Symphytum* 'Goldsmith' x 7

A Low-Maintenance Border

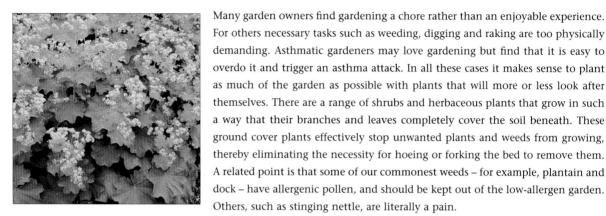

ABOVE: Alchemilla mollis, *which grows in sun or shade, is one of the easiest and most attractive plants for the low-allergen garden.*

BELOW: Lamium maculatum, *with its striped leaves and pink flowers, forms a low carpeting ground cover and survives poor soils and dry shade.*

Many garden owners find gardening a chore rather than an enjoyable experience. For others necessary tasks such as weeding, digging and raking are too physically demanding. Asthmatic gardeners may love gardening but find that it is easy to overdo it and trigger an asthma attack. In all these cases it makes sense to plant as much of the garden as possible with plants that will more or less look after themselves. There are a range of shrubs and herbaceous plants that grow in such a way that their branches and leaves completely cover the soil beneath. These ground cover plants effectively stop unwanted plants and weeds from growing, thereby eliminating the necessity for hoeing or forking the bed to remove them. A related point is that some of our commonest weeds – for example, plantain and dock – have allergenic pollen, and should be kept out of the low-allergen garden. Others, such as stinging nettle, are literally a pain.

Whenever you use ground cover plants in the low-allergen garden you must make sure that the plants selected are absolutely right for the soil, degree of shade and the amount of moisture in the bed to be planted. If you choose the wrong plants – for example, you put catmint in damp shade or hostas in dry sun – they cannot thrive and will never make the leaf cover that you need.

Ground cover plants

There are a number of ways in which to use ground cover plants, ranging from substituting a mass of *Vinca* for a lawn to using a highly ornamental planting of herbaceous geraniums and catmint. The point to remember, when using ground cover plants to reduce weeds, is that weeds find it difficult to grow within a clump of the same plant but will take advantage of the space created when two different plants meet. Therefore the larger the clump of any one type of plant the less will be the risk of weeds. Conversely, this will reduce visual interest if what you really want is to enjoy a variety of different plants.

I greatly enjoy using ground cover plants, for both their practical and their ornamental value. In the low-maintenance bed on the opposite page I have included some of my favourite plants to create a bed which will look attractive throughout most of the year and require very little maintenance. There are several plants with attractive coloured leaves as these will give interest for much longer than flowers of the same colour.

A LOW-MAINTENANCE BORDER

This is a border designed for a sunny area and all the plants selected will need little attention once they are established. The paved path allows both easy access to the border and acts as a mowing strip for the lawn, which will also eliminate the task of clipping the edge of the grass after mowing.

1 *Eryngium tripartitum* x 3

2 *Prunus cistena* x 1

3 *Perovskia atriplicifolia* 'Blue Spire' x 3

4 *Fuchsia magellanica* 'Versicolor' x 3

5 *Salvia sylvestris* 'Indigo' x 3

6 *Weigela florida* 'Foliis Purpureis' x 1

7 *Nepeta faassenii* x 6

8 *Geranium pratense* 'Blue Skies' x 5

9 *Origanum laevigatum* 'Herrenhausen' x 6

10 *Cistus* x *pulverulentus* 'Sunset' x 1

11 *Heuchera micrantha* 'Palace Purple' x 5

12 *Scabiosa caucasica* 'Clive Greaves' x 5

13 *Cistus* 'Silver Pink' x 1

14 *Astrantia major* x 5

15 *Hebe* 'Red Edge' x 1

16 *Armeria maritima* 'Splendens' x 5

17 *Heuchera micrantha* 'Palace Purple' x 5

18 *Helianthemum* 'Annabel' x 5

19 *Veronica spicata incana* x 5

20 *Helianthemum* 'Wisley Park' x 6

21 *Geranium traversii* 'Crug Strain' x 5

22 *Veronica peduncularis* 'Georgia Blue' x 6

A Bog Garden

ABOVE: Astilbe chinensis *var.* taquetii *'Purpurlanze' is one of the many astilbes which grow well in moist soils.*

BELOW: Iris sibirica *is seen at its best in damp conditions.*

There are often wet areas within a garden, particularly where there happens to be a clay subsoil, or if the water-table is very near the surface of the ground. In some cases these wet areas are low places in which drainage water collects after a rainstorm and then slowly disappears. Where the clay is near the surface the water may not drain away and a natural pond forms in the hollow. Other wet areas may be found on either side of a stream flowing along the boundary of a garden.

Natural boggy areas may not be wet all year round; often they will be very wet in winter and merely damp in summer. If this is the case, you should select plants which will grow in these conditions, such as hosta and astilbes. Several moisture-loving plants will tolerate a certain amount of drying out in summer if there is some shade overhead. For example, a boggy area under a group of deciduous trees can be relatively easy to plant as the denser shade of the tree, when in full leaf in summer, compensates for the lack of moisture at this time of year.

Moisture levels

Before planting wet areas you must monitor the area for a full year to ascertain the precise moisture levels. Many plants are specific as to the amount of moisture they need and the degree of dryness they will tolerate. At one extreme of the moisture scale are water plants or marginal plants that grow in the water around ponds and lakes, most of which must have their roots permanently covered with water. At the other end of the scale are grey-leaved plants, which need an almost dry soil. In between are plants which need constant moisture at root level but do not like standing in water, and plants which like moisture but will survive dry soil for part of the year.

A few plants are tolerant of almost any amount of moisture, from standing in water to almost dry soil. These include purple loosestrife and Queen Anne's lace, which are very useful when a winter pond dries up during the summer months.

If you want to eliminate the boggy areas from your garden because of an allergy, it is usually possible to install a drainage system to take the water away from the site, or to build a soakaway below ground at the lowest point.

In the plan on the opposite page I have shown a bed for a moist area of the garden – possibly a low site where water collects in wet weather, but then drains away leaving a permanent but not water-logged soil.

A BED FOR MOIST SOILS

This bed is planned for a damp sunken area in full sun or very light shade, where the soil retains moisture throughout the year but is never under water. The stepping stones allow access through the border on even the wettest days.

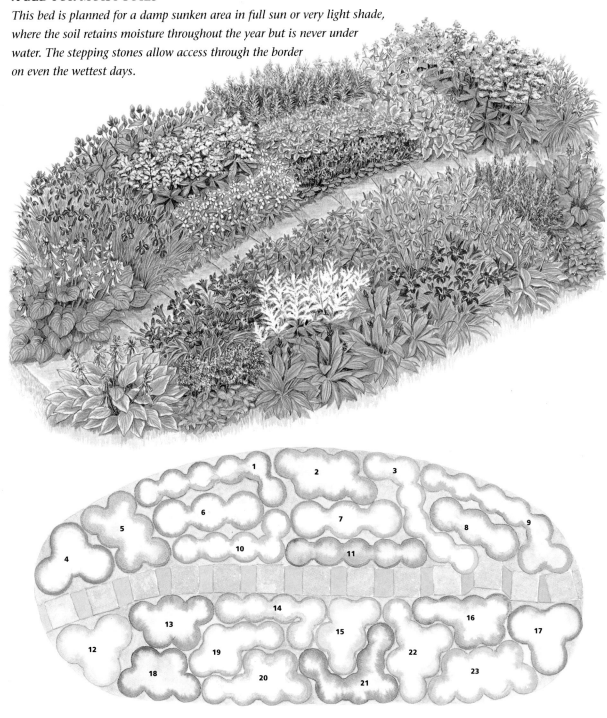

1. *Tricyrtis formosana* x 6
2. *Astilbe* 'Rhineland' x 6
3. *Hosta* 'Shade Fanfare' x 6
4. *Hosta sieboldiana* x 3
5. *Iris sibirica* 'Tropic Night' x 6
6. *Rodgersia pinnata* 'Elegans' x 3
7. *Scrophularia aquatica*
   'Variegata' x 3
8. *Rodgersia pinnata* 'Superba' x 3
9. *Hemerocallis*
   'Children's Festival' x 7
10. *Gentiana asclepiadea alba* x 5
11. *Geum rivale*
    'Leonard's Variety' x 5
12. *Hosta* 'Francee' x 3
13. *Hemerocallis*
    'Chicago Royal Robe' x 5
14. *Gentiana asclepiadea* x 5
15. *Iris sibirica* x 5
16. *Astilbe* 'Fanal' x 6
17. *Hosta* 'Halcyon' x 3
18. *Filipendula* 'Kahome' x 5
19. *Astilbe* 'Snowdrift' x 5
20. *Hosta lancifolia* x 6
21. *Hemerocallis* 'Black Magic' x 6
22. *Hosta* 'Thomas Hogg' x 6
23. *Houttuynia cordata*
    'Flora Pleno' x 7

A Rose Garden

ABOVE: *The shrub rose 'Frau Karl Druschki' has large pure white flowers and is very robust. It has no scent so is a useful addition to the low-allergen rose garden.*

BELOW: *If you are allergic to the scent of roses, avoid planting them over an arch where they will be at 'nose' level.*

Roses are among the loveliest of all plants and there are literally thousands of species, hybrids and cultivars from which to choose. At one extreme are the species roses: the naturally occurring 'wild' roses such as *Rosa moyesii*, which are graceful in habit, have simple flowers in mid-summer and usually produce hips in autumn. Species roses do not as a rule require pruning and are generally resistant to the more common rose pests and diseases. However, they do need lots of space and look most natural in the less formal areas of the garden.

At the other end of the rose spectrum are the bedding roses, which include the the floribunda roses, which have clusters of flowers, and the hybrid tea roses, with their large, formal flowers and rigid branches. Bedding roses bloom almost continuously from mid-summer throughout autumn and frequently well into winter, but they must be pruned annually and in almost all cases require regular spraying. These roses are best grown on their own in rose beds, with just an edging of low-growing herbaceous plants to hide their stems. Suitable edging plants are the herbaceous geraniums, catmint or ladies mantle.

Between these two extremes are the shrub roses, which range from the old varieties, such as the gallicas, albas and damask roses, to the recently hybridized English roses. Most shrub roses have beautifully formed flowers which bloom for most of the summer, and need to be pruned and sprayed only occasionally. They fit in happily with the more ornamental herbaceous plants, such as delphiniums, campanulas and peonies, to create some of the loveliest borders and beds in our gardens. Alternatively, you can plant them together in rose beds or in mixed shrub borders.

Bedding roses

The plan opposite is a very simple way of including bedding roses in the low-allergen garden. As the roses selected have little or no scent, they should not act as triggers for asthma attacks. The roses shown here must be pruned and if you are allergic to rose thorns it will be essential to get someone else to prune the roses and carefully dispose of all the rose prunings. I have tried to include disease-resistant roses to reduce or eliminate the need for spraying, but if you live in an area where black spot and mildew are often major problems you must either forgo the pleasures of a rose garden or use some of the more disease-resistant shrub roses.

A ROSE GARDEN

Below is a rose garden for a sunny area in front of a brick wall. The colour scheme is based on the orange and brown colours of the patio rose 'Free As Air', which was a feature of the 1996 low-allergen garden at the Chelsea Flower Show. Cream coloured roses have been planted to brighten up the back of the garden and an edging of blue plants completes the scheme. The roses chosen have little or no fragrance. We have shown a garden that would fit into a very small area, but if you have more space then the plan can easily be enlarged by adding two or more beds of roses and moving the sundial, plus its surround of roses, to the centre of the garden.

1 *Rosa* 'Free as Air' x 7

2 *Rosa* 'Warm Welcome' x 1

3 *Rosa* 'Peace' x 3

4 *Rosa* 'Chanelle' x 1 as standard

5 *Rosa* 'L'Oréal Trophy' x 2

6 *Veronica austriaca* spp. *teucrium* 'Crater Lake Blue' x 7

7 *Rosa* 'Wandering Minstrel' x 8

8 *Geranium* 'Johnson's Blue' x 14

Banks and Rock Gardens

Low-Allergen Plants for Covering Banks

These plants can all be used for covering banks which are difficult to maintain. Choose a plant that will thrive in the soil, drainage and aspect of the site and then plant the whole area with the one species. For a more ornamental effect select two or three compatible species to plant together in large drifts. An asterisk indicates the plant must be grown in acid soil.

Arctostaphylos
  *uva-ursi**
Cotoneaster
  dammeri
Cotoneaster
  microphyllus
Epimedium
  perralderianum
*Erica carnea**
Genista lydia
Geranium macrorrhizum
Helianthemum
  nummularium
Hypericum calycinum
Lamium galeobdolon
  'Florentinum'
Lamium maculatum
Rubus tricolor
Stachys macrantha
Stephanandra
  incisa 'Crispa'
Thymus serpyllum
Vinca major
Vinca minor
Waldsteinia ternata

I have spent much of my gardening career in the south west of England, where a good number of houses are built on the side of hills with steeply sloping gardens. While these sloping sites can make gardening difficult and in some cases even dangerous, they have the potential for exciting changes of level. Rock banks and waterfalls become a possibility for an informal garden, and grand flights of steps and flat terraces for a formal garden.

There is also a marked difference between gardens sloping to face the sun, which will be beautifully warm and sunny, and gardens facing away from the sun, which will be correspondingly cooler and more shady. These factors may affect how you use and plant the garden.

Banks

In a sloping garden you may decide to leave steep banks between more level areas, rather than go to the expense of building retaining walls. You will then need to clothe the bank, but it is frequently impractical to use the obvious remedy, grass, and in the low-allergen garden it is in any case undesirable. One alternative is a rock bank or garden of the kind described below, although a simpler approach is to use a prostrate plant as a ground cover. It is essential to choose a plant that will thrive, as quick growth is the main objective. Banks tend to be well drained, or even rather dry, and drought-tolerant plants should be considered. It may well be difficult to walk on the bank to carry out maintenance, in which case you should use a dense planting of a single species to keep weeding to an absolute minimum. Suitable plants include *Cotoneaster dammeri*, *Lamium galeobdolon*, *Vinca minor* or possibly a ground cover rose, such as *Rosa* 'Flower Carpet'. An approach which can be relied upon to give a weed-free area is to cover the bank with a stabilizing blanket, such as a geo-textile material, and then cut holes for plants as needed.

RIGHT: *A stone retaining wall supports a bank well covered in low-growing perennials. When planting a bank like this, it is a good idea to add some rocks or paving slabs to allow easy access for maintenance.*

Steps

If a garden slopes you may need to build steps to gain access between the different levels. It is important in planning these that they should be easy to climb without over-exertion, as this can trigger an asthma attack. There is a well-established formula for calculating the size of steps to ensure that they are comfortable to climb up and down. In this formula, twice the measurement of the riser plus the tread depth equals 65cm (26in). This ratio of riser to tread means that the effort needed to both lift the leg and move forward along the steps is not excessive. It can be translated into a riser of 15cm (6in) and a tread depth of 35cm (14in), so that twice the riser (2 x 15cm = 30cm) plus the tread (35cm) gives a total of 65cm (26in). Another help is to provide a resting place or landing between every eight to ten steps, to give the climber the opportunity to stop to take breath. A change in the steps' direction at the landing gives even more reason to pause and take a rest. Further help can be provided by installing discreet handrails along the edges of the steps. These can be made more ornamental by planting a climbing plant, such as *Clematis montana*, to cover the supports.

ABOVE: *These shallow steps constructed from wooden sleepers and gravel make a gradual and easy climb through the garden.*

BELOW: *A rock garden with large rocks deeply embedded, and the spaces filled with alpines.*

Rock gardens

A rock garden may be on the list of features that you would like to include in your garden. Bear in mind that this feature will look far more natural if your garden is already sloping, as rock outcrops are usually found on the sides of mountains and hills. Choose a local rock, if possible, and get the largest rocks that you can handle. When you have selected where you are going to build the garden, place the rocks carefully with the largest ones at the base and the smaller ones above. Bury at least half of each rock in the bank, making sure that any lines visible in the rocks all run in the same direction, and leave ample room between the rocks for planting. To make future maintenance easier incorporate some flat rocks to form a series of stepping stones through the garden.

The plants which you include in your rock garden are a matter of personal choice, but you should consider the time you have available for looking after this area. If you adore pottering about nurturing tiny plants, by all means cover the whole bank with an assortment of alpines. But if your greatest pleasure comes from the visual impact of the stones themselves, consider a more natural approach using drifts of heathers with low-growing conifers. For a more ornamental, but relatively low-maintenance planting, use large groups of ground cover plants, such as *Campanula carpatica* or *Helianthemum nummularium*.

Container Gardening

The containers used for growing plants range from a purpose-built box to an old chimney-pot, an elaborate eighteenth-century urn or an inside-out tyre. Almost every garden has at least one plant growing in a container and some gardens are full of them. Where container gardening comes into its own is in the small urban garden or backyard which is covered with concrete or paving, making it impossible to put plants directly into the soil. Roof gardens and balconies are other areas where, if you want to grow plants, they will need to be in a container.

There are lots of advantages to growing plants in containers. It allows you to use a soil suitable for the plant and also to place the pot in an aspect suited to the plant, for example a camellia can be placed to avoid the early morning sun. Also, you can move the container if the plants need more or less light, and when the plant is passed its best you can put away the container or replace the plant with one at its peak. An advantage for the gardener with a back problem is that containerized plants can be at a level which minimizes bending.

Planting a container

There are two main ways of planting a container. You can use the container like a flowerpot, planting a single specimen plant in the middle; an example would be a mopheaded bay tree. Alternatively, you can plant the container with annuals and half-hardy perennials to create a floral display which provides a blaze of colour for the whole of the summer. There is one further type of container gardening: the miniature garden. A trough is used and planted with alpines, and decorated with rocks. Decide whether you want a collection of individual plants each in its own container, floral arrangements, or a combination of the two, and then select the plants you are going to use before finding the most suitable container.

Some containers are best left unplanted and enjoyed as ornaments, and these include narrow-topped urns and oil jars whose shapes are best left unadorned.

RIGHT: *The large green leaves and bright pink flowers of* Bergenia *'Ballawley Hybrids' filling a trough with colour and textural interest.*

For planting specimen plants choose a container which allows plenty of space for the plant roots, both at the time of planting and as the plant grows, since it may remain there for several years. Square containers and those shaped like the traditional flowerpot are excellent for this purpose. Arrangements look wonderful in shallower containers such as urns and bowls. You will only need to make sure that there is space for a season's growth as most arrangements are replaced at the end of each season.

Choosing plants for containers

Evergreen shrubs work very well in containers, as do climbers, which can be mounted on a frame attached to the container if no wall is available. Other good choices are plants with spiky shapes – for example, phormium and yucca – and almost all the herbs. Mint planted in a container is an excellent idea as it cannot invade the rest of the herb garden. To create a formal look, use one of the various mophead trees, such as bay or photinia, but investigate them thoroughly as several of these plants are allergenic.

Containerized flower arrangements for summer are best created by using annuals with a half-hardy perennial or a shrub, such as a fuchsia, at the centre. Plant annuals in circles, with those chosen for their mass colour – for

ABOVE: *A wooden barrel filled with fuchsias and petunias creating a bright splash of colour in the corner of the courtyard.*

example, petunias – inside a circle of trailing plants such as lobelia and nepeta to cover the edge of the container. For a particularly impressive arrangement pack in as many plants as possible, and then water and feed the container throughout summer. Use only low-allergen plants and avoid scented plants as perfume is much nearer nose level when plants are containerized.

Successful winter arrangements are much more difficult to achieve as many of the most useful plants, such as ivies, are allergenic. It is hard to get as full an arrangement as you can in summer, but winter-flowering pansies give plenty of colour and you can include some spring-flowering bulbs for extra effect. Suitable bulbs are the early-flowering *Iris reticulata* and species crocuses. Exclude hyacinths from the low-allergen garden as they have a strong scent and their bulbs cause nasty skin allergies. The bulbs of narcissi can also cause skin allergies but if you wear gloves while planting, and remember to select varieties with little or no scent, you might include a few in your garden.

Trees and Shrubs

ABOVE: Pieris *'Forest Flame'*, with its bright pink young leaves in spring and early summer, is a lovely shrub for low-allergen gardens with lime-free soil.

BELOW: *One of the best flowering cherries,* Prunus avium *'Plena' in full bloom.*

Both trees and shrubs give height, structure, a sense of scale, as well as a feeling of permanence to our gardens, and no garden is complete without them. All trees and shrubs contain woody tissue which forms the skeleton of the plant and stays unchanged throughout the year. They can be either deciduous, losing their leaves in winter, or evergreen, retaining them through the seasons. Trees have a single trunk supporting a branching head, while shrubs have several stems at ground level.

Tree pollen is a major allergen and causes asthma and hay fever in a great many people. However, only wind-pollinated trees produce enough buoyant pollen to be a problem, and then only certain trees produce pollen which is also allergenic. The following families of trees and shrubs are known to produce large quantities of allergenic pollen: Aceraceae (maples), Betulaceae (alder, birch and hazel), Fagaceae (beech, oak and sweet chestnut), Juglandaceae (hickories and walnuts), Moraceae (mulberries), Oleaceae (ash, olive and privet), Salicaceae (poplars and willows) and Ulmaceae (elms). All wind-pollinated plants from the these families should be considered suspect as far as the low-allergen garden is concerned. Either exclude them to be completely safe, or investigate the reactions of you or members of your family to each such plant before allowing them to remain in, or introducing them into, your garden.

Selecting and using low-allergen shrubs

Shrubs provide a great deal of the living structure for the smaller garden, particularly where there is little room for trees. In larger gardens they provide the middle layer of plants, linking the lower-growing herbaceous plants and the trees. Shrubs are used in all parts of the garden and can form hedges, lend impact to ornamental beds and borders, or act as focal points. Evergreen shrubs are particularly useful for providing a green background to gardens throughout the year.

Harmful shrubs

In the low-allergen garden there are some shrubs to avoid as they are known to provoke allergic reactions. Among the worst culprits is privet, *Ligustrum* spp., a member of the Oleaceae family. Other problem shrubs are those that produce highly-scented blossom, which acts as a trigger for allergies. These include the mock orange, *Philadelphus* spp.; flowering currant, *Ribes sanguineum*; lilac, *Syringa* spp.; and the butterfly bush *Buddleja davidii*, any of which may need to be excluded.

Skin allergies may be caused by the various daphnes, many of which are both beautifully scented and toxic, and therefore must be treated with extreme caution. Rue has already been mentioned as a major cause of photodermatitis (see p.23). The other main offenders in this respect are the various species of Rhus, one of which, *Rhus radicans*, is the notorious 'poison ivy', which causes severe blistering dermatitis. Other, less obnoxious plants which may nevertheless cause problems in susceptible people are the hairy, prickly and grey-leaved plants. The key to choosing shrubs is to avoid the real villains and then exclude only such other plants as you know affect you or any member of your family.

Selecting and planting trees

As well as contributing to the structure and scale of gardens, trees provide shade and display blossom, fruit and autumn leaf colour, adding interest in the different seasons. They also bring birds and insects into our gardens and, when mature, will provide the support for a swing or a tree house and make a natural climbing frame for children.

Unfortunately, trees can cause severe problems in the low-allergen garden, particularly where a member of the family is allergic to tree pollen. If you study the list of allergenic plants mentioned on page 80 you will find the majority of Britain's most common trees included among them: the alder, ash, beech, elm, oak, poplar, sycamore and willow, which are all known to cause problems. One of the

ABOVE: *The red stems of the dogwood* Cornus alba *'Sibirica' are capable of brightening up even the dullest of winter gardens.*

BELOW: Sorbus sargentiana, *a wonderful tree for autumn colour in the low-allergen garden.*

worst culprits is the silver birch. For at least three months of the year throughout the spring, one or more of these trees is bound to be dispersing pollen.

Fortunately, not all who suffer from tree-pollen allergy are allergic to all trees. You may have a single allergy – to silver birch, for example – in which case removing these trees from your garden makes sense. But if you suffer from a general allergy to all tree pollen, you should either avoid all the trees listed on page 80 when they are producing pollen or remove them all from your garden. This is an extreme course of action, so check your symptoms carefully and decide which species are the worst offenders before thinking about disposing of any of the trees in your garden.

Planning permission

If, like most people, you live in a town or city or in a designated conservation area, the problem is complicated by the fact that all your trees will be protected

Tree Preservation Orders (TPOs)

● A tree preservation order is an order made by a local planning authority which makes it an offence wilfully to damage or destroy or to fell, top, lop or uproot a tree or trees specified in that order without the authority's consent.

● The purpose of a tree preservation order is to protect trees in the interests of amenity, the amenity should normally be one that is capable of enjoyment by the general public. An order may cover any single tree or trees, groups of trees or woodlands but not hedges or shrubs.

● You can check if there are any TPOs on your existing trees by looking in the local land charges registry at your local planning offices or town hall. If you are considering removing a tree or trees which are, or may be, covered by a TPO, then seek the advice of your planning authority first, they are usually very helpful.

by preservation orders (see left). These make it an offence to remove any tree without seeking permission from the local authority. Usually the planning officials will not allow the removal of a tree unless it is dead, dangerous or growing in such a way as to be liable to damage an adjacent tree. I have yet to propose allergen avoidance as grounds for removing a large oak tree. However, you may receive permission to take out a scrubby planting of willows and poplars, provided you can show that you intend to replace them with low-allergenic trees.

In the heart of the countryside there may be no such preservation orders to negotiate, but even so the decision to remove a mature tree, being irreversible, is not one to rush into. Again the answer may be to decide which species causes the most trouble and remove only those.

If you decide to keep trees that are potentially troublesome, check the pollen counts in the spring and stay indoors when they are high or when the weather is windy. It might seem as though there are no trees that you can plant in the low-allergen garden, but in fact the choice is wide. Most of our blossom trees are insect-pollinated and so are safe to include; among these are the crab-apples, cherries, pears, rowans and whitebeam. Of the larger-growing trees which are suitable there are the tulip tree and horse chestnuts, although the second are poisonous so you might prefer to exclude these. You could also use some more exotic trees, including the large-leaved catalpas and paulownias.

RIGHT: *The London plane,* Platanus x hispanica *produces masses of allergenic pollen and should be excluded from the low-allergen garden.*

Conifers for the Low-Allergen Garden

Many of the conifers commonly found in gardens belong to the family Cupressaceae and produce potentially allergenic pollen, and as well as being poisonous, they are likely to cause contact irritant dermatitis. If you want to exclude the Cupressaceae but still want to enjoy a range of beautiful conifers then the following are worth considering. Omitted from the list are *Cedrus* spp. and *Ginkgo biloba* both of which can irritate the skin.

Conifers for use as specimens
– height 15–30m (50–90ft)

Abies concolor 'Violacea'
Abies koreana
Metasequoia glyptostroboides
Picea breweriana
Picea omorika 'Pendula'
Pinus wallichiana
Taxodium distichum

Conifers for ornamental use
– height 2.4–9m (8–30ft)

Cryptomeria japonica 'Elegans'
Picea glauca albertiana 'Conica'
Picea pungens 'Koster'
Pinus densiflora 'Umbraculifera'
Pinus parviflora 'Glauca'
Pinus strobus 'Nana'

Dwarf conifers for the rock garden
– height 30cm–1.2m (1–4ft)

Abies balsamea hudsonia
Cryptomeria japonica 'Vilminiriana'
Picea abies 'Nidiformis'
Picea mariana 'Nana'
Pinus mugo 'Gnom'
Tsuga canadensis 'Jeddeloh'

Ground cover conifers
– spread 3–6m (10–20ft)

Picea abies 'Procumbens'
Picea abies 'Reflexa'
Tsuga canadensis 'Cole's Prostrate'
Tsuga canadensis 'Pendula'

Trees in neighbouring gardens

It seems pointless to remove all the wind-pollinated trees from your own garden when the same species are flourishing in your neighbour's garden, and capable of spreading their pollen over your garden whenever the wind blows in your direction. However, while it is true that pollen can be blown for many miles, most of it falls in the area in which the parent plant is growing.

Pollen checks taken from pollen traps set up in gardens have shown that most of the pollen present has come from trees in those gardens or from those of near neighbours. So removing trees in your own garden will reduce pollen levels and if you can persuade your neighbours to take down trees on your boundary it will help the situation. If this second remedy is ruled out, remember that you may legally remove any branches of a neighbouring tree that hang over your property. The only condition to this is that you must not thereby cause the death of the tree and you must return the severed limb to the owner of the tree!

Problems with conifers

Conifers differ from all other trees and shrubs in that they have cones as their fruiting structure and needles in place of leaves. They are all wind-pollinated and produce masses of buoyant pollen. Fortunately, much of this pollen is only slightly allergenic and, with the exception of pollen from the Cupressaceae family, should not be a problem. This family includes the *Chamaecyparis*, *Cupressus*, *Juniperus* and *Thuja* species, and of these the last are by far the most harmful. Most *Cupressus* species are not fully hardy so are not often seen in north European gardens, although in southern Europe and the southern states of Australasia *Cupressus macrocarpa* will survive. The junipers have been known to provoke allergic reactions, but don't exclude them without checking whether they affect you or anyone in your family.

Vegetables and Fruit

ABOVE: *The attractive, ripe, red fruits of gooseberry 'Winham Industry'.*

BELOW: *Lettuce is a safe salad crop for the low-allergen garden and looks very effective when grown in rows, as seen here in the potager at Le Manoir aux Quatre Saisons, Oxfordshire, central England.*

Having the space to grow vegetables and fruit is one of the great pleasures of having a garden. Most of us relish the idea of digging our own carrots, cutting our own crisp lettuces or picking the first apple of the autumn. There is also the opportunity to grow more exotic varieties of vegetables and fruit, which may have a lovely taste but are not on sale in the supermarket as they are not commercially viable. There are now several specialist vegetable seed suppliers for unusual varieties (see Useful Addresses, p.124).

Health benefits

Asthmatics are encouraged to eat plenty of fresh fruit and vegetables, but in fact it is healthy for everyone to do the same. Growing your own vegetables and fruit is one way to be certain exactly how the crop has been grown – there are no nasty residual chemicals on their skins when they are homegrown – and it will probably save you money as well.

Vegetables need a site in full sun and a soil that is rich and well-drained but retains moisture. So, if you want to create a reasonably sized vegetable garden you need to find the right place for it while you are designing your garden. Fruits do not need full sun all day long, but neither will they flourish in deep shade. Also, if you are planning to use a fruit cage to protect fruit from birds, you may prefer to position the cage so that it can be screened from your view.

Selecting and planting vegetables

Most vegetables can be included in the low-allergen garden, but a few have been known to cause problems. Sweet corn and spinach produce pollen in abundance, so they may affect asthma and hay fever sufferers. Among vegetables known to cause skin reactions are asparagus, celery, parsnips, radishes, rhubarb and tomatoes. The latter seem to be among the worst offenders, but the sap of both celery and parsnip are known to have caused photodermatitis and should be treated with caution. When we included a vegetable garden in our second low-allergen garden at Chelsea Flower Show in 1994 some visitors mentioned that they were allergic to courgettes, broad beans and even potatoes. Eating tomatoes and celery frequently causes welts in sufferers from urticaria, and beans, particularly broad beans, can stimulate the same reaction. The best approach is to eliminate only those vegetables that you know cause problems for you or your family.

Growing vegetables

I find that the most satisfactory way of growing vegetables is in raised beds 1.2m (4ft) wide, with 60cm (2ft) wide paths between adjacent beds. The narrow width of the beds allows you to reach over them to look after the plants without walking on and trampling down the soil.

Vegetables need plenty of food and this means adding fertilizer, inorganic or organic, to the soil before planting, or digging in plenty of organic matter; both will ensure a healthy and abundant crop. This is where having a good compost heap pays dividends, but see the advice given on page 33.

Selecting and planting fruit

Growing your own fruit can involve a great deal of time and effort, as planting is followed by the indispensable tasks of training, pruning, tying-in and feeding. One of our aims in creating the low-allergen garden has been to reduce maintenance, whereas tending a large orchard will certainly entail a lot of work. On the other hand, a few fruit bushes and some cordon apples will provide you with all the fruit you need for very little effort.

Cordon apples and pears can be bought ready trained and, once planted against a wall or fence, just need pruning back to fruiting buds once a year. Pruning is best done on a winter's day when there is no frost – a perfect time for the asthmatic gardener, provided he or she wraps up warmly. Cordon trees should be kept pruned to about 1–1.2m (3–4ft) high, which is just the right height to work at without risk of straining your back. Place a fence along the edge of one of the vegetable beds and you can feed the fruit whenever the vegetables are fed.

BELOW: *Cordon trained fruit trees make an attractive division in the low-allergen garden.*

Soft fruits

Summer-fruiting raspberries require a considerable amount of work each year – in particular, tying in the canes – but this is well compensated for by the pleasure of enjoying your own crop. Currant bushes are easier to maintain, needing the odd trim to keep them under control and they seem to attract fewer fruit-eating birds than raspberries. Gooseberries can be left as bushes or trained into mopheads, but their prickles may cause a problem. Many people are allergic to both handling and eating strawberries, and if you are in this category you should keep them out of your garden. Figs have also been known to be problematic, causing photodermatitis (see p.23).

Herbs

ABOVE: *Mixed cultivars of thyme make a colourful display in a corner of a herb garden.*

BELOW: *Curly-leaved parsley makes an attractive edging for herb beds in sun or shade.*

Herbs in the low-allergen garden

The large group known as herbs embraces a wide range of plants, including trees, shrubs, herbaceous perennials, biennials and annuals. The only thing that links them is that they are all useful to man: as medicines, cosmetics, insect repellents or in the kitchen. Many herbs are not only useful but also attractive and merit a place in any garden for either reason.

We have included herbs in all our low-allergen gardens, and in our first garden for the Chelsea Flower Show, in 1993, a small herb garden was a major feature. In the garden for the following year's show herbs were planted on all levels. These included rows in the vegetable garden, pots of mint, and some of the more ornamental herbs planted among the flowering plants in the rest of the garden. Herbs that prefer sunny positions were planted in the open spaces and herbs that thrive in shade were placed with other shade lovers. In the third low-allergen garden we used herbs simply for their ornamental value, planting them in the borders and beds rather than including them in specific herb areas.

Growing herbs

If you would like to grow herbs in your garden, decide whether they will be for use in the kitchen, for their ornamental value, or both. Plant herbs that you will need for culinary purposes in pots close to the kitchen door. However, if you plan to use large quantities of herbs, either in the kitchen, or to make pot-pourri or cosmetics, the most practical arrangement is to plant rows of your favourite varieties alongside the vegetables in the vegetable garden. Ornamental herbs, such as lemon balm, rosemary and sage, can be grown in mixed borders if you intend to use them only occasionally, or included with a larger range of herbs within a herb garden.

Herb gardens

As well as providing fresh herbs whenever you require them, the herb garden takes up relatively little space and is a visually pleasing feature in almost any garden. Herb gardens date back to the fifteenth century when all gardens were laid out formally, and many gardeners still follow this tradition. However, there is no reason why you shouldn't try an informal, less geometrical arrangement of beds,

ABOVE: *A large pot of variegated lemon balm,* Melissa officinalis *'Aurea' forms the focal point for a small formal herb garden.*

although in this instance you will need a fairly large area in which to create attractive curves. It is important to be able to reach the herbs easily and without treading on other plants or too much soil, so small beds are more practical than large ones. It is also a good idea to pave the herb garden as this will allow you mud-free access to the beds in wet weather. When selecting the plants for your herb garden choose several evergreen herbs, such as thyme and marjoram, as these look attractive all year round.

Problems with herbs

Herbs are a marvellous group of plants but they are not without their problem members. Some cause skin allergies, some are wind-pollinated, while others belong to the family Asteraceae and therefore may affect susceptible asthmatics (see p.21). Several of our loveliest herbs are very attractive to bees, particularly lemon balm which has been used over the centuries by beekeepers to attract a swarm of bees into the hive. This is definitely not a plant to include if you are allergic to bee stings. When making your choice of herbs, consult the list on page 122 of those that you should avoid.

A–Z
PLANTS TO USE

Annuals and Biennials

Snapdragon

Antirrhinum majus
SCROPHULARIACEAE

An attractive, short-lived perennial usually grown as a half-hardy annual. Upright spikes of lipped, tubular flowers 'snap' open when squeezed. There are a wide range of flower colours and shapes, including double-flowered and 'open-faced' varieties. Snapdragons flower all summer and are useful for bedding schemes, filling gaps in the mixed border and for containers. Cultivars range in size from 'Little Gem' at 10–15cm (4–6in) high and 'Coronette' at 35–40cm (14–16in) high, up to 'Bright Butterflies' at 60–90cm (24–36in). Grow in full sun and any well-drained soil.
Height **10–90cm (4–36in)**
Spread **20–45cm (8–18in)**
Hardiness **Half-hardy annual**
• older cultivars are susceptible to the disease known as rust, so be sure to select rust-resistant cultivars

Fibrous-rooted begonia

Begonia x *carrierei*
BEGONIACEAE

A popular half-hardy annual which is particularly useful for providing summer colour under trees and in shady areas. It forms mounds of shiny, rounded leaves covered all summer by masses of white, pink, salmon or red flowers. There are cultivars with bronze-coloured leaves which provide an attractive background to some of the more vibrant flower colours. It is useful as low edging for beds and borders, in containers, and there are pendant cultivars suitable for hanging baskets. Cultivars include 'Devon Gems' with bronze foliage and 'Pink Avalanche', a pendant form with abundant pink flowers. Grow in fertile, well-drained soil, preferably with plenty of organic matter. Partial to full shade is best.
Height **15–30cm (6–12in)**
Spread **15–30cm (6–12in)**
Hardiness **Half-hardy annual**
• can be difficult to germinate

Busy lizzie

Impatiens walleriana
BALSAMINACEAE

One of the most versatile bedding plants available, tolerating sun or shade and moist or dry soils, although its preference is for semi-shade and plenty of water. The plants form domes of green, bronze or variegated leaves smothered in a sheet of flowers all summer. Flower colours include white, pink, red, orange, lavender and bicolours. An excellent plant for shade whether in beds, pots or hanging baskets, it looks most attractive when planted with hostas and hemerocallis. Cultivars include the 'Accent' range, which have larger flowers and increased vigour, and the 'New Guinea' hybrids with coloured foliage, 'Tango' having deep orange flowers and dark bronze leaves.
Height **15–40cm (6–16in)**
Spread **25–45cm (10–18in)**
Hardiness **Tender perennial grown as half-hardy annual**
• best if planted in single-colour groups, as some colour combinations are harsh

Lobelia

Lobelia erinus
CAMPANULACEAE

The familiar blue-flowered bedding lobelia used since Victorian times for edging bedding schemes. A spreading plant with small, bronze or green leaves and blue, white, pink or lilac flowers, which cover the plant from early summer until the hard frosts. Use standard forms for edging planting schemes or filling gaps in the rockery and the trailing forms for hanging baskets, edges of containers or cascading over walls. Cultivars include 'Crystal Palace' with deep blue flowers and bronze foliage, 'Cambridge Blue' with light blue flowers and green leaves and 'White Fountain' with white flowers and light green leaves.
Height **10–20cm (4–8in)**
Spread **15–25cm (6–10in)**
Hardiness **Tender perennial used as half-hardy annual**
• all parts are poisonous if eaten

Forget-me-not

Myosotis alpestris
BORAGINACEAE

A biennial with clusters of small, blue flowers which is available in dwarf compact forms suitable for edging and as white- and pink-flowered cultivars. This is one of the best plants for spring bedding when combined with tulips in contrasting colours, or used as low edging for beds and borders. It tends to naturalize and reappear year after year. Compact varieties include 'Ultramarine' with rich blue flowers and 'Carmine King' with pink flowers, both only 15cm (6in) high. 'Royal Blue', 30cm (12in) high and with deep blue flowers, is an excellent choice for planting with bulbs.

ABOVE: *The startling New Guinea range of* Impatiens *with bright flowers and variegated leaves.*
FAR LEFT: *A colourful mixed bed of snapdragons,* Antirrhinum *'Coronet Mixed'.*
LEFT: *'Love Me' is the name of this attractive bright pink-flowered begonia.*

Height **15–45cm (6–18in)**
Spread **30cm (12in)**
Hardiness **Hardy**
• mildew can be a problem in dry weather

Love-in-a-mist

Nigella damascena
RANUNCULACEAE

A lovely annual with delicate, finely divided foliage and blue, starry flowers followed by seedpods which are almost as ornamental as the flowers. It readily self-seeds and is seen at its best when 'popping up' among cottage-garden perennials like peonies. Apart from the familiar blue; pink, white and lavender flowers are also available, either in the mixture 'Persian Jewels' or separately – the cultivar 'Miss Jekyll' is cornflower blue with bright green leaves and 'Mulberry Rose' is pink. Grow in almost any well-drained soil in sun or partial shade, but it prefers plenty of organic matter.
Height **45–50cm (18–20in)**
Spread **30cm (12in)**
Hardiness **Hardy**
• flowers short lived and plants quickly go to seed, but this can be delayed by regular deadheading

Petunia

Petunia x *hybrida*
SOLANACEAE

Brilliantly colourful flowers providing a wonderful splash of colour for bedding schemes and containers. Soft green leaves are covered in large, funnel-shaped flowers from early summer to the first frost. The flowers come in a range of colours from salmon-pink to lavender and purple and can be double, striped or picoteed. Good cultivars include the 'Fantasy' range, of which 'Fantasy Blue' is a deep blue and 'Fantasy Ivory' a veined creamy white. Multiflora types have double flowers and grandifloras have larger flowers. The 'Surfinia' petunias are trailing cultivars and superb plants for hanging baskets. All prefer fertile, well-drained soil and full sun.
Height **20–45cm (8–18in)**
Spread **30–45cm (12–18in)**
Hardiness **Tender perennial grown as half-hardy annual**
• protect from slugs

Annual phlox

Phlox drummondii
POLEMONIACEAE

Low-growing annual with large clusters of flowers in a wide range of colours from white, pink through lavender to blue and occasionally yellow. The flower may be a simple colour or have a distinctive eye in a different colour. A good plant for mixed planting schemes, for cutting and for containers. The dwarf forms are excellent for edging beds and the rockery. The cultivar 'Chanal' has double pink flowers, 'Blue Beauty' is a dwarf form with lovely blue flowers, 'Twinkle Stars' is a dwarf form with masses of starry flowers and 'Carnival' has larger flowers with contrasting centres. Grow in fertile, moist but well-drained soil and preferably in full sun.
Height **15–45cm (6–18in)**
Spread **20–30cm (8–12in)**
Hardiness **Half-hardy annual**
• avoid overwatering

Salvia

Salvia farinacea
LAMIACEAE

The most frequently used annual salvia is *S. splendens,* the scarlet sage, and it is very popular where bright red is wanted but the purple annual salvia, *S. farinacea,* deserves to be just as widely used. Long-lasting, narrow spikes of purple-blue flowers are carried above grey-green, strap-like foliage. They are most attractive used for bedding schemes with pink and white petunias, and are a useful addition to the mixed border or as a central feature in containers. The cultivar 'Victoria' has blue-purple flowers and 'Strata' has bicoloured white and blue flowers. Grow in any well-drained soil in full sun, although it will tolerate light shade.
Height **45–60cm (18–24in)**
Spread **30–45cm (12–18in)**
Hardiness **Tender perennial grown as half-hardy annual**
• no problems

Pansy

Viola x *wittrockiana*
VIOLACEAE

The familiar flat-faced pansy can be found in flower throughout the year. It is most useful as part of winter-spring bedding schemes, to provide a splash of colour in the darkest months of the year, and will flower for up to six months if left undisturbed. Colours range from pure white to jet black and can be single or with a change of colour at the centre of the flower, or bicoloured. Use with spring bulbs in beds and containers, and for adding colour to the cottage garden. Cultivars include the 'Universal' series, with the best forms for winter flowers, and the 'Turbo' series, which is better for spring flowering. Grow in any reasonable garden soil in sun or partial shade.
Height **15–25cm (6–10in)**
Spread **20–30cm (8–12in)**
Hardiness **Hardy**
• protect from slugs; deadhead often

ADDITIONAL ANNUALS AND BIENNIALS

Common name	Botanical name	Family name
Bacopa	*Bacopa* 'Snowflake'	SCROPHULARIACEAE
	Browallia speciosa	SOLANACEAE
	Calceolaria integrifolia	SCROPHULARIACEA
Canterbury bells	*Campanula medium*	CAMPANULACEAE
	Canna indica	CANNACEAE
	Clarkia elegans	ONAGRACEAE
	Cobaea scandens	COBAEACEAE
	Coleus spp.	LABIATAE
	Convolvulus tricolor	CONVOLVULACEAE
	Delphinium ajacis	RANUNCULACEAE
	Diascia rigescens	SCROPHULARIACEAE
California poppy	*Eschscholzia californicum*	PAPAVERACEAE
	Eustoma grandiflorum	GENTIANACEAE
	Gilia capitata	POLEMONIACEAE
	Godetia spp.	ONAGRACEAE
Tree mallow	*Lavatera trimestris*	MALVACEAE
	Limnanthes douglasii	LIMNANTHACEAE
Monkey flower	*Mimulus luteus*	SCROPHULARIACEAE
	Nemesia strumosa	SCROPHULARIACEAE
	Nemophila menziesii	HYDROPHYLLACEAE
	Nierembergia caerulea	SOLANACEAE
	Nolana paradoxa	SOLANACEAE
	Phacelia campanularia	HYDROPHYLLACEAE
Poppy	*Papaver rhoeas*	PAPAVERACEAE
	Salpiglossis sinuata	SOLANACEAE
Sage	*Salvia splendens*	LABIATAE
Scabious	*Scabiosa atropurpurea*	DIPSACEAE
Butterfly flower, Poor man's orchid	*Schizanthus* spp.	SOLANACEAE
Black-eyed Susan	*Thunbergia alata*	ACANTHACEAE
Nasturtium	*Tropaeolum majus*	TROPAEOLACEAE
Verbena	*Verbena* x *hybrida*	VERBENACEAE

Herbaceous Perennials

Bear's breeches

Acanthus mollis
ACANTHACEAE

A wonderful architectural plant grown as much for its large, shiny, evergreen leaves as for its spikes of mauve and white flowers in late summer. Best planted on the corner of a border or alone so that you can enjoy the shape of the plant as a whole; it also makes a good plant for larger containers. The cultivar 'Latifolius' has larger leaves and is even more dramatic. Grow in full sun to light shade in well-drained, sandy soil.

Height **90cm–1.2m (36in–4ft)**
Spread **90cm (36in)**
Hardiness **Hardy**
• **can be invasive**

African lily

Agapanthus campanulatus
ALLIACEAE

A lovely plant with clumps of bright green, arching, strap-like leaves with rounded clusters of blue, lily-like flowers in mid- to late summer. It adds an exotic touch to the flower border and in less favoured areas makes an excellent container plant. Hybrids between the different agapanthus include the deep blue 'Bressingham Blue', the white 'Bressingham White' and the lower-growing 'Lilliput' with bright blue flowers. Must have a sheltered position in full sun and well-drained neutral to alkaline soil.

Height **60–75cm (24–30in)**
Spread **45cm (18in)**
Hardiness **Hardy to –10°C (14°F)**
• **mulch for winter protection**

Japanese anemone

Anemone x *hybrida*
RANUNCULACEAE

An elegant plant with clusters of pink or white, cup-shaped single, semi-double or double flowers borne on upright stems for long periods in late summer, above clumps of handsome, palmate leaves. Long lived, vigorous and easy to grow, it makes an excellent plant for the back of the late-summer border and is a useful cut flower. It can also look good in open woodland and informal areas. The range of cultivars includes 'Honorine Jobert' with single white flowers and 'Queen Charlotte' with semi-double pink flowers. A similar plant is *A. hupehensis*, which includes the cultivar 'September Charm', a lower-growing plant with single pink flowers. Grow in full sun to medium shade and almost any soil, though it grows best in deep, fertile, neutral to alkaline soil.

Height **45cm–1.2m (18in–4ft)**
Spread **45–60cm (18–24in)**
Hardiness **Hardy**
• **all anemones are mildly poisonous**

Columbine

Aquilegia vulgaris
RANUNCULACEAE

Aquilegias form mounds of grey-green, fern-like leaves from which rise stems of delicate, spurred flowers in late spring to early summer. Almost every colour is available and there are many bicoloured and double-flowered forms. An essential plant for the cottage garden and for any early-summer flower border. The best cultivars include 'Hensol Harebell' with nodding, purple, short-spurred flowers, 'Magpie' with dark purple and white flowers and the double-flowered pink and white 'Nora Barlow'. Grow in full sun to light shade and in well-drained soil.

Height **60–90cm (24–36in)**
Spread **45–60cm (18–24in)**
Hardiness **Hardy**
• **all parts are mildly poisonous**

LEFT: *The blue flowers of* Agapanthus campanulatus *create a strong impact in the flower border.* **ABOVE**: *The pink* Anemone hupehensis *'Splendens' is good for brightening up dull corners.*

Astilbe

Astilbe x *arendsii*
SAXIFRAGACEAE

The domes of ferny, cut-leaved foliage give rise to upright flower stems with plumes of red, pink or white flowers in summer. One of the prettiest plants for damp borders and bog gardens, it is suitable for the flower border only if the soil is damp all summer. Some of the best cultivars include 'Irrlicht' with white flowers, 'Fanal' with deep red flowers carried in short, dense spikes, and 'Venus' with large flowers of rosy-pink. Grow in full sun to light shade and in rich, moist soil, which must retain moisture throughout the growing season. They grow best if placed next to a pool or stream.

Height **60–90cm (24–36in)**
Spread **30–45cm (12–18in)**
Hardiness **Hardy**
• **leaves and flowers shrivel in dry soil**

Bellflower

Campanula persicifolia
CAMPANULACEAE

One of the many campanulas which provide us with a range of excellent border plants, it produces mounds of narrow, evergreen leaves with tall spikes of lavender-blue, open, bell-shaped flowers in summer. Plant with yellow daylilies or with pink peonies; it also makes a long-lasting cut flower. Among dozens of cultivars are 'Alba' with pure white flowers, the double-flowered 'Fleur de Neige', 'Chettle Charm' with pretty white flowers edged with blue, 'Hampstead White' with semi-double white flowers and 'Telham Beauty' with tall, large lavender-blue flowers. Grow in full sun or very light shade in well-drained, humus-rich soil.

Height **60–90cm (24–36in)**
Spread **60cm (24in)**
Hardiness **Hardy**
• **attracts bees, so avoid if allergic to bee stings**
• **may need staking**

RIGHT: *The bright blue flowers of* Campanula latiloba, *typical of the many beautiful bellflowers.*
FAR RIGHT: Eryngium giganteum *is a useful foil to yellow flowers in the sunny border and also looks attractive planted in gravel.*
BELOW: Astilbe *x* arendsii *'Fanal' is useful for bringing dramatic colour to a border over a long period.*

Delphinium

Delphinium elatum
RANUNCULACEAE

Tall, stately plants which are an indispensable part of any flower border, with stems of showy flowers rising above deeply cut green leaves. Flowers are usually blue, but pink, white and purple hybrids are readily available. Flowering from early summer, some varieties rebloom in late summer and early autumn. Hybrids include 'Black Knight' with dark blue flowers, 'Galahad' with white flowers and 'Astolat', which is lavender with a darker centre. Grow in full sun in well-drained, fertile soil.
Height **1.2–1.8m (4ft–6ft)**
Spread **60cm (24in)**
Hardiness **Hardy**
• all parts are poisonous

Bleeding heart

Dicentra spectabilis
PAPAVERACEAE

An interesting plant with graceful foliage and flowers. The leaves are deeply divided and a light grey-green colour. The pink and white flowers are heart-shaped and hang down from red, arching flower stems in late spring and early summer. A good plant for the early border or for shade planting, although it tends to die down after flowering and so should be placed where later flowering plants will take over the space. The form *alba* is pure white, which is equally lovely. Grow in full sun or light shade and in moist, but well-drained, humus-rich soil.
Height **40–50cm (16–20in)**
Spread **30–45cm (12–18in)**
Hardiness **Hardy**
• all parts are mildly poisonous

Sea holly

Eryngium x *tripartitum*
APIACEAE

An elegant plant with deeply-lobed, greyish-green, spiny foliage and small, teasel-like flower cones ringed by steely-blue, spiny bracts from early to mid-summer. A useful foil to yellow flowers in the sunny border and also attractive planted in gravel. There are other closely related species, including *E. giganteum* with blue-white flowers and grey foliage and *E. amethystinum* with dark blue flowers and silver-blue foliage. Grow in full sun in sandy, well-drained soil with plenty of organic matter.
Height **60–75cm (24–30in)**
Spread **45cm (18in)**
Hardiness **Hardy**
• prickly plant to handle
• may attract bees, so avoid if allergic to bee stings

Geum

Geum chiloense
ROSACEAE

A plant which is useful for its bright orange, scarlet and yellow flowers. The flowers are round and bloom from late spring to mid-summer and are held up above the attractive domes of bright green, lobed and indented leaves. A good front or mid-border plant and best grouped for effect. 'Fire Opal' has orange-flame flowers, 'Lady Stratheden' has double yellow flowers and 'Mrs J Bradshaw' has double red flowers. Easy to grow in full sun or light shade and in any well-fed soil.
Height **40–60cm (16–24in)**
Spread **45cm (18in)**
Hardiness **Hardy**
• can be short lived

Daylily

Hemerocallis hybrids
HEMEROCALLIDACEAE

The daylily is a handsome, robust and trouble-free plant that deserves a place in every garden. The foliage is very attractive with long, green, arching, strap-shaped leaves. The flowers are large and trumpet-shaped, and although each lasts only a day, many more blooms always follow. There are dozens of hybrids, varying from the very popular, low-growing, yellow-flowered 'Stella de Oro' to the tall, deep red 'Stafford' which reaches 90cm (36in), and 'Pink Damask' at 75cm (30in) high. Easily grown, daylilies tolerate full sun or medium shade and soil ranging from well-drained and dry to constantly moist.
Height **30–90cm (12–36in)**
Spread **45–60cm (18–24in)**
Hardiness **Hardy**
• some yellow cultivars are scented

Siberian iris

Iris sibirica
IRIDACEAE

A graceful plant with tall, narrow, arching, green leaves and typical iris flowers on tall, slender stalks in early summer. Although the flowers are relatively short-lived, the foliage looks good all summer. Plant in the middle or back of the flower border or in damp areas and edges of bog gardens. Colours range from white, cream and yellow to all shades of blue and purple. Attractive cultivars include the smaller 'Flight of Butterflies' with blue and white flowers, 'Papillon' with pale blue flowers and 'Tropic Night' with dark purple flowers. Grow in full sun or light shade in humus-rich, moisture-retentive soil.
Height **60cm–1.2m (24in–4ft)**
Spread **45–60cm (18–24in)**
Hardiness **Hardy**
• all parts of most irises are poisonous and the sap of some is known to cause mild skin irritation

Peony

Paeonia officinalis
PAEONIACEAE

One of the most popular border plants with its single or, more usually, double, large, round flowers and wide domes of compound, shiny green leaves. Place in the middle of the border, where the flowers can have maximum impact, and mix with delphinium and shrub roses. Flower colours range from white, cream or pink to deep red and burgundy. Among the large number of cultivars and hybrids are 'Alba Plena' with double white flowers and 'Rubra Plena', the old-fashioned double red peony. Grow in full sun to very light shade and in deep, rich, well-drained soil.
Height **60–90cm (24–36in)**
Spread **75cm–1.2m (30in–4ft)**
Hardiness **Hardy**
• some cultivars are scented

Oriental poppy

Papaver orientale
PAPAVERACEAE

A spectacular flowering plant with large, cup-shaped flowers. The large hairy leaves are light green with a grey sheen and can look untidy towards the end of summer. Plant near the back of the border with later-flowering asters in front to cover the foliage in late summer. Colours range from the astonishing black and white flowers of 'Black and White' to 'Helen Elisabeth' with salmon-pink flowers and 'Curlilocks' with orange and black flowers. Grow in full sun or light shade in soil with plenty of organic matter.

Height **75–90cm (30–36in)**
Spread **75–90cm (30–36in)**
Hardiness **Hardy**
• may attract bees, so avoid if allergic to bee stings

Penstemon hybrids

Penstemon
SCROPHULARIACEAE

Penstemons are one of the loveliest of all garden plants and one of the most floriferous. Spikes of funnel-shaped flowers appear from early to late summer and come in a wide range of colours from pink to blue and deep purple. Plant in the front or middle of the border with other summer flowers like polemoniums and geraniums. Hybrids include 'Garnet' with dark red flowers, 'Sour Grapes' with pale blue flowers flushed lilac-purple and 'White Bedder', which is white with a tinge of pink. Easy to grow in sun or partial shade in any well-drained soil.
Height **45–60cm (18–24in)**
Spread **38cm (15in)**
Hardiness **Depends on hybrid**
• no problems

Garden phlox

Phlox paniculata
POLEMONIACEAE

An almost essential plant for the late-summer flower border with its tall domes of pink, white or lavender flowers held up above its rather dull green leaves. The large range of cultivars includes 'Norah Leigh' with white-edged foliage and lavender flowers, the white-flowered 'Fujiyama' and 'Mother of Pearl' with soft pink flowers. Grow in full sun to light shade in deep, moist but well-drained, rich soil.
Height **90cm–1.2m (36in–4ft)**
Spread **45–60cm (18–24in)**
Hardiness **Hardy**
• some white-flowered phlox are scented

Jacob's ladder

Polemonium caeruleum
POLEMONIACEAE

The common name for this flower comes from the arrangement of the light green leaves, which are opposite each other and suggest a ladder.

The upright flower stems have clusters of bright blue flowers in late spring and early summer. A lovely plant for the middle of the flower border and a useful addition to the shade garden. The form *album* has white flowers and 'Brise d'Anjou' is a new cultivar with cream edges to the green leaves and blue flowers. Easy to grow in sun or partial shade in any reasonable well-drained soil.
Height **45–90cm (18–36in)**
Spread **45cm (18in)**
Hardiness **Hardy**
• attractive to bees, so avoid if allergic to bee stings

Rodgersia

Rodgersia pinnata
SAXIFRAGACEAE

A majestic plant with large, bronze-green, deeply veined, compound leaves and erect stems with a plume-like cluster of small, creamy flowers in early to late summer. They need plenty of room but look wonderful when planted in damp soil beside ponds and streams and mix well with

ABOVE LEFT: *The large, round, deep red flowers of* Paeonia officinalis *'Rubra Plena'.*
LEFT: *The dramatic sugary pink and black flowers of the*

oriental poppy Papaver orientale *'Turkish Delight'.*
ABOVE: Phlox paniculata *'Barnwell' makes a very attractive addition to the late summer border.*

astilbes and hostas. The cultivar 'Elegans' has larger leaves and creamy flowers and 'Superba' has brilliant pink flowers and a bronzier leaf colour. Grow in partial to full shade in moist, humus-rich soil.

Height **90cm–1.2m (36in–4ft)**
Spread **90cm–1.2m (36in–4ft)**
Hardiness **Hardy**
• **must have the right soil and moisture conditions**

Sisyrinchium striatum

IRIDACEAE

A very useful plant with upright, grey-green, sword-shaped leaves and spikes of pale yellow flowers in summer. The leaves are evergreen and their strong shape makes this an excellent plant for planting in gravel and for beds near the house. The subtle shade of the flowers blends with almost any colour scheme and there is an even better cultivar with striped, pale yellow and green leaves, 'Aunt May', which deserves a place in every garden. Grow in full sun in a light, well-drained soil with plenty of added organic matter.

Height **45–60cm (18–24in)**
Spread **45cm (18in)**
Hardiness **Hardy**
• **seedlings can be a nuisance**

Spiked speedwell

Veronica spicata
SCROPHULARIACEAE

A semi-evergreen plant forming domes of deep green leaves from which arise intense blue flowers in tall, erect spikes in mid- to late summer. A good plant for any flower border but perhaps seen at its best in a well-drained bed beside a pond or stream. The subspecies *incana* has silvery-grey, felt-like leaves and bright blue flowers. There are many other veronicas, including the lower-growing *V. austriaca* spp. *teucrium* 'Crater Lake Blue', which has navy-blue flowers in arching spikes. Grow in full sun to light shade in well-drained soil.

Height **45–60cm (18–24in)**
Spread **45cm (18in)**
Hardiness **Hardy**
• **attractive to bees, so avoid if allergic to bee stings**

ABOVE: *The pretty blue flowers of* Veronica austriaca *spp.* teucrium *'Crater Lake Blue' appear in early summer.*

LEFT: Polemonium foliosissimum *is very similar to the more usually planted Jacob's ladder* P. caeruleum.

ADDITIONAL HERBACEOUS PERENNIALS

Common name	Botanical name	Family name
Hollyhock	*Alcea rosea*	MALVACEAE
Onion	*Allium karataviense*	ALLIACEAE
	Anchusa azurea	BORAGINACEAE
	Armeria maritima	PLUMBAGINACEAE
	Aruncus dioicus	ROSACEAE
	Asphodeline lutea	ASPHODELACEAE
	Baptisia australis	PAPILIONACEAE
	Camassia cusickii	HYACINTHACEAE
Bitter cress	*Cardamine trifolia*	BRASSICACEAE
	Corydalis flexuosa	PAPAVERACEAE
	Crambe maritima	BRASSICACEAE
Montbretia	*Crocosmia masoniorum*	IRIDACEAE
Angel's fishing rod, Wandflower	*Dierama pulcherrimum*	IRIDACEAE
Willow herb	*Epilobium glabellum*	ONAGRACEAE
Foxtail lily, King's spear	*Eremurus robustus*	ASPHODELACEAE
Meadowsweet	*Filipendula ulmaria*	ROSACEAE
	Galtonia candicans	HYACINTHACEAE
Gentian	*Gentiana asclepiadea*	GENTIANACEAE
Cranesbill	*Geranium* 'Johnson's Blue'	GERANIACEAE
	Gladiolus hybrids	IRIDACEAE
	Kirengeshoma palmata	HYDRANGEACEAE
Red-hot poker, Torch lily	*Kniphofia citrina*	ASPHODELACEAE
	Linum perenne	LINACEAE
Lilyturf	*Liriope muscari*	CONVALLARIACEAE
Loosestrife	*Lysimachia clethroides*	PRIMULACEAE
Purple loosestrife	*Lythrum salicaria*	LYTHRACEAE
Plume poppy	*Macleaya cordata*	PAPAVERACEAE
Poppy	*Meconopsis betonicifolia*	PAPAVERACEAE
	Mertensia pulmonarioides	BORAGINACEAE
	Penstemon heterophyllus	SCROPHULARIACEAE
Obedient plant	*Physostegia virginiana*	LAMIACEAE
Balloon flower	*Platycodon grandiflorus*	CAMPANULACEAE
	Potentilla recta	ROSACEAE
Sage	*Salvia* x *superba*	LAMIACEAE
Scabious	*Scabiosa caucasica*	DIPSACEAE
Kaffir lily	*Schizostylis coccinea*	IRIDACEAE
Figwort	*Scrophularia auriculata*	SCROPHULARIACEAE
	Sidalcea candida	MALVACEAE
Meadow rue	*Thalictrum aquilegiifolium*	RANUNCULACEAE
Spiderwort	*Tradescantia* x *andersoniana*	COMMELINACEAE
Globeflower	*Trollius* x *cultorum*	RANUNCULACEAE

Ground Cover Plants

Bugle

Ajuga reptans
LAMIACEAE

A really useful plant for an evergreen carpeting effect. The stems, covered by round, shiny, almost metallic leaves, run horizontally over the ground, rising only to produce tiered whorls of intense blue flowers on 15cm (6in) stems in late spring and early summer. Good as ground cover below shrubs or trees, provided the soil is moist. The coloured-leaved varieties make an attractive edging for a border of low-growing plants. 'Atropurpurea' has deep purple leaves and blue flowers, 'Burgundy Glow' has foliage that is a mixture of pink and burgundy, edged with cream, 'Rainbow' has multicoloured leaves in purple, green and cream, and 'Variegata' has green and white variegated leaves. Grow in full sun or partial shade in moist, humus-rich soil.
Height **10–25cm (4–10in) when in flower**
Spread **45–60cm (18–24in)**
Hardiness **Hardy**
• **will not tolerate drought**

Lady's mantle

Alchemilla mollis
ROSACEAE

One of the essential plants for every garden as it will grow virtually anywhere and flowers almost continuously all summer. The soft green, rounded leaves collect water around their edges like a string of jewels and the tiny greenish flowers are carried in foamy clusters. Use it as edging for rose beds and flower borders, as massed ground cover or in gravel, where it will happily self-seed. Grow in either sun or shade and in any soil.
Height **30–40cm (12–16in)**
Spread **45–60cm (18–24in)**
Hardiness **Hardy**
• **can become invasive through self-seeding**

Masterwort

Astrantia major
APIACEAE

A very showy plant with neat mounds of palmate foliage and erect stems of starry domes of pinky-white flowers in early summer. An excellent border plant for front or middle rows, or massed in the semi-wild garden. The range of newer, more ornamental cultivars includes 'Sunningdale Variegated' with cream and green variegated leaves, 'Shaggy' with large, greenish-pink flowers, and *rubra* with deep red flowers. Grow in full sun or partial shade and moisture-retentive, rich soil.
Height **60–75cm (24–30in)**
Spread **45–60cm (18–24in)**
Hardiness **Hardy**
• **no problems**

Elephant's ears

Bergenia cordifolia
SAXIFRAGACEAE

A handsome plant with large, rounded, shiny, bright green, evergreen leaves and thick stems with clusters of nodding pink flowers in early spring. An excellent edging plant for rose gardens and flower borders in either sun or shade. The cultivar 'Purpurea' has deeper pink flowers and leaves that turn purple-red in winter. Grow in sun or partial shade; it prefers moist, humus-rich soil, but it will tolerate any garden soil.
Height **30cm (12in)**
Spread **45–60cm (18–24in)**
Hardiness **Hardy (benefits from winter protection in cold areas)**
• **may need lifting and dividing every five years**

Cotoneaster dammeri
ROSACEAE

An evergreen shrub that has horizontal branches covered with tiny, shiny, dark green leaves and minute white flowers in spring, followed by red berries in autumn. The growth is totally flat, hugging the ground, or hanging down over a wall or bank. It will grow in sun or

LEFT: *Bugle,* Ajuga reptans, *carpets the ground with blue flowers in spring and summer.*

ABOVE: *The soft green leaves of* Alchemilla mollis *catch drops of rain on its soft foliage.*

RIGHT: *The deep pink, star-like flowers of masterwort* Astrantia major rosea.

FAR RIGHT: *The yellow flowers and tiny leaves of the rock rose* Helianthemum nummularium *which loves a sunny position (see p.98).*

BELOW: *A mixed planting of heathers* Erica carnea *'Springwood White' complementing the deep pink flowers of* E. c. *'Vivellii'.*

shade, particularly that cast by buildings, and in almost any soil, although it grows best in heavy, limy soil. A very useful plant and my first choice for growing on banks or over walls.

Height **10cm (4in)**
Spread **90cm–1.2m (36in–4ft)**
Hardiness **Hardy**
• may attract bees, so avoid if allergic to bee stings

Barrenwort

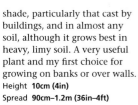

Epimedium perralderianum
BERBERIDACEAE

A very attractive ground cover for the shady garden, with domes of evergreen, heart-shaped leaves and distinctive hanging clusters of yellow flowers which arise just above the new leaves in spring. Very similar is *E. perralchicum* 'Frohnleiten', but the green leaves are tinged with red. Other

useful epimediums are *E.* x *rubrum* with pink flowers and *E.* x *youngianum* 'Niveum' with white flowers. Grow in partial or full shade; prefers moist, humus-rich soil, although it tolerates dry shade.

Height **25–30cm (10–12in)**
Spread **45–60cm (18–24in)**
Hardiness **Hardy**
• no problems

Winter-flowering heather

Erica carnea
ERICACEAE

An extremely useful winter-flowering carpeting plant. The upright branches are hidden by the tiny leaves and masses of small, pink or white flowers cover the tips from late autumn right through winter. It is very attractive as mass planting on

banks or in rock gardens. The innumerable cultivars range from the dwarf 'Vivellii' with dark bronze-green foliage and deep pink flowers to the golden foliage and pink flowers of 'Aurea', and the spreading green branches and large white flowers of 'Springwood White'. Best grown in full sun to light shade and moist, neutral to acid soil, although it tolerates mild alkalinity.

Height **30–45cm (12–18in)**
Spread **45–60cm (18–24in)**
Hardiness **Hardy**
• will not tolerate drought

Cranesbill

Geranium spp.
GERANIACEAE

The herbaceous geraniums are among the best and most useful of all garden plants. An extensive range of species is

available, most of which are fully hardy and tolerant of a wide variety of soils and flower over a long period of time. *G. macrorrhizum* is probably the best for general ground cover being fast growing and tough. The lobed, soft green leaves are semi-evergreen and form a dense mat of foliage from which arise sparse clusters of round, bright pink flowers in mid-summer. There are several good cultivars, including *G. m.* 'Album' with white flowers and *G. m.* 'Ingwersen's Variety' with soft pink flowers. They all provide excellent ground cover for shady areas. Among the other species are several fine border plants, including the blue-flowered *G.* 'Johnson's Blue' and the salmon-pink flowered *G.* x *oxonianum* 'Wargrave Pink', both of which flower for a long time in summer and are perfect edging for almost any border. *G. phaeum* with deep purple flowers, *G. nodosum* with lilac-pink flowers and the white-flowered *G. sylvaticum* 'Album' are all good in deep shade. For the smaller border or rock garden, use the various forms of *G. sanguineum* and the even smaller *G. cinereum*. Check the amount of sun required for the chosen species and plant in any well-drained garden soil.

Height **20–45cm (8–18in)**
Spread **30–60cm (12–24in)**
Hardiness **Hardy**
• many geraniums attract bees, so choose carefully if you are allergic to bee stings

Rock rose

Helianthemum nummularium
CISTACEAE

This is the best carpeting plant for dry soils and full sun, with evergreen grey or green, hairy leaves and small, rose-like flowers in myriads of colours all summer. Use them as a carpet between paving slabs, for covering a sunny bank, or at the front of raised beds or a sunny border. Popular hybrids include *H.* 'Wisley Primrose' with grey leaves and soft yellow flowers, *H.* 'Rhodanthe Carneum' with grey foliage and pink flowers, *H.* 'The Bride' with grey leaves and white flowers, and *H.* 'Jubilee' with green foliage and double yellow flowers. Grow in full sun and sandy, well-drained, alkaline soil.
Height 15cm (6in)
Spread 45–60cm (18–24in)
Hardiness Hardy
• may attract bees, so avoid if allergic to bee stings

Coral bells

Heuchera sanguinea
SAXIFRAGACEAE

Long-lived evergreen plants for edging beds whether in sun or partial shade. Rounded, glossy leaves form domes of foliage from which rise thin, wiry stems carrying open clusters of tiny pink flowers in late spring and into summer. They look lovely planted with aquilegia, catmint and geraniums. One of the most useful heucheras is the purple-leaved *H. micrantha* 'Palace Purple' and *H.* 'Pewter Moon' with purple leaves shot with silver. There is also a green-flowered hybrid, *H.* 'Green Ivory', and *H.* 'Firefly' with vermilion-red flowers. Grow in full sun to partial shade in well-drained, humus-rich soil.
Height 30–45cm (12–18in)
Spread 45cm (18in)
Hardiness Hardy
• lift and replant regularly

Plantain lily

Hosta spp.
HOSTACEAE

There are an enormous number of hostas from which to choose. All are excellent plants for any garden with an area of moist soil or shade, and, apart from a few with scented flowers, they are good low-allergen plants. All have large, arching, cone-shaped leaves with deeply indented veins which form elegant mounds of foliage. The lavender or white tubular flowers hang down from slender, upright stems in early to mid-summer. They are all excellent plants for the shade garden or beside water and the more dramatic species are good planted in containers. Apart from attracting slugs, the only problem is that they look rather untidy in late autumn when the leaves die down. The most dramatic species is *H. sieboldiana* with very large, blue-green leaves and lilac-blue flowers; given adequate moisture, it makes a striking display. The form *H. s.* var. *elegans* has rounder foliage and a bluer leaf colour. *H.* 'Frances Williams' has a pale creamy edge to the leaves. Among the smaller-leaved hostas are many with variegated leaves, including *H. undulata albomarginata* with green leaves edged with white, *H.* 'Francee' with dark green foliage and a white margin, and *H. fortunei* var. *albopicta* with yellow-centred leaves. For small gardens there are smaller hostas, including *H.* 'Halcyon' with blue-green leaves and *H.* 'Ground Master' with green leaves edged with a wide band of cream. Grow in light to full shade in moist, humus-rich soil.
Height 30–90cm (12–36in)
Spread 30cm–1.2m (12in–4ft)
Hardiness Hardy
• protect from slugs
• some cultivars have scented flowers

Yellow archangel

Lamium galeobdolon 'Florentinum'
LAMIACEAE

This is the perfect choice for planting in dry shade under trees where very few other plants will survive. In these conditions the green and white marbled leaves form a luxuriant evergreen carpet. Yellow-lipped flowers appear above the leaves in early summer. The cultivar 'Hermann's Pride', with more dramatic, silver-speckled leaves, is less invasive. A closely related species, *L. maculatum* has an almost completely flat habit and is available in several varieties. There is also a range of cultivars with variegated leaves and white, pink or mauve flowers. Grow in partial or full shade in any ordinary garden soil.
Height 30–45cm (12–18in)
Spread 60cm (24in)
Hardiness Hardy
• invasive

Catmint

Nepeta racemosa
LAMIACEAE

Catmint is the perfect plant for a sunny site at the front of a border, where it can spread itself on to the adjacent path or terrace. Small, hairy, grey-green leaves on arching stems are topped with whorls of lavender-blue flowers all summer. It is a good edging plant for rose beds and an excellent addition to a grey-leaved border. Grow in full sun and well-drained soil, although it tolerates both partial shade and poor, dry soil.
Height 30–45cm (12–18in)
Spread 60–90cm (24–36in)
Hardiness Hardy
• attracts bees, so avoid if allergic to bee stings

Lungwort

Pulmonaria saccharata
BORAGINACEAE

Lovely spring-flowering plants with large, rough-textured, green leaves variously spotted or dotted with silver, and pendulous blue and pink bell-shaped flowers. They are good in shade, forming a dense, impenetrable carpet of leaves all year round. For more ornamental planting, mix with comfrey, tiarella and dicentras. 'Leopard' has even more dramatic spots on its leaves and pink-red flowers, 'Alba' has white flowers and *P. angustifolia* has narrow green leaves and gentian-blue flowers. Grow in partial to full shade and moist, humus-rich soil.

ABOVE: *The dead nettle* Lamium maculatum *'Beacon Silver' forming a carpet of silver and pink.*
LEFT: *A lovely ground cover plant for shade and moisture* Hosta fortunei *var.* albopicta.

Height **25–40cm (10–16in)**
Spread **45cm (18in)**
Hardiness **Hardy**
• **no problems**

Comfrey

Symphytum grandiflorum
BORAGINACEAE

The comfreys are really tough plants for difficult areas like heavy soils in shade where nothing else will grow. They form a carpet of large, rich green leaves with arching stems of hanging tubular flowers. There are some attractive cultivars, including 'Goldsmith' with bright cream and green variegated leaves and pale blue flowers and 'Hidcote Blue' with green leaves and pink buds opening to blue flowers. Grow in partial to full shade in any soil.
Height **30cm (12in)**
Spread **60–90cm (24–36in)**
Hardiness **Hardy**
• **invasive**

Foamflower

Tiarella cordifolia
SAXIFRAGACEAE

A very pretty, low-growing carpeting plant for shady areas, with rosettes of triangular, soft-textured, light green leaves and clouds of tiny cream flowers borne on short, upright stems in late spring to mid-summer. It forms a weed-free mat of leaves, looks wonderful under shrubs and trees and combines well with comfrey and dicentras. *T. wherryi* has flowers with a pink tinge. Grow in partial or full shade in moist, humus-rich, neutral soil.
Height **20–30cm (8–12in) when in flower**
Spread **45cm (18in)**
Hardiness **Hardy**
• **needs shade or moisture**

Periwinkle

Vinca minor
APOCYNACEAE

An evergreen plant which forms a flat carpet of foliage all year round. The small, shiny, dark green leaves are covered with blue-violet starry flowers in spring. It will grow almost

anywhere, but is best used as ground cover under trees and shrubs or covering a bank. It is too rampant to be grown in beds and borders unless you use the variegated cultivars, such as 'Argenteovariegata' with green and white leaves or 'Aureovariegata' with cream and green leaves. Cultivars are available with white, purple and pale blue flowers and also double flowers; all are worth growing. It does best in partial or full shade in a well-drained, humus-rich soil.
Height **10cm (4in)**
Spread **90cm (36in) – indefinite**
Hardiness **Hardy**
• **can become invasive**

LEFT: *Catmint,* Nepeta racemosa, *one of the best ground cover plants for sunny beds and borders.*
BELOW LEFT: *The yellow variegated leaves of* Symphytum *'Goldsmith' will brighten up the darkest corner of any garden.*
BELOW: *The pure white flowers and green and yellow variegated foliage of* Vinca minor *'Argenteovariegata'.*

ADDITIONAL GROUND COVER PLANTS

Common name	Botanical name	Family name
Bishop's weed, Gout weed, Ground elder	*Aegopodium podagraria* 'Variegatum'	APIACEAE
Masterwort	*Brunnera macrophylla*	BORAGINACEAE
Scotch heather	*Calluna vulgaris*	ERICACEAE
St Dabeoc's heath	*Daboecia cantabrica*	ERICACEAE
Mountain avens	*Dryas octopetala*	ERICACEAE
	Glechoma hederacea 'Variegata'	LAMIACEAE
	X *Heucherella tiarelloides*	SAXIFRAGACEAE
	Houttuynia cordata	SAURURACEAE
	Hypericum calycinum	CLUSIACEAE
	Iberis sempervirens	BRASSICACEAE
Loosestrife	*Lysimachia nummularia*	PRIMULACEAE
	Omphalodes cappadocica	BORAGINACEAE
	Pachysandra terminalis	BUXACEAE
Self-heal	*Prunella grandiflora*	LAMIACEAE
Blackberry, Bramble	*Rubus tricolor*	ROSACEAE
Saxifraga	*Saxifraga umbrosa*	SAXIFRAGACEAE
	Stachys macrantha	LAMIACEAE
	Stephanandra incisa	ROSACEAE
	Symphoricarpos x *chenaultii* 'Hancock'	CAPRIFOLIACEAE
	Tellima grandiflora	SAXIFRAGACEAE
	Viburnum davidii	CAPRIFOLIACEAE
	Waldsteinia ternata	ROSACEAE

Climbers

Actinidia kolomikta

ACTINIDIACEAE

A showy deciduous climber with large, heart-shaped, shiny leaves which are purplish when young but, on becoming green, develop a white and pink blotch on the apex. The white flowers in early summer are almost completely hidden by the foliage and occasionally give rise to large, oval, yellow fruit. A climber for sunny walls and fences, it is best seen on its own rather than at the back of a border where the unusual colouring is hard to match. It prefers a sheltered position in full sun, although it tolerates light shade, and needs a well-drained, well-fed soil which does not dry out.

Height **6m (20ft)**
Spread **6m (20ft)**
Hardiness **Hardy**
• **no problems**

Clematis hybrids

RANUNCULACEAE

The sap of clematis can cause slight skin irritation, but with so few climbers available for the low-allergen garden they are included with the suggestion that gloves are worn when handling them. The other problem is that some clematis species are scented and therefore need to be excluded; however, most of the large-flowered hybrids are scent-free. These are twining climbers with tendrils and dull green leaves and large, open, plate-like starry flowers, which may be single, semi-double or double and come in a wide range of colours. Many flower from late spring and through the summer. These are superb climbers for walls, fences, pillars, pergolas or over arches, and particularly attractive at the back of a flower border planted with complementary flower colours. Among the most popular are C. 'Comtesse de Bouchaud' with single pink flowers, C. 'Perle d'Azur' with blue flowers, C. 'Marie Boisselot' with large, white flowers, and C. 'The President' with rich purple flowers. Most grow in sun or shade and in any well-fed soil, preferably slightly alkaline.

Height **5m (16ft)**
Spread **5m (16ft)**
Hardiness **Hardy**
• **leaves and sap may irritate skin**

Climbing hydrangea

Hydrangea anomala petiolaris

HYDRANGEACEAE

This is of the best self-clinging climbers for walls and buildings and its only drawback is that it loses its leaves in winter. To compensate, the bright green, shiny leaves appear quite early in spring and last well into autumn, remaining green until they fall. The clusters of flowers appear as flat, white domes and what look to be petals are, in fact, large, white bracts; the overall effect when in flower is magnificent. Apart from walls and buildings, it will clothe arbours and pergolas. Grows in sun to full shade, and does well on a sunless wall, in rich, well-drained, moist soil.

Height **Up to 12m (40ft)**
Spread **Up to 12m (40ft)**
Hardiness **Hardy**
• **may attract bees, so avoid if allergic to bee stings**

Chinese woodbine

Lonicera tragophylla

CAPRIFOLIACEAE

A great many honeysuckles have to be excluded from the low-allergen garden because of their strong scent but it is worth searching out the non-scented species. This is one of them: a spectacular deciduous climber with light grey-green leaves and whorls of bright yellow, tubular flowers on the ends of side stems in mid-summer. It climbs by twining around adjacent plants and is seen at its best climbing through large shrubs or trees, although it can be trained to cover an arbour or pergola. Grow in light shade and a moist, rich soil with protection from strong winds.

Height **Up to 12m (40ft)**
Spread **Up to 9m (30ft)**
Hardiness **Hardy**
• **can become very untidy**

Virginia creeper

Parthenocissus quinquefolia

VITACEAE

One of the favourite climbers for growing up the walls of old houses, where its brilliant autumn colour is unsurpassable. A fast-growing climber which clings to walls with small sucker pads, it has large, green leaves, divided into five leaflets, which turn vivid orange and crimson in autumn. The flowers are small and insignificant. Use it to cover large banks, walls and fences and the windowless walls of buildings. It can also be grown as ground cover. Another similar species is P. henryana, which has more attractive leaves in

ABOVE: *Pink, green and white large, heart-shaped leaves of* Actinidia kolomikta.

RIGHT: Clematis *'Perle d'Azur' is one of the best blue clematis and will grow in sun or shade.*

RIGHT: Rosa 'Climbing Iceberg'
with clusters of white flowers
throughout the summer.
BELOW RIGHT: The soft plum
foliage of Vitis vinifera 'Purpurea'
makes a perfect background for
almost any flower border.
BELOW: The unique blue and
white blooms of the passion
flower Passiflora caerulea.

Passion flower

Passiflora caerulea
PASSIFLORACEAE

The flowers of passion flower are slightly fragrant but probably not enough to act as a trigger, so I feel fairly safe including it in the low-allergen garden. This is a fast-growing, deciduous, woody-stemmed, twining climber with green, finger-like leaflets. The large, unique, white flowers, sometimes pink-flushed, have blue- or purple-banded crowns in mid- to late summer, followed by oval orange or yellow, fleshy,

summer. These are dark green with a distinctive silver-white veining, and then turn purple and red in autumn. Grow in any aspect in any reasonable well-drained garden soil.
Height **12m (40ft)**
Spread **12m (40ft)**
Hardiness **Hardy**
• **attracts bees, so avoid if allergic to bee stings**
• **berries and leaves mildly poisonous**

edible fruit in hot seasons. It looks its best when grown in sheltered gardens climbing up pergolas, pillars, walls and fences. There is a white-flowered cultivar, 'Constance Elliott', with even less fragrance. It needs a sheltered sunny position and fertile, well-drained soil. Water freely in full growth.
Height **6m (20ft)**
Spread **6m (20ft)**
Hardiness **Hardy to –5°C (23°F)**
• **may die back to ground in a hard winter**

Climbing rose

Rosa 'Climbing Iceberg'
ROSACEAE

Climbing roses have to be carefully selected for the low-allergen garden, as so many are strongly fragrant. 'Climbing Iceberg', with its healthy green leaves and sprays of white flowers, is only lightly scented, so it should not cause any problems unless you are allergic to rose thorns. The flowers are produced all summer. This is a very useful rose for training on house walls, fences, pillars and pergolas. An alternative lightly scented climbing rose is the pink and white double-flowered 'Handel', whose shapely flowers appear from summer to autumn. Where a larger, more rampant rose is needed – for example, on a large pergola or climbing into an apple tree – 'Seagull' or 'Rambling Rector' could be considered. 'Climbing Iceberg' can be grown in sun and shade in any well-fed soil.
Height **3m (10ft)**
Spread **3m (10ft)**
Hardiness **Hardy**
• **needs training**

Vitis coignetiae

VITACEAE

One of the best climbers for autumn colour, with large, heart-shaped, glabrous leaves that turn brilliant orange and scarlet in autumn. It naturally climbs into large shrubs, but it needs to be trained along wires fixed to walls, fences or pergolas. Best when used to cover low walls or allowed to scramble among conifers. It can be slow to establish but once settled grows very rapidly. Grow in any aspect and in any reasonable garden soil.
Height **12m (40ft)**
Spread **12m (40ft)**
Hardiness **Hardy**
• **can outgrow its allocated area**

Purple-leaved vine

Vitis vinifera 'Purpurea'
VITACEAE

An attractive vine with five-lobed claret leaves with a purple/blue underside. It is a form of the grapevine which has insignificant flowers but produces bunches of small, purple grapes in autumn. A wonderful climber used as a backdrop to a flower border with a pink, blue and plum colour scheme or used as a dark background behind an urn, statue or, for real drama, a white-painted seat. Train it with wires fixed to the wall or fence. It tolerates all aspects, but is best in full sun in any reasonable garden soil.
Height **6m (20ft)**
Spread **6m (20ft)**
Hardiness **Hardy**
• **may be visited by bees, so avoid if allergic to bee stings**

ADDITIONAL CLIMBERS

Common name	Botanical name	Family name
	Akebia quinata	LARDIZABALACEAE
	Ampelopsis brevipe dunculata	VITACEAE
Birthwort	*Aristolochia durior*	ARISTOLOCHIACEAE
	Celastrus orbiculatus	CELASTRACEAE
	Decumaria barbaras	AXIFRAGACEAE
	Eccremocarpus scaber	BIGNONIACEAE
	Pileostegia viburnoides	HYDRANGEACEAE
	Schisandra grandiflora	MAGNOLIACEAE
	Schizophragma integrifolium	HYDRANGEACEAE
Nasturtium	*Tropaeolum speciosum*	TROPAEOLACEAE

Herbs

Chives

Allium schoenoprasum
ALLIACEAE

A low-growing herbaceous perennial which forms clumps of grass-like foliage with small, neat silvery-pink balls of flowers in summer. A very useful edging plant for the herb garden and also a good container or window-box plant. The leaves can be cut all summer for use in salads, soups and omelettes. For culinary purposes it is best to remove all the flowers before flowering. Easy to grow in sun or light shade and any reasonable garden soil.

Height **30cm (12in)**
Spread **30cm (12in)**
Hardiness **Hardy**
• **attractive to bees, so avoid if allergic to bee stings**
• **the sap can be a mild skin irritant**

Fennel

Foeniculum vulgare
APIACEAE

This is a lovely herbaceous perennial which forms tall drifts of feathery foliage topped by flat domes of tiny yellow flowers in late summer. Planted at the back of the border, it makes a good foil for brightly coloured herbaceous plants and roses. It is also very useful for adding height and airiness to the herb garden. Bronze fennel, 'Purpureum', is an even more elegant form with bronze-coloured leaves throughout summer and a mass of seedheads. It seems particularly robust and is one of the first plants to appear in the spring. Both leaves and seed are used in cooking. Grow in full sun in a fertile, well-drained, neutral to alkaline soil.

Height **1.2–1.8m (4–6ft)**
Spread **60cm (24in)**
Hardiness **Hardy**
• **seedlings may become a problem, so remove flower heads after flowering**
• **attracts bees, so avoid if allergic to bee stings**

Sweet bay

Laurus nobilis
LAURACEAE

A useful evergreen tree which can be trained to form mopheaded small trees or kept clipped as a rounded bush. It can be used as a central feature in a herb garden or placed in a pot and used almost anywhere in the garden as a small focal point. The dark green leaves are used in cooking and for making pot-pourri. There is a golden-leaved cultivar, 'Aurea', which can be used to brighten up a shady corner. Grow in a sheltered position in full sun to medium shade in rich, well-drained soil.

Height **Up to 6m (20ft) if unclipped**
Spread **Up to 4m (13ft) if unclipped**
Hardiness **Hardy to –5°C (23°F)**
• **can suffer frost damage in a hard winter**

Lemon balm

Melissa officinalis
LAMIACEAE

Lemon balm is a wonderful lemon-scented herbaceous perennial that will grow almost anywhere. It has bright green, deeply veined leaves with small, white flowers in summer. The leaves are used as a garnish for salads, summer drinks and desserts. The green form is invasive, so it is best planted in a pot. There is a yellow and green variegated-leaf variety, 'Aurea',

and an all-yellow variety, 'All Gold'. Both of these are lovely additions to the flower border or the herb garden. Grow in full sun or partial shade in any well-drained soil.

Height **45–60cm (18–24in)**
Spread **45–60cm (18–24in)**
Hardiness **Hardy**
• **can be invasive**
• **very attractive to bees, so avoid if allergic to bee stings**

Mint

Mentha spp.
LAMIACEAE

Most of the mints are rampant herbaceous perennials with shiny green leaves and pale purple flowers in summer. There is a wide variety of mints, but the most useful are *M. spicata*, spearmint, which is used in cooking and *M.* x *piperita*, peppermint, which is used for herb teas. The more attractive mints for planting in the garden include the yellow and green variegated *M.* x *gracilis* 'Variegata', ginger mint, and the green and white variegated *M. suaveolens* 'Variegata', pineapple mint. Mints are best planted in their own area or in open-bottomed containers sunk into the bed or border – this helps to keep them under control. Grow in rich, moist soil in sun or part shade.

Height **30–45cm (12–18in)**
Spread **Unlimited**
Hardiness **Hardy**
• **invasive**
• **the sap may cause skin irritation**

Basil

Ocimum basilicum
LAMIACEAE

This is a tender perennial which is usually treated as a half-hardy annual. It has bright green leaves and small, white flowers in summer. A wonderful herb

ABOVE: *The round flower heads of chives* Allium schoenoprasum *will enhance any herb garden.*
FAR LEFT: *The bright green foliage of spearmint* Mentha spicata *is the best for use in cooking.*
LEFT: *The lemon scented leaves of the variegated lemon balm* Melissa officinalis *'Aurea'.*

for using in salads, it is worth the effort of growing each year either in pots or in the herb garden. Miniature basil forms compact low domes and is useful as an edging plant. Purple-leaved basil, var. *purpurascens,* with its dark purple leaves and deep pink flowers, adds dramatic colour to summer borders. It must have warm, sunny conditions and well-drained, neutral to alkaline soil.

Height **50cm (20in)**
Spread **30cm (12in)**
Hardiness **Tender**
• **difficult to grow in chilly, damp summers**
• **attracts bees, so avoid if allergic to bee stings**

Marjoram

Origanum vulgare
LAMIACEAE

This herbaceous perennial has soft green leaves and violet flowers in mid-summer and is a very popular culinary herb. It is an excellent plant for the front of the bed or border, particularly the yellow-leaved cultivars like 'Aureum', whose evergreen leaves become a rich yellow all summer, and 'Gold Tip', which has pointed, oval leaves with yellow tips. A good plant to attract butterflies. Green-leaved varieties require full sun, but golden-leaved varieties do better in light shade. Grow in well-drained, neutral to alkaline soil.

Height **30cm (12in)**
Spread **45cm (18in)**
Hardiness **Hardy**
• **attracts bees, so avoid if allergic to bee stings**

Parsley

Petroselinum crispum
APIACEAE

A hardy biennial with bright green, curly leaves which are a popular garnish for salads and sandwiches. It makes an attractive edging plant for the herb garden and does best in a sunny position in moist, well-drained soil.

Height **60cm (24in)**
Spread **45cm (18in)**
Hardiness **Hardy**
• **can be difficult to germinate; cover seeds with boiling water before sowing to ensure germination**

Rosemary

Rosmarinus officinalis
LAMIACEAE

An evergreen shrub with narrow grey-green leaves and pale blue flowers in spring. It is an essential plant for every herb garden and is much loved by butterflies. It also makes a useful foil for bright pink or yellow flowers in the mixed border. Low-growing prostrate cultivars such as 'Prostratus' are good for dry, sunny banks. 'Miss Jessopp's Upright' is a taller shrub and looks lovely planted either side of an entrance. It is best grown in full sun in well-drained, neutral to alkaline soil.

Height **1.5m (5ft)**
Spread **1.2m (4ft)**
Hardiness **Hardy to –10°C (14°F)**
• **not fully hardy in cold areas**
• **attracts bees, so avoid if allergic to bee stings**

Sage

Salvia officinalis
LAMIACEAE

This aromatic evergreen shrub has large, velvety, grey-green leaves and pale purple flowers in summer. The leaves are used for culinary and medicinal purposes. It is an excellent front to mid-border shrub and should be included in any herb garden. It has a long flowering season and is attractive to butterflies. 'Icterina' is the golden sage, with grey-green

and yellow variegated leaves; 'Purpurascens' has deeper coloured flowers with purple-grey leaves; 'Tricolor' is a smaller variety with grey, white and pink foliage. Grow in full sun in well-drained, neutral to alkaline soil.

Height **75cm (30in)**
Spread **75cm (30in)**
Hardiness **Hardy**
• **attracts bees, so avoid if allergic to bee stings**

Thyme

Thymus vulgaris
LAMIACEAE

The habit of this evergreen sub-shrub makes it perfect for use as ground cover. Pinkish-mauve flowers appear in summer, covering the tiny green leaves. It forms a good edging to herb gardens and is also an attractive

LEFT: *One of the most decorative of herbs the golden marjoram* Origanum vulgare *'Aureum'.*
BELOW: *The dusky deep purple leaves of the purple sage Salvia officinalis 'Purpurascens'.*

plant for growing in paving or in the rock garden. The leaves are an essential part of the *bouquet garni* used in cooking. Thyme is also a good butterfly plant. Attractive cultivars are the gold and silver thymes, *aureus* and 'Silver Posie' respectively. It is does best if grown in full sun in almost dry, neutral to alkaline soil.

Height **15cm (6in)**
Spread **30cm (12in)**
Hardiness **Hardy**
• **attracts bees, so avoid if allergic to bee stings**
• **dislikes damp, cold weather in spring**

ADDITIONAL HERBS

Common name	Botanical name	Family name
Dill	*Anethum graveolens*	APIACEAE
Chervil	*Anthriscus cerefolium*	APIACEAE
Caraway	*Carum carvi*	APIACEAE
Coriander	*Coriandrum sativum*	APIACEAE
Cumin	*Cuminum cyminum*	APIACEAE
Liquorice	*Glycyrrhiza glabra*	PAPILIONACEAE
Hyssop	*Hyssopus officinalis*	LAMIACEAE
Lovage	*Levisticum officinale*	APIACEAE
Bergamot	*Monarda didyma*	LAMIACEAE
Sweet Cicely	*Myrrhis odorata*	APIACEAE
Anise	*Pimpinella anisum*	APIACEAE
Purslane	*Portulaca oleracea*	PORTULACACEAE
Clary	*Salvia sclarea*	LAMIACEAE
Savory	*Satureja montana*	LAMIACEAE
Betony	*Stachys officinalis*	LAMIACEAE
Comfrey	*Symphytum officinale*	BORAGINACEAE
Valerian	*Valeriana officinalis*	VALERIANACEAE
Verbena	*Verbena*	VERBENACEAE

Shrubs

Japanese laurel

Aucuba japonica
CORNACEAE

A very useful evergreen shrub for planting in shady areas, where few other plants survive. The rounded bushes have dark, glossy green leaves with sulphur-yellow flowers, followed by red berries. Individual plants are either male or female, so at least one of each sex is needed to ensure berrying. The green-leaved species is very handsome, but there are a number of variegated forms, the best of which is 'Crotonifolia' with golden spots and blotches. 'Roxannie' is a free-fruiting

cultivar with a more compact habit and is the best form for most planting schemes. Plant in any soil in partial or full shade and sheltered from cold winds.
Height **3m (10ft)**
Spread **2–3m (6–10ft)**
Hardiness **Hardy**
• fruits mildly poisonous

Camellia japonica

THEACEAE

A superb plant that requires the right soil and position to thrive. Large, rounded, shiny, evergreen leaves and beautiful white, pink or red single or double flowers. It makes an excellent container plant or a wall shrub when planted to avoid the early morning sun. There are hundreds of cultivars from which to choose but among the best are 'Alba Simplex' with large, single, pure white flowers with prominent yellow stamens; 'Adolphe Audusson' with large, semi-double, rich red flowers; 'Elegans' with large, peach-pink flowers; and the glamorous 'Lady Vansittart' with red- and white-striped semi-double flowers. Camellias must be planted in a moist, acid soil, preferably high in organic matter, and in light shade sheltered from cold winds.

Height **3m (10ft)**
Spread **2–3m (6–10ft)**
Hardiness **Hardy**
• flowers damaged by frost in exposed areas

Japanese quince

Chaenomeles speciosa
ROSACEAE

A vigorous deciduous shrub with cup-shaped flowers in early spring which cover the bare branches just before the oval, dark green leaves appear. In autumn large pear-shaped fruit appear which ripen to an attractive yellow. It is best used as a wall shrub, so that its untidy habit can be kept pruned and trained to a neat shape. There is a large number of cultivars with different coloured single or double flowers, including 'Moerloosei' with pink and white single flowers similar to apple blossom, 'Nivalis' with

ABOVE: *The flowers of the japanese quince,* Chaenomeles japonica, *appear before the leaves in spring.*
ABOVE LEFT: *The shiny leaves of* Aucuba japonica *will grow in almost complete shade.*
LEFT: *One of the loveliest of spring flowers, the scarlet blooms of* Camellia japonica *'Bob's Tinsie'.*

pure white flowers and 'Phylis Moore' with lovely double coral-pink flowers. Easy to grow in any but poor alkaline soil and does well in sun or shade.
Height **2–3m (6–10ft)**
Spread **2–3m (6–10ft)**
Hardiness **Hardy**
• thorns on some branches
• may attract bees, so avoid if allergic to bee stings

Rock rose

Cistus x hybridus
CISTACEAE

A first-class evergreen shrub with oval, dark green leaves and masses of small, white flowers from early to late summer. Good for sunny borders and rock gardens. This is one of the hardiest and easiest to grow of all the cistus, but there are many other species and cultivars, including the enchanting C. 'Silver Pink' with grey, downy leaves and pale pink flowers and the bright coloured C. x *pulverulentus* 'Sunset' with cerise flowers and grey-green foliage. There is also the useful ground-covering C. x *dansereaui* 'Decumbens' with arching branches of tiny dark green leaves almost covered in small, white flowers with crimson basal blotches. Best grown in full sun and any fairly dry soil.
Height **1.2m (4ft)**
Spread **1.5m (5ft)**
Hardiness **Hardy to –5°C (23°F)**
• may attract bees, so avoid if allergic to bee stings

Smoke bush

Cotinus coggygria
ANACARDIACEAE

One of the best foliage shrubs, with mid-green leaves turning to vivid orange and yellow in autumn. The pale pink, plume-like flowers appear in summer and persist into autumn, when they become smoky-grey. Good as a specimen shrub in the lawn or with other autumn colour plants in a large border. The cultivar *C.* 'Flame' has even brighter and better autumn colour, and there are several purple-leaved forms, including 'Royal Purple', whose deep plum leaves turn scarlet-red in the autumn. Easy to grow, but prefers a rich, well-fertilized soil and full sun.

Height **3–5m (10–16ft)**
Spread **3–5m (10–16ft)**
Hardiness **Hardy**
• no problems

Cotoneaster spp.

ROSACEAE

There are many cotoneasters from which to choose, almost all of which make good garden plants. However, among the most useful and attractive are the taller-growing, evergreen species, many of which can be trained to form small trees. They all have oval, mid-green leaves, with the veins clearly visible, and small white flowers in early summer, followed by neat, round, red, orange or yellow fruit in autumn. All are good for planting as screens or as a background to other plants. Some of the best are *C. frigidus* 'Cornubia' with large clusters of flowers and fruits, *C. salicifolius* with graceful branches of long, narrow leaves and its cultivar 'Rothschildianus' with pale yellow fruits. Plant in any good garden soil and in full sun to medium shade.

Height **3–5m (10–16ft)**
Spread **3–5m (10–16ft)**
Hardiness **Hardy**
• attracts bees, so avoid if allergic to bee stings

Deutzia scabra

HYDRANGEACEAE

A free-flowering deciduous shrub with medium olive-green leaves, and clusters of bell-shaped white or pink flowers which appear from late spring into early summer. It is graceful as an addition to the mixed border or as a specimen shrub if regularly pruned. Among the more attractive forms are 'Candidissima' with double, pure white flowers and the double rose-purple flowering 'Plena'. Plant in moist soil in sun or light shade.

Height **3m (10ft)**
Spread **2–3m (6–10ft)**
Hardiness **Hardy**
• dislikes drought

Escallonia rubra

ESCALLONIACEAE

A useful evergreen shrub for milder areas and particularly for coastal gardens. It has arching branches of oval, shiny, deep green leaves covered in pinky-red flowers in summer. The best form is var. *macrantha*, with glossy, dark, aromatic leaves and deep, rosy-red flowers. There is also 'Crimson Spire', which has crimson flowers and an upright growth habit and makes an excellent informal hedge. For a smaller garden, try 'Woodside', a much smaller cultivar with tiny leaves and small, deep red flowers. Grow in any but extremely alkaline soil and in full sun.

Height **3m (10ft)**
Spread **2–3m (6–10ft)**
Hardiness **Hardy to –10°C (14°F)**
• attracts bees, so avoid if allergic to bee stings

Exochorda x *macrantha*

ROSACEAE

Graceful deciduous flowering shrubs with arching branches of grey-green leaves hung with pendulous bunches of open white flowers in late spring. For maximum effect use as a specimen shrub in the lawn underplanted with daffodils. The loveliest cultivar is 'The Bride', which forms a low mound of arching branches covered with an abundance of large white flowers amid dark green foliage, and it is worth a place in every garden. Plant in any but extremely alkaline, shallow soil in full sun to light shade.

Height **2.4m (8ft)**
Spread **3m (10ft)**
Hardiness **Hardy**
• no problems

Forsythia x *intermedia*

OLEACEAE

Easily grown, large, deciduous shrub with bright yellow, bell-shaped flowers in early spring, which flower along the bare branches before the leaves appear. They are, however, rather dull shrubs after flowering, so are best planted at the back of the border, where they can provide a green background to summer-flowering herbaceous plants and shrubs. One of the best flowering and most popular forms is 'Spectabilis' with golden-yellow flowers and there is also 'Lynwood' with even larger rich yellow flowers. Grow in any soil in full sun to medium shade.

Height **3.6m (12ft)**
Spread **3.6m (12ft)**
Hardiness **Hardy**
• no problems

LEFT: *In summer clouds of pink, fluffy flowers cover the smoke bush* Cotinus coggyria.
BELOW: *The bright yellow flowers of* Forsythia suspensa *open from early to mid-spring, before the leaves appear.*

Fuchsia magellanica

ONAGRACEAE

For continuous flowers from mid-summer until the first frosts there is almost no plant to surpass the hardy fuchsias, with their bright green leaves and pendulous red and purple flowers. They are not fully hardy and are often best planted in containers in colder areas and brought inside during the winter. In more favoured areas they are lovely in summer and autumn borders or as a graceful, informal hedge, particularly in warm coastal gardens. There are many different forms, some with golden or variegated leaves and with a range of flower colours. *F. m* var. *gracilis* has lovely arching branches with long, slender flowers. 'Versicolor' has coppery-pink young leaves turning to grey-green as the summer advances, a perfect foil to its red and purple flowers. *F. m.* var. *molinae* has delicate white flowers. Grow in any well-drained soil in full sun.

Height **1.5m (5ft)**
Spread **1.5m (5ft)**
Hardiness **Hardy to –10°C (14°F)**
• protect in winter in colder areas

Shrubby veronica

Hebe albicans
SCROPHULARIACEAE

This is one of the hardiest of the many available hebe species. It makes a low, rounded dome of round, glaucous leaves with bell-shaped clusters of white flowers in late spring and throughout the summer. An excellent plant for the front of the border, the rock garden or for growing in a container. 'Red Edge' is a most attractive form with grey foliage edged deep red and the cultivar 'Pewter Dome' has grey-green leaves. Plant in any well-drained, open soil in full sun.

Height **60cm (24in)**
Spread **90cm (36in)**
Hardiness **Hardy to −5°C (23°F)**
• **relatively short lived**

Hydrangea macrophylla

HYDRANGEACEAE

One of the best plants for late-summer flowers, with bushes of rounded, dark green leaves and large mopheads of flowers which last well into the winter. Use in the mixed border, in containers, or, even more effectively, massed in a bed or on a bank. The flower colour varies with soil acidity: many cultivars have pink flowers in alkaline soil but are red in neutral and blue in acid conditions. Among my favourite cultivars are 'Générale Vicomtesse de Vibraye', which is a clear blue in acid soil and pink in alkaline, 'Madame Emile Mouillère', which is white, and 'Ayesha' with lilac flowers in acid and pink flowers in alkaline conditions. There are also 'Lacecap' varieties that form flat domes of flowers and include the cultivar 'Tricolor', which has green leaves with creamy outer variegation. Prefers rich, deep, acid soil and light shade.

Height **1.8m (6ft)**
Spread **2.4m (8ft)**
Hardiness **Hardy**
• **dislikes drought**

Beauty bush

Kolkwitzia amabilis
CAPRIFOLIACEAE

A graceful, medium-sized, deciduous shrub with soft green leaves and pale pink, bell-shaped flowers with yellow throats in late spring through to mid-summer. It is lovely planted on its own or to enhance the summer-flowering border, or it can be planted in a row as an informal hedge. Easy to grow in any soil and full sun.

Height **3m (10ft)**
Spread **3m (10ft)**
Hardiness **Hardy**
• **no problems**

New Zealand flax

Phormium tenax
AGAVACEAE

An excellent plant for providing a focal point whether in the corner of a border, planted in gravel or in a container. The large, upright, sword-shaped, green leaves form a dramatic fan of foliage with spikes of bronze-red flowers in mid-summer. The species is too big for any except the very largest garden and it is usually better to select one of the many interesting cultivars and hybrids. 'Purpureum' has bronze-purple foliage and is nearly as large as the green form, whereas the hybrid P. 'Sundowner' is smaller and has interesting purple, cream and green striped foliage. P. 'Bronze Baby' is about one-third the size, with bronze-purple foliage. It needs a well-drained, light soil and full sun.

Height **1.8m (6ft)**
Spread **2.1m (7ft)**
Hardiness **Hardy to −10°C (14°F)**
• **takes several years to flower**

Photinia x *fraseri*

ROSACEAE

An evergreen shrub for late autumn, when its new large, glossy leaves emerge as dark red, becoming brilliant red in the winter and early spring, fading to bronze in the late spring and finally turning dark green in the summer. It rarely produces its clusters of white flowers except in very hot areas. Use for winter colour at the back of the border or fan-train against a wall, where pruning will ensure a plentiful supply of new leaves. 'Red Robin' is the best cultivar, with even brighter winter colour. Grows in any except extremely alkaline soil, in full sun to light shade.

Height **4m (13ft)**
Spread **3m (10ft)**
Hardiness **Hardy**
• **young plants can suffer from cold winters**

Spiraea japonica

ROSACEAE

A very popular deciduous shrub for the garden, providing mounds of oval leaves topped with flat domes of pink or white flowers in early to mid-summer. Useful for the front of the border, for a low, unclipped hedge and for mass planting. Among the most ornamental cultivars are 'Anthony Waterer' with new foliage frequently variegated green, and pink, cream and dark pink-red flowers, 'Goldflame' with new foliage orange-apricot becoming orange and finally gold with pink-red

ABOVE: *One of the lovely lacecap hydrangeas,* Hydrangea macrophylla *'Mariesii Perfecta'.*
LEFT: Hebe salicifolia, *an evergreen shrub with white, lilac-tinged flowers in summer.*

ABOVE: *The beauty bush,* Kolkwitzia amabilis *with pale pink flowers in late spring.*

flowers, and 'Shirobana', which has plain green leaves and pink, white or half white and half pink flowers. Plant in any good garden soil in full sun, although it tolerates light shade.

Height **75cm (30in)**
Spread **75cm (30in)**
Hardiness **Hardy**
• **no problems**

Laurustinus

Viburnum tinus
CAPRIFOLIACEAE

The winter-flowering viburnum, with evergreen leaves and domes of small, white flowers, pink in bud, from late autumn to late spring, is excellent for screening, mass planting or in the winter border. There are several cultivars, including 'Eve Price', which is smaller growing and the flowers flushed with pink, and 'Variegatum' with beautiful green and cream variegated foliage but not as hardy as the other forms. Plant in well-drained soil and light shade, although it tolerates full sun and medium shade.

Height **3m (10ft)**
Spread **3m (10ft)**
Hardiness **Hardy to –10°C (14°F)**
• **suffers in severe winters**
• **may be visited by bees**

Weigela florida

CAPRIFOLIACEAE

One of the best and easiest of all shrubs for the garden, with a neat, rounded shape, mid-green foliage and funnel-shaped pink flowers in late spring to mid-summer. A useful plant for the shrub border with coloured-leaved cultivars which are particularly effective in the mixed border as a foil to the pinks and reds of peonies and roses. 'Foliis Purpureis' has purple-flushed leaves and darker pink flowers. 'Aureovariegata' has green and cream leaves with pale pink flowers. Among the hybrids are W. 'Bristol Ruby' with ruby-red flowers and W. 'Candida' with white flowers. Easy to grow in any soil, preferably in full sun, although it tolerates some shade.

Height **2m (6ft)**
Spread **2m (6ft)**
Hardiness **Hardy**
• **may attract bees, so avoid if allergic**

LEFT: *The flowers of the evergreen shrub* Viburnum tinus *'Gwenllian' which bloom from late summer through the winter to early spring.*

FAR LEFT: Spiraea japonica *'Anthony Waterer' with bright pink flowers and sometimes variegated leaves.*

ADDITIONAL SHRUBS

Common name	Botanical name	Family name
	Abelia x *grandiflora*	CAPRIFOLIACEAE
	Abutilon x *hybridum*	MALVACEAE
Chokeberry	*Aronia arbutifolia*	ROSACEAE
Barberry	*Berberis thunbergii*	BERBERIDACEAE
	Callicarpa bodinieri	VERBENACEAE
	Carpenteria californica	HYDRANGEACEAE
	Caryopteris incana	VERBENACEAE
	Ceratostigma willmottianum	PLUMBAGINACEAE
	Choisya ternata	RUTACEAE
	Colutea arborescens	PAPILIONACEAE
	Convolvulus cneorum	CONVOLVULACEAE
Dogwood	*Cornus alba*	CORNACEAE
	Coronilla valentina glauca	PAPILIONACEAE
	Cotoneaster conspicuus	ROSACEAE
	Crinodendron hookerianum	ELAEOCARPACEAE
Broom	*Cytisus* x *kewensis*	PAPILIONACEAE
	Deutzia x *rosea*	PHILADELPHIACEAE
	Diervilla sessilifolia	CAPRIFOLIACEAE
	Enkianthus campanulatus	ERICACEAE
	Forsythia suspensa	OLEACEAE
Broom	*Genista lydia*	PAPILIONACEAE
	Griselinia littoralis	CORNACEAE
Silver bell, snowdrop tree	*Halesia monticola*	STYRACACEAE
	Hebe salicifolia	SCROPHULARIACEAE
	Hibiscus syriacus	MALVACEAE
	Indigofera heterantha	PAPILIONACEAE
	Kerria japonica	ROSACEAE
Tree mallow	*Lavatera olbia*	MALVACEAE
	Leycesteria formosa	CAPRIFOLIACEAE
	Magnolia stellata	MAGNOLIACEAE
	Nandina domestica	BERBERIDACEAE
	Neillia thibetica	ROSACEAE
Peony	*Paeonia delavayi*	PAEONIACEAE
Russian sage	*Perovskia atriplicifolia*	LAMIACEAE
	Phygelius capensis	SCROPHULARIACEAE
	Physocarpus opulifolius	ROSACEAE
	Piptanthus nepalensis	PAPILIONACEAE
	Potentilla fruticosa	ROSACEAE
Cherry	*Prunus* x *cistena*	ROSACEAE
	Pyracantha 'Teton'	ROSACEAE
Firethorn	*Rhododendron* hybrids	ERICACEAE
	Romneya coulteri	PAPAVERACEAE
Californian poppy	*Rubus* 'Beneden'	ROSACEAE
Blackberry, bramble	*Stachyurus chinensis*	STACHYURACEAE
	Symphoricarpos orbiculatus	CAPRIFOLIACEAE
Tamarisk	*Tamarix tetrandra*	TAMARICACEAE
	Teucrium fruticans	LAMIACEAE
	Yucca flaccida	AGAVACEAE

Trees

Snowy mespilus

Amelanchier lamarckii
ROSACEAE

Amelanchiers are frequently seen as shrubs in our gardens, but this species can be grown as a single-stemmed tree. It forms an attractive rounded canopy of upright branches which are covered by a cloud of white, starry flowers in spring, followed by small, soft green leaves which turn red and orange in the early autumn. Beautiful in all seasons, this is a small enough tree to be given a space in every garden. Easy to grow in any soil, including damp but not water-logged conditions, and prefers full sun but tolerates shade.

Height **7m (23ft)**
Spread **6m (20ft)**
Hardiness **Hardy**
• **no problems**

Strawberry tree

Arbutus unedo
ERICACEAE

An evergreen shrub that makes a very attractive small tree. A native of Southern Ireland, it needs a sheltered position where it is protected from the worst of the frosts. The leathery, oval, dark green leaves have purple veins and the white, pitcher-shaped flowers hang down in clusters throughout the spring and early summer. Strawberry-like, round, red fruits, edible but insipid, are produced in the autumn but frequently held on the tree until the next summer. It makes a good container plant or small specimen tree. The cultivar *A. u.* f. *rubra* has dark pink flowers and more abundant fruits. It prefers a rich, organic soil and light shade.

Height **5m (16ft)**
Spread **5m (16ft)**
Hardiness **Hardy to −10°C (14°F)**
• **may attract bees, so avoid if allergic to bee stings**

Judas tree

Cercis siliquastrum
CAESALPINIACEAE

A slow-growing, dome-shaped tree with bare branches covered in rosy-purple, pea-shaped

flowers in late spring, followed by attractive, heart-shaped leaves and in warm seasons by long, pale grey-green pods in late summer. In its early years it is best used as a shrub, either at the back of the border, where it can eventually grow into a tree, or fan-trained as a wall shrub. The cultivar *C. s.* f. *albida* has white flowers. Grows best on neutral to acid soil, although it tolerates some alkalinity, in full sun to medium shade.

Height **6m (20ft)**
Spread **6m (20ft)**
Hardiness **Hardy**
• **may attract bees, so avoid if allergic to bee stings**

Hawthorn

Crataegus laevigata
ROSACEAE

All the hawthorns are tough, easily grown trees that seem to thrive in almost any conditions, including cold, exposed sites. They are small, round-topped

LEFT: *The springtime cloud of white blossom of the snowy mespilus* Amelanchier lamarckii.
TOP: *The strawberry-like fruits and evergreen leaves of the beautiful* strawberry tree Arbutus unedo *in autumn.*
ABOVE: *The small purple flowers that cover the Judas tree* Cercis siliquastrum *in late spring.*

LEFT: *The dark pink flowers of the hawthorn* Crataegus laevigata *'Paul's Scarlet'.*

BELOW: *The large pendulous flowers of the handkerchief tree* Davidia involucrata.

trees with deeply lobed green leaves and clusters of white, pink or red flowers in late spring, followed by small, dull, red fruits in autumn. Among the cultivars are 'Paul's Scarlet' with dark pink to red double flowers and 'Rosea Flore Pleno' with double pink flowers. Several other species of crataegus are useful in the garden, notably *C. persimilis* 'Prunifolia', which has large clusters of white flowers and smooth green leaves that turn bright yellow and orange in the autumn. Plant in any soil in full sun to medium shade.

Height **6m (20ft)**
Spread **6m (20ft)**
Hardiness **Hardy**
• attracts bees, so avoid if allergic to bee stings
• large thorns

Handkerchief tree

Davidia involucrata
DAVIDIACEAE

This eventually becomes a large tree, so is best suited to the medium or large garden. The leaves are large and mid-green with felted undersides which turn yellow in the autumn. The flowers, in late spring, are the main attraction, consisting of two uneven, large, white bracts around the small, central, black flowers, the bracts looking like white pocket handkerchiefs. No other tree, low- or high-allergen, equals this when it is in full bloom. It grows best in rich, deep loam, although it tolerates a wide range of soils, and is best in light shade.

Height **12m (40ft)**
Spread **6m (20ft)**
Hardiness **Hardy**
• slow growing and takes years to produce flowers, but it is well worth the wait

Golden rain tree

Koelreuteria paniculata
SAPINDACEAE

An attractive small tree with pale green pinnate leaves with long-toothed leaflets and open sprays of small, yellow flowers in mid-summer, followed by large, inflated fruits in autumn. Use as an alternative to laburnum in the low-allergen garden, or as a specimen to provide light shade. Plant in any except thin, alkaline soil and in full sun.

Height **12m (40ft)**
Spread **6m (20ft)**
Hardiness **Hardy**
• may attract bees, so avoid if allergic to bee stings

Tulip tree

Liriodendron tulipifera
MAGNOLIACEAE

This majestic tree has extraordinary large, grey-green, square-shaped leaves which turn yellow in autumn and it eventually bears tulip-shaped yellow and green flowers. It is a good substitute for beech or oak as a specimen tree in the larger low-allergen garden. The cultivar 'Aureomarginatum' has wide, yellow-green leaf margins and is smaller then the type and makes a more interesting garden specimen. 'Fastigiatum' is a useful form for smaller areas, with a narrow columnar shape when young, becoming more oval in later years. Grow in any good soil in full sun.

Height **30m (100ft)**
Spread **15m (50ft)**
Hardiness **Hardy**
• may attract bees, so avoid if allergic to bee stings

Magnolia x *soulangeana*

MAGNOLIACEAE

Although usually considered a large shrub, this magnolia makes a good specimen tree when grown on a single stem. The large, goblet-shaped, pink-flushed purple flowers are produced in spring, followed by large, soft green leaves which turn yellow in autumn. It needs a sheltered site where the blossoms are shaded from the morning sun but with enough room to allow its spectacular beauty to be enjoyed to the full. There are a number of good cultivars, including 'Brozzoni' with large, white flowers with a purple base, which appear rather late and so may escape the late frosts; 'Lennei' with dark purple flowers which are white inside and larger leaves; and 'Rustica Rubra', a stronger-growing form with rosy-red flowers. It prefers a rich, deep neutral to acid loam and light shade protected from early morning sun.

Height **10m (30ft)**
Spread **8m (26ft)**
Hardiness **Hardy**
• some cultivars are scented

Crab apple

Malus tschonoskii
ROSACEAE

There are many crab apples, most of which are good plants for the low-allergen garden, and I consider this to be one of the most useful. It makes a neat, upright, rounded tree rather like a lollipop with grey-green leaves which turn orange-red for a long period in the autumn. The flowers are pink at first, turning white, and produced in small clusters in late spring, followed by small, brown-yellow fruit in autumn. A very neat, reliable, small tree which can be used as a specimen or with other plants for autumn colour. There are many other attractive crab apples, including the floriferous *M. floribunda*, which forms a spreading dome of branches with masses of rose-red buds opening to pink flowers which fade to white. Among the varieties grown for their fruit is *M.* x *zumi* 'Golden Hornet' with white flowers, followed by a heavy crop of bright yellow fruit that hang on the tree well into the winter. There are also some good purple-leaved crab apples,

one of the best being *M.* 'Royalty' with wine coloured foliage and wine-red flowers, followed by purple-red crab apples. Grow in any good, well-drained soil in full sun.

Height **8m (26ft)**
Spread **6m (20ft)**
Hardiness **Hardy**
• attracts bees, so avoid if allergic to bee stings

Medlar

Mespilus germanica
ROSACEAE

The medlar is one of the oldest trees in cultivation and worth planting in almost any garden, not just the low-allergen garden. It forms a low, wide-topped tree with large green leaves which turn first yellow and then rich brown in the autumn. The atractively white-fringed flowers appear in late spring, followed by the unusual 'medlar' fruits in late summer and autumn. The cultivar 'Nottingham' is said to have better fruit, but as the fruit are rarely eaten the species would seem to be just as good. Grow in all but extremely alkaline soils and in full sun.

Height **6m (20ft)**
Spread **6m (20ft)**
Hardiness **Hardy**
• may attract bees, so avoid if allergic to bees stings
• may need support, particularly when laden with fruit

Purple-leaved plum

Prunus cerasifera 'Pissardii'
ROSACEAE

There are very few purple-leaved trees which can be planted in the low-allergen garden, as the copper beech and purple maples have to be excluded. However, the purple plum should cause no problems. A small to medium tree that can be pruned to any size or shape, it has thin branches covered in masses of pink buds which open to white flowers in early spring, followed by oval, shiny leaves which become a deep red and then turn purple-black in summer. It can be used as a dramatic screen or background or as a single specimen. There are several other cultivars, including 'Nigra' with darker leaves, black stems and pink flowers. *P.* 'Trailblazer'

is similar, with white flowers and larger but greener leaves, and produces a crop of edible purple plums in the autumn. Plant in good soil in full sun.

Height **8m (26ft)**
Spread **5m (16ft)**
Hardiness **Hardy**
• attracts bees, so avoid if allergic to bee stings

Japanese cherry

Prunus serrulata
ROSACEAE

This is the parent species from which most of the large range of Japanese cherries were selected. They are medium-sized deciduous trees with serrated, oval, green leaves, which in many instances turn bright red, orange or yellow in autumn. All produce a profusion of pink or white blossoms in early to late spring, depending on the variety. They make good specimen trees or can be used for avenues or in groups behind beds and borders. Some of the best varieties are *P.* 'Shirofugen', a round-topped tree with flowers in late spring which are deep pink in bud opening to pink and fading to white. The foliage is a coppery colour when young, becoming light green and with some autumn colour. *P.* 'Taihaku' has the largest flowers of all the cherries; these are single and pure white and appear to smother the upright-growing tree in mid-spring. *P.* 'Kiku-shidare-zakura', also known as Cheal's weeping cherry, is a weeping tree with frilly, double pink flowers in early spring. *P.* 'Ukon' is a dome-shaped tree with hanging, pale green, semi-double flowers fading to white. The leaves are coppery when young, green through the summer and red, yellow and orange in the autumn. For a small garden there is the columnar *P.* 'Amanogawa' with semi-double pale pink flowers in late spring and leaves which turn orange and yellow in the autumn. It prefers to be grown in full sun and in any, but waterlogged soil.

Height **8m (26ft)**
Spread **8m (26ft)**
Hardiness **Hardy**
• Cherries with single flowers attract bees, so choose double-flowered varieties if allergic to bee stings

ABOVE: *The purple-leaved crab apple* Malus *'Royalty' with its deep pink blossom in spring.*
ABOVE RIGHT: *The extraordinary edible, brown fruits and long* grey-green leaves of the medlar Mespilus germanica.
RIGHT: *The double white flowers of the ornamental cherry* Prunus avium *'Plena' in spring.*

Winter-flowering cherry

Prunus x *subhirtella* 'Autumnalis'

ROSACEAE

This is the only tree with winter blossoms and it deserves a place in every garden. The fine tracery of branches, usually forming a flat dome shape, is covered by small pink blossoms from late autumn through the winter and into the spring, only stopping in very cold weather. The small, pale green leaves usually turn yellow in autumn. Place as a specimen where it can be seen from the windows, preferably silhouetted against the sky. There is a form with deeper pink flowers, *P. s.* 'Autumnalis Rosea'. Grow in fertile soil in full sun or light shade.

Height **7m (23ft)**
Spread **7m (23ft)**
Hardiness **Hardy**
• attracts bees, so avoid if allergic to bee stings

Ornamental pear

Pyrus spp.

ROSACEAE

Several ornamental pear trees are suitable for the low-allergen garden, including the popular *P. salicifolia* 'Pendula', which has pendulous branches with hanging, narrow, grey leaves and white cup-shaped blossoms that may be followed by hard, green 'pears' in the autumn. If kept pruned to form a tidy shape, it makes an excellent specimen tree for the smaller garden, particularly when placed beside a water feature. A rather more choice tree is *P. calleryana* 'Chanticleer' which has an oval shape and upright branches of bright, glossy green leaves that stay on the tree for much of the winter. The flowers, single white and cup-shaped, cover the branches in mid-spring. A good tree for avenues or placed either side of an opening or singly as a focal point. Pears are happy grown in most soils, including damp, and in full sun.

Height **7m (23ft)**
Spread **5m (16ft)**
Hardiness **Hardy**
• attracts bees, so avoid if allergic to bee stings

Mountain ash

Sorbus aucuparia

ROSACEAE

A small native tree with dark green pinnate leaves and clusters of white flowers followed by red fruit much enjoyed by birds. The leaves turn orange-red or yellow in the autumn. A good tree for providing wind shelter or for use in the wild garden. It has several more ornamental cultivars, including 'Aspleniifolia' with elegant cut leaves, 'Beissneri' with an orange stem that adds colour to the winter garden, and 'Fastigiata', which forms a tall pillar with masses of sealing-wax-red berries in autumn. There are also some similar-looking *Sorbus* species, including the beautiful *S. vilmorinii,* which has delicate grey-green leaves and white flowers, followed by rose-red fruits fading to white. *S.* 'Joseph Rock' is a lovely small tree with green leaves turning yellow and orange in autumn and clusters of yellow fruit which hang on the tree well into the winter. Another gem of a small tree is *S. cashmiriana,* which has bunches of pendulous pearly-white fruit in late summer. Grow in any good garden soil in full sun.

Height **12m (40ft)**
Spread **9m (30ft)**
Hardiness **Hardy**
• may attract bees, so avoid if allergic to bee stings

Whitebeam

Sorbus aria

ROSACEAE

The whitebeam is one of the best of our garden trees, having a beautifully round shape even when young and large, round, grey-green leaves with downy white undersides. The dome-shaped clusters of white fluffy flowers in spring are followed by bunches of bright red fruits in autumn. It is a native tree and can be used for tree screens and background planting or trained to form an arch or a fan against a wall. It also makes a good formal avenue tree. Some of the cultivars are more ornamental and include 'Lutescens' with bright, silvery-white foliage and

LEFT: *The white flowers and soft, grey leaves of the ornamental pear,* Pyrus salicifolia *'Pendula'.*
BELOW: *The bright orange, red and yellow leaves of* Parrotia persica *in autumn.*

orange berries – an absolute joy in spring when the white buds first emerge and a beautiful foil to brighter coloured foliage. 'Chrysophylla' has leaves which are almost yellow and become deeper in colour in the autumn, and orange-red fruits. 'Majestica' has larger, grey-green leaves and slightly bigger fruits than the species. Grow in any soil, including extremely alkaline, and in full sun.

Height **12m (40ft)**
Spread **8m (26ft)**
Hardiness **Hardy**
• may attract bees, so avoid if allergic to bee stings

ADDITIONAL TREES

Common name	Botanical name	Family name
Buckeye, horse chestnut	*Aesculus* x *carnea*	HIPPOCASTANACEAE
	Caragana arborescens	PAPILIONACEAE
	Catalpa bignonioides	BIGNONIACEAE
	Cercidiphyllum japonicum	CERCIDIPHYLLACEAE
	Cladastris lutea	LEGUMINOSAE
	Cotoneaster salicifolius 'Pendulus'	ROSACEAE
Hawthorn, thorn	*Crataegus oxyacantha*	ROSACEAE
	Gleditsia triacanthos	CAESALPINIACEAE
	Gymnocladus dioicus	CAESALPINIACEAE
Tupelo	*Nyssa sylvatica*	NYSSACEAE
	Oxydendrum arboreum	ERICACEAE
	Parrotia persica	HAMAMELIDACEAE
	Paulownia tomentosa	SCROPHULARIACEAE
Cherry	*Prunus avium* 'Plena'	ROSACEAE
	Sassafras albidum	LAURACEAE
Kowhai	*Sophora japonica*	PAPILIONACEAE
	Stewartia pseudocamellia	THEACEAE
	Styrax japonicus	STYRACACEAE

Plants to Avoid

The symbols:

Problem plants for those with asthma and/or hay fever ✺

Plants that cause skin and/or eye irritation 🍃

Plants with prickles and thorns 🌿

Poisonous plants if eaten ✪

This section of the plant directory is devoted to plants that should be excluded from the low-allergen garden. Plants are categorized as Annuals and Biennials, Herbaceous Perennials and Ground Cover Plants, Climbers, Shrubs, Trees and Herbs. In addition, there are separate lists of vegetables, fruit, grasses and weeds. In each subsection there is a list of many of the plants which may cause allergies. Wherever a plant name is followed by 'spp.' (subspecies), this indicates that the allergenic properties may be found in all plants belonging to that genera. Where a specific name is given, many of the other plants in the genera are safe to use.

The major allergenic plants in each subsection are given a separate, detailed description, including suggested low-allergen plants that could be used as an alternative to their allergenic counterparts. The lists may seem to comprise a dauntingly large number of plants, but you will need to exclude only those that are likely to cause allergic problems for you or your family.

I have tried to include all plants known to cause allergies, but as the research in this area remains incomplete I may have left out a plant that you know causes you problems. I apologize for any such omission.

GRASSES

ABOVE: *The feathery plumes of one of the smaller pampas grasses,* Cortaderia selloana *'Pumila'.*

ABOVE: *Variegated leaves of the ornamental grass called gardener's garters* Phalaris arundinacea *'Picta'.*

Grass pollens are the most common cause of hay fever and a frequent cause of asthma attacks, and may cause skin rashes. If possible, they should be excluded from the low-allergen garden. This means not only avoiding grass lawns, but also checking your beds and borders for ornamental grasses and replacing them with non-allergenic plants.

All the grasses found in our lawns should be avoided (see pp.48–51 for alternatives). However, a list of every kind of grass that is found in our gardens would be endless, so in the table below I have selected the more frequently used ornamental grasses grown in beds and borders. All of these are members of the Poaceae family.

Pampas grass ✺

Cortaderia selloana
POACEAE
A large, evergreen, clump-forming grass with plumes of silvery flowers.
ALTERNATIVE
New Zealand flax Hardy to –10°C (14°F)
Phormium tenax
Sword-shaped, stiff, dark green leaves.

Blue fescue grass ✺

Festuca glauca
POACEAE
A small evergreen, tuft-forming, perennial. It is frequently planted in the front of the border for its steely, narrow blue-green leaves.
ALTERNATIVE
Thrift Hardy
Armeria maritima
Best used in the front of a border.

Gardener's garters ✺

Phalaris arundinaria picta 'Picta'
POACEAE
An invasive green and white variegated grass commonly found in garden beds and borders.
ALTERNATIVE
Daylily Hardy
Hemerocallis fulva 'Kwanso Variegata'
This vigorous clump-forming perennial has attractive foliage but also has large, orange flowers.

Feather grass ✺

Stipa gigantea
POACEAE
A tall grass becoming very popular, with feathery foliage and flowers. It is used as a specimen or at the back of the border.
ALTERNATIVE
Gypsophila paniculata Hardy
It bears numerous small flowers in summer.

ADDITIONAL GRASSES TO AVOID

Common name	Botanical name	
	Hakonechloa acra 'Alboaurea'	*Note:* All these grasses may cause both
Oat grass	*Helictotrichon sempervirens*	asthma and hay fever, while the sap may
Creeping soft grass	*Holcus mollis* 'Albovariegatus'	cause dermatitis and other skin allergies.
Bowles golden grass	*Milium effusum* 'Aureum'	
Maiden grass	*Miscanthus sinensis*	
Fountain grass	*Pennisetum orientale*	

ANNUALS AND BIENNIALS

This section includes annuals and biennials, and also tender perennials used as bedding plants. Many popular annuals are members of the Asteraceae family and have daisy-like flowers and allergenic

pollen, and will need to be excluded. If scented plants act as a trigger to your asthma and hay fever then select non-scented cultivars from the plants listed below with the scented flower symbol.

Marigold ✺ ✇

Calendula officinalis
ASTERACEAE

This familiar marigold, with its sticky, green leaves and bright orange flowers, must be eliminated from the low-allergen garden. Not only does the pollen cause attacks of asthma and hay fever, but the sap and leaves may cause dermatitis and urticaria.
ALTERNATIVES
Calceolaria integrifolia Perennial treated as annual
Clusters of yellow to orange flowers in summer.
Monkey Musk Annual
Mimulus luteus
Snapdragon-like bright yellow flowers.

Geranium ✺ ✇

Pelargonium hybrids
GERANIACEAE

These large, tender geraniums are popular as summer bedding and pot plants. Pelargoniums

cause attacks of asthma and hay fever – their musky scent probably acts as a trigger – and contact with the leaves may cause dermatitis.
ALTERNATIVE
Fuchsia Annual
Fuchsia
Cultivars display a similar colour range and are attractive for both bedding and pots.

Castor oil plant ✇ ⊗

Ricinus communis
EUPHORBIACEAE

Like many of the other members of the Euphorbia family, this plant may cause problems. Large, shiny red leaves and 'spiny' flowers, it contains ricin one of the most potent toxins known. Handling the plant may cause soreness of the skin. It should never be grown where there are children.
ALTERNATIVE
Canna indica Tender perennial
This robust perennial has large, handsome leaves and brightly coloured flowers.

ABOVE: *The bright orange flowers of the common English marigold* Calendula officinalis.

ABOVE: *The richly scented flowers of the biennial evening primrose.*

ADDITIONAL ANNUALS, BIENNIALS AND TENDER PERENNIALS TO AVOID

Common name	Botanical name	Family name
Floss flower ✺	*Ageratum houstonianum*	CAPPARACEAE
Love-lies-bleeding ✺ ✇	*Amaranthus caudatus*	AMARANTHACEAE
African daisy ✺	*Arctotis x hybrida*	ASTERACEAE
Marguerite ✺ ✇	*Argyranthemum frutescens*	ASTERACEAE
Daisy ✺	*Bellis perennis*	ASTERACEAE
Straw flower ✺	*Bracteantha bracteata*	ASTERACEAE
China aster ✺	*Calendula officinalis*	ASTERACEAE
Cornflower ✺	*Centaurea cyanus*	ASTERACEAE
Spider flower ✇	*Cleome hassleriana*	ASTERACEAE
Cosmea ✺	*Cosmos bipinnatus*	ASTERACEAE
Wallflower ✺ ✇	*Erysimum cheiri*	BRASSICACEAE
Dahlia hybrids ✺	*Dahlia*	SCROPHULARIACEAE
Carnations, pinks ✺	*Dianthus* spp.	CARYOPHYLLACEAE
Foxglove ⊗	*Digitalis purpurea*	BORANGINACEAE
Annual borage ✇	*Echium plantagineum*	ASTERACEAE
Gazania hybrids ✺	*Gazania*	ASTERACEAE
Sunflower ✺	*Helianthus annuus*	BORANGINACEAE
Heliotrope ✺ ✇	*Heliotropium arborescens*	BALSAMINACEAE
Balsam ✇	*Impatiens balsamina*	ASTERACEAE
Lantana ✇ ⊗	*Lantana camara*	VERBENACEAE
Sweet pea ✇ ⊗	*Lathyrus odoratus*	PAPILIONACEAE
Stocks ✺	*Matthiola* spp.	BRASSICACEAE
Tobacco plant ✺ ✇	*Nicotiana alata*	SOLANACEAE
Evening primrose ✺ ✇	*Oenothera biennis*	ONAGRACEAE
Osteospermum ✺ ✇	*Osteospermum jucundum*	ASTERACEAE
Polyanthus ✇	*Primula x polyantha*	PRIMULACEAE
Mignonette ✺	*Reseda odorata*	RESEDACEAE
Dusty miller ✺ ✇	*Senecio cineraria*	ASTERACEAE
French marigold ✺	*Tagetes* spp.	ASTERACEAE
Zinnia ✺	*Zinnia elegans*	ASTERACEAE

HERBACEOUS PERENNIALS AND GROUND COVER PLANTS

I have combined herbaceous perennials and ground cover plants as so many ground cover plants can be used in the flower border. The plants which are most likely to cause problems are given detailed entries and these should be excluded from the low-allergen garden. Some of the plants listed in the table are scented, others produce allergenic pollen, and the rest may cause skin allergies. Try growing your favourites and see if they cause you problems before eliminating them from your garden.

Yarrow

Achillea millefolium
ASTERACEAE

Yarrow is an old-fashioned plant with grey-green, ferny foliage and flat heads of tiny flowers in a wide variety of colours. The white-flowered species is often found as a weed in lawns. The pollen is allergenic and may cause attacks of asthma and hay fever, and the sap may irritate the skin. This is not a suitable plant for the low-allergen garden.
ALTERNATIVES
Daylily Hardy
Hemerocallis 'Stella de Oro'
Large, trumpet-shaped yellow flowers.
Red-hot poker, Torch lily Hardy
Kniphofia 'Bee's Lemon'
Citron-yellow flowers on stout stems.
Phlox paniculata Hardy
This has larger flower heads but looks similar to the pink yarrows.

Monkshood

Aconitum spp.
RANUNCULACEAE

Monkshood is a useful plant, providing tall spikes of blue, helmet-like flowers for the shade garden. Also available are cream, white and bicoloured cultivars. Monkshood is one of the most poisonous plants known, containing aconitine throughout, particularly in the roots. It is possible to absorb the poison through the skin if there is prolonged contact with the plant. Great care should be taken when disposing of this plant. Although it is not strictly an allergenic plant, it should be excluded from any garden where there are children.
ALTERNATIVES
Bell flower Hardy
Campanula persicifolia
Not quite so tall as monkshood, but similar coloured spikes of flowers.
Delphinium hybrids Hardy
Very similar to monkshood in size and leaf shape, with almost identical spikes of blue flowers.

Carnations and pinks

Dianthus spp.
CARYOPHYLLACEAE

The genus Dianthus includes some lovely garden plants, among them the annuals pinks and carnations, and the biennial Sweet William. All have white, pink, or red flowers and either grey or green leaves, and most have very strongly scented flowers. The scent often triggers attacks of asthma and hay fever, so you should exclude the plants from the low-allergen garden. Non-scented plants are probably safe.
ALTERNATIVES
Armeria maritima Hardy
This has similar leaves and round pink flowers.
Helianthemum 'Rhodanthe Carneum' Hardy to −10ºC (14°F)
This has grey leaves and pink flowers, and is a good choice in place of pinks in the rock garden.

Burning bush

Dictamnus albus
RUTACEAE

'Dittany' is an interesting plant with tall spikes of pink or white flowers above scented, deeply divided foliage. The ripening seedpods release a gas that burns when lit, giving it the familiar name 'burning bush'. Contact with the sap in sunny weather may cause a nasty skin rash.
ALTERNATIVES
Campanula lactiflora 'Loddon Anna' Hardy
Similar spikes of upright soft pink flowers.
Campanula latifolia 'White Ladies' Hardy
Tall spikes of white-flowers.

Spurge

Euphorbia spp.
EUPHORBIACEAE

Euphorbias have become very popular with gardeners in recent years, as they have foliage that is interesting throughout the year, and they can be used on their own or in a combination with a wide range of other plants. One of the best is *E. characias*, with upright stems of horizontal, grey-green leaves surmounted by enormous, rounded heads of yellow-green flowers. Another useful form is *E. amygdaloides* 'Purpurea', with red shoots, deep plum leaves and greenish-yellow flowers. All euphorbias have a milky sap that is highly allergenic and may cause skin irritation and dermatitis. Avoid rubbing the eyes after handling the plant, as the sap may seriously damage them. Either take great care when handling the plant or remove it from the low-allergen garden.
ALTERNATIVES
Lady's mantle Hardy
Alchemilla mollis
This has the same colour as *E. characias* but is smaller. It bears small sprays of tiny, bright greenish-yellow flowers in mid-summer.

ABOVE: *One of the many michaelmas daisies, Aster* x *frikartii 'Jungfrau' all of which have allergenic pollen.*

ABOVE: *The dramatic yellow spikes and large dissected leaves of Ligularia 'The Rocket' which needs a moist soil.*

Alum root Hardy
Heuchera micrantha 'Palace Purple'
This has dark plum foliage similar to that of
E. amygdaloides 'Purpurea'.

Christmas rose ⊗

Helleborus spp.
RANUNCULACEAE

These are lovely plants with evergreen leaves and saucer-shaped white, pink or pale green flowers in winter or early spring. They are very good for shady areas. However, the sap may cause serious blistering of the skin if the plant is handled in sunlight and all parts of the plant are poisonous. Therefore they may have to be eliminated from the low-allergen garden.
ALTERNATIVES
Cranesbill Hardy
Geranium sylvaticum 'Album'
There is no good alternative for winter flowers, but for flowers in shade use the above and for good foliage use hostas and bergenias.

Shasta daisy ❀

Leucanthemum spp.
ASTERACEAE

This is one of the plants that used to be listed as chrysanthemums but are now available under a variety of names. The shasta daisy, which has coarse, green leaves and large double white, daisy flowers in summer, seems to survive complete

neglect. All chrysanthemums have highly allergenic pollen, which can be a problem for sufferers of asthma and hay fever, and the leaves and sap may cause dermatitis. None of them should be included in the low-allergen garden.
ALTERNATIVE
Windflower Hardy
Anemone x *hybrida*
All plants with daisy flowers have allergenic pollen, so they cannot be used in the low-allergen garden. Instead, the white flowers of the variety 'Whirlwind' could be used. The flowers are shallowly cup-shaped and appear in late summer and early autumn.

Primroses and primulas

Primula spp.
PRIMULACEAE

There are lots of primulas in our gardens, ranging from the humble primrose, *P. vulgaris* to the glamorous *P. japonica*. Contact with most primula leaves may cause dermatitis, although some are more allergenic than others. The worst offender is the indoor *P. obconica*, but most garden primulas can cause problems in susceptible individuals.
ALTERNATIVES
Purple loosestrife Hardy
Lythrum salicaria
For *P. japonica*, use this clump-forming perennial, which has similarly coloured flowers.
Waldsteinia ternata Hardy
Semi-evergreen perennial with low domes of saucer-shaped yellow flowers.

ABOVE: *The exotic flowers of Alstroemeria 'Apollo'; sadly, repeated contact with these plants may cause allergic dermatitis.*

ADDITIONAL HERBACEOUS PERENNIALS AND GROUND COVER PLANTS TO AVOID

Common name	Botanical name	Family name
Peruvian Lily	*Alstroemeria* hybrids	ALSTROEMERIACEAE
Pearl everlasting ❀	*Anaphalis* spp.	ASTERACEAE
Wood anemone ⊗	*Anemone nemorosa*	RANUNCULACEAE
Cuckoo pint ⊗	*Arum maculatum*	ARACEAE
Michaelmas daisies ❀	*Aster* spp.	ASTERACEAE
Kingcup	*Caltha palustris*	RANUNCULACEAE
Cupid's dart ❀	*Catanache caerulea*	ASTERACEAE
Knapweed ❀	*Centaurea* spp.	ASTERACEAE
Tickseed ❀	*Coreopsis* spp.	ASTERACEAE
Carnations, Pinks ❀	*Dianthus* spp.	CARYOPHYLLACEAE
Purple coneflower ❀	*Echinacea purpurea*	ASTERACEAE
Globe thistle ❀	*Echinops* spp.	ASTERACEAE
Fleabane ❀	*Erigeron* spp.	ASTERACEAE
Wallflower ❀	*Erysimum* spp.	BRASSICACEAE
Blanket flower	*Gaillardia* x *grandiflora*	ASTERACEAE
Sneezewort ❀	*Helenium autumnale*	ASTERACEAE
Sunflower ❀	*Helianthus* spp.	ASTERACEAE
Ligularia ❀	*Ligularia* spp.	ASTERACEAE
Lily ❀	*Lilium* hybrids	LILIACEAE
Lupin ❀ ⊗	*Lupinus* spp.	PAPILIONACEAE
Knotweed ❀	*Persicaria* spp.	POLYGONACEAE
Pasque flower ⊗	*Pulsatilla vulgaris*	RANUNCULACEAE
Buttercup ⊗	*Ranunculus* spp.	RANUNCULACEAE
Coneflower ❀	*Rudbeckia* spp.	ASTERACEAE
Golden rod ❀	*Solidago* spp.	ASTERACEAE
Stoke's aster ❀	*Stokesia laevis*	ASTERACEAE
False helleborine ⊗	*Veratrum* spp.	MELANTHIACEAE
Arum lily ⊗	*Zantedeschia aethiopica*	ARACEAE

CLIMBERS

The major problem with using climbers in the low-allergen garden is that many have scented flowers which may trigger attacks of asthma and hay fever. Where the flowering season is short it may be feasible to grow the climber at the back of the flower border so it is far away from frequented areas of the garden. Avoid gardening near it when it is in flower. Many of the scented climbers listed here have prolonged or repeated flowering and are best excluded from the low-allergen garden.

ABOVE: *The triangular leaves and round flowers of one of the many variegated ivies,* Hedera helix *'Angularis Aurea'.*

ABOVE: *The small white, fragrant flowers of* Jasminum officinale *which appear from late summer to early autumn.*

Clematis ✼

Clematis spp.
RANUNCULACEAE

Clematis hybrids are included in *Plants to Use* (see p.100) as they have little or no scent. However, several species have strongly scented flowers that may trigger attacks of asthma and hay fever. These include the evergreen *C. armandii,* with large, fragrant, white or pink flowers in spring; the rampant spring-flowering *C. montana;* Fragrant Virgin's Bower, *C. flammula,* with very sweet-scented creamy flowers in summer; and *C. rehderiana,* with flowers redolent of cowslips.
ALTERNATIVES
Various **clematis hybrids** Hardy (see p.100)

Ivy 🍃 ⊗

Hedera helix
ARALIACEAE

The most commonly seen climbing plant in both garden and countryside, this is capable of growing almost anywhere. It has evergreen leaves on self-clinging stems and there is a range of variegated forms. The sap from all parts of the plant is harmful and may cause skin reactions ranging from a mild rash to blistering and swelling. All parts of the plant are poisonous, particularly the sap and young leaves.
ALTERNATIVE
Hydrangea anomala petiolaris Hardy
This self-clinging climber is not evergreen, but it keeps its shiny leaves until late autumn (see p.100).

Jasmine ✼

Jasminum officinale
OLEACEAE

This is a vigorous climber with dark green leaves and clusters of sweet-scented white flowers from mid-summer to early autumn. The scent of jasmine is very distinctive and, although enjoyed by most people, in some it triggers attacks of asthma or hay fever. All white-flowered jasmines tend to be strongly scented, but some species with yellow flowers have little or no fragrance.
ALTERNATIVE
Yellow winter-flowering jasmine
Jasminum nudiflorum Hardy
This has little or no scent. Although a shrub, it is easy to train against a wall.

Japanese honeysuckle ✼ 🍃

Lonicera japonica 'Halliana'
CAPRIFOLIACEAE

This is one of the loveliest and most useful of the range of honeysuckles that can be grown in the garden. It has vigorous twining stems, evergreen leaves and creamy flowers throughout the summer. However, the strong scent of the flowers may trigger attacks of asthma and hay fever, and contact with the plant may irritate the skin.
ALTERNATIVE
Honeysuckle Hardy
Lonicera
Several climbing honeysuckles have little or no scent, including *L. tragophylla* (see p.100).

Japanese wisteria ✼ ⊗

Wisteria floribunda
PAPILIONACEAE

The wisteria is attractive in all seasons, with contorted stems in winter, large, hanging racemes of violet-blue flowers in late spring and fresh, green leaves in summer. However, the flowers are very fragrant and may trigger attacks of asthma and hay fever. All parts of the plant are poisonous, especially the seeds and pods.
ALTERNATIVE
Clematis Hardy
Clematis 'Perle d'Azur'
The above variety or other similar coloured clematis.

ADDITIONAL CLIMBERS TO AVOID

Common name	Botanical name	Family name
Trumpet creeper 🍃	*Campsis radicans*	BIGNONIACEAE
Russian vine ✼	*Fallopia baldschuanica*	POLYGONACEAE
Hop 🍃	*Humulus lupulus*	CANNABACEAE
Morning glory ⊗ (seed contains hallucinogens)	*Ipomoea tricolor*	CONVOLVULACEAE
Sweet pea ✼ (seeds may cause temporary paralysis)	*Lathyrus odoratus*	PAPILIONACEAE
Climbing rose ✼	*Rosa* 'Compassion'	ROSACEAE
Jasmine nightshade ✼	*Solanum jasminoides*	SOLANACEAE
	Trachelospermum jasminoides ✼	APOCYNACEAE

SHRUBS

The shrubs detailed below are well known to cause allergies and should be excluded from the low-allergen garden. Rue is another plant that should be removed and details of it can be found on page 122.

Most of the other shrubs listed in the table have scented flowers and only need to be excluded from the garden if the scent of that particular plant is a problem for you or any member of your family.

ABOVE: *The soft blue flowers of* Ceanothus *'Pin Cushion' completely covering the foliage in summer.*

Mezereon

Daphne mezereum
RHAMNACEAE

A very popular deciduous shrub for its bright pink, scented flowers, which appear clustered on the bare stems in early spring. These are followed in autumn by vibrant red, poisonous berries. The sap and juice of the berries may cause dermatitis.

ALTERNATIVE
Cherry Hardy
Prunus tenella
This bushy shrub has similar pink flowers in early spring and is easy to grow.

Fremontia

Fremontodendron californicum
STERCULIACEAE

This is a lovely shrub, with heart-shaped grey-green leaves and saucer-shaped yellow flowers all summer. All parts of the plant have tiny hairs that are extremely irritant and when touched may affect the skin, mouth, nose and eyes.

ALTERNATIVES
Hypericum **'Hidcote'** Hardy
This large shrub has similar yellow, saucer-shaped flowers all summer. For covering a wall one of the yellow-flowered climbing roses such as *Rosa* 'Golden Showers', which is only lightly scented, would give the same overall effect.

Privet

Ligustrum ovalifolium
OLEACEAE

This is one of the most popular plants for hedging, with semi-evergreen, shiny leaves and fluffy, cream-coloured, honey-scented flowers in summer. However, the scent of the flowers is a major trigger of attacks of asthma and hay fever, the pollen is allergenic and contact with leaves and bark may cause irritant dermatitis. In addition to this the black berries are poisonous.

ALTERNATIVE
Viburnum tinus Hardy to –10ºC (14°F)
This has larger evergreen leaves and white flowers. It can be used for an informal hedge.

Elder

Sambucus nigra
CAPRIFOLIACEAE

This tall shrub has furrowed bark, green, pinnate leaves and creamy flowers in summer, followed by hanging bunches of black berries. All parts of the plant are poisonous. The scent of the flowers frequently triggers attacks of asthma and hay fever.

ALTERNATIVES
Sorbaria sorbifolia Hardy
For similar clusters of flower use the above.
Weigela florida Hardy
For coloured-leaved varieties, use cultivars (see p.107).

ABOVE: *The variegated leaves and richly scented and allergenic flowers of golden privet* Ligustrum ovalifolium *'Aureum'.*

ADDITIONAL SHRUBS TO AVOID

Common name	Botanical name	Family name
Japanese maple	*Acer palmatum*	ACERACEAE
Shrubby ragwort	*Brachyglottis* spp.	ASTERACEAE
Butterfly bush	*Buddleja* spp.	BUDDLEJACEAE
California lilac	*Ceanothus* spp.	RHAMNACEAE
Sweet pepper	*Clethra alnifolia*	CLETHRACEAE
Dogwood	*Cornus sanguinea*	CORNACEAE
	Daphne spp.	THYMELAEACEAE
	Elaeagnus spp.	ELAEAGNACEAE
	Grevillea spp.	PROTEACEAE
Holly	*Ilex aquifolium*	AQUIFOLIACEAE
Winter honeysuckle	*Lonicera* x *purpusii*	CAPRIFOLIACEAE
	Mahonia japonica	BERBERIDACEAE
Daisy bush	*Olearia* spp.	ASTERACEAE
	Osmanthus delavayi	OLEACEAE
Mock orange	*Philadelphus* spp.	HYDRANGEACEAE
Jerusalem sage	*Phlomis fruticosa*	LAMIACEAE
	Rhododendron and *Azaleas*	ERICACEAE
Flowering currant	*Ribes sanguineum*	GROSSULARIACEAE
Rue	*Ruta graveolens*	RUTACEAE
Sweet box	*Sarcococca* spp.	BUXACEAE
Lilac	*Syringa vulgaris*	OLEACEAE
	Viburnum carlesii	CAPRIFOLIACEAE

TREES

Trees can be a problem if your asthma or hay fever is caused by tree pollen as many of our larger trees are wind-pollinated and have allergenic pollen. Many of these trees can be recognized by the flowers being reduced to catkins or similar structures. A full list of these trees is included in the table, but details are given of some of the most commonly found ornamental species or cultivars.

ABOVE: *The typical trifoliate leaves and peeling bark of* Acer griseum. *The uncovered stem is a rich mahogany colour.*

ABOVE: *The bright yellow flowers of* Laburnum alpinum *'Pendulum' which, as in all laburnums, are followed by poisonous seeds.*

Paperbark maple ❈

Acer griseum
ACERACEAE

There are several good maples that provide autumn colour and winter bark interest, and this is among the best. It is a lovely medium-sized tree with trifoliate, soft green leaves that turn vivid scarlet and orange in autumn. Another major feature is the peeling, orange-brown bark that develops as the tree matures. All the maples produce allergenic pollen.

ALTERNATIVES
Crab apple Hardy
Malus tschonoskii
Brilliant shades of orange, red and purple in the autumn colour (see p.110).
Cherry Hardy
Prunus serrula
For winter bark use this attractive early flowering cherry with a shiny mahogany bark.

Variegated Norway maple ❈

Acer platanoides 'Drummondii'
ACERACEAE

This is a medium-sized tree with a rounded shape and dramatic green and white, variegated leaves. It is easy to grow but the leaves are apt to revert to green and must be removed. See above for reasons to exclude from the low-allergen garden.

ALTERNATIVES
Dogwood Hardy
Cornus controversa 'Variegata'
A small, variegated tree with horizontal branches. Small white flowers in summer.
Liriodendron tulipifera 'Aureomarginatum' Hardy
A large, dramatic, variegated-leaved tree, with greenish-white flowers in mid-summer.

Weeping silver birch ❈

Betula pendula 'Youngii'
BETULACEAE

The lovely umbrella shape of the weeping birch is seen in many gardens as a specimen tree on the lawn or, perhaps at its prettiest, framing a pool. All birches have pendulous catkins full of allergenic pollen, one of the major causes of hay fever and asthma in spring.

ALTERNATIVES
Cherry Hardy
Prunus 'Kiku-shidare-Sakura'
A medium-sized, weeping tree with a wide-domed shape and double pink flowers in spring.
Cherry Hardy
Prunus x subhirtella 'Pendula Rubra'
A small, weeping tree with branches hanging to the ground and pink flowers in spring.

Upright hornbeam ❈

Carpinus betulus 'Fastigiata'
CORYLACEAE

The hornbeam is a native tree often used as a hedge, but the fastigiate form makes an excellent avenue tree or formal specimen. It has neat, upright branches and shiny, oval leaves that turn yellow in the autumn. Sadly, it produces clouds of allergenic pollen in the spring and must be removed from the low-allergen garden.

ALTERNATIVE
Whitebeam Hardy
Sorbus aria
A medium-sized tree with rounded, upright shape (see p.111). The leaves are silver-grey when young, maturing to dark green above, white-felted beneath. Clusters of small white flowers in spring are followed by deep red, rounded fruits.

Purple beech ❈

Fagus sylvatica 'Riversii'
FAGACEAE

The beech is ultimately a large forest tree and this, the darkest purple of the 'copper' beeches, will eventually outgrow all but the largest garden. However, it is often planted as a specimen tree on lawns and also used as a clipped hedge. Beech produces allergenic pollen in spring and so is not suitable for the low-allergen garden.

ALTERNATIVE
Cherry plum Hardy
Prunus cerasifera 'Pissardii'
This round-headed tree has equally dark purple leaves and is of a more suitable size for most gardens (see p.110). Pale pink flowers in spring are followed by edible red fruit.

Golden ash ❈

Fraxinus excelsior 'Jaspidea'
OLEACEAE

This is a most attractive form of the European ash, and has the same furrowed bark, black buds and pinnate leaves as the common ash. However, the young branches are bright yellow and the new leaves are yellow, becoming light green in summer and turning golden in the autumn. All ash trees produce allergenic pollen and should be excluded from the low-allergen garden.

ALTERNATIVE
Honey locust Hardy
Gleditsia triacanthos 'Sunburst'
A similar tree to the golden ash but with rather smaller, more attractive, glossy pinnate leaves that remain yellow all summer and into autumn. In mid-summer bunches of pretty, greeny-white blossoms appear.

Golden chain tree ✪

Laburnum x *watereri* 'Vossii'
PAPILIONACEAE

There are three commonly grown laburnums, all of which are lovely small trees with dark green, trifoliate leaves and pendulous racemes of golden-yellow flowers in late spring. The flowers are followed by long, grey-green pods containing black, shiny, highly toxic seeds that are very attractive to children. Although they cause no specific allergic reaction, laburnums should be removed from any garden where there are children, as there is a high risk of accidental poisoning. *L. x w.* 'Vossii' is supposed to have fewer seedpods than other laburnums, but even one seedpod is one too many for safety.

ALTERNATIVE
Golden rain tree, Pride of India Hardy
Koelreuteria paniculata
A spreading tree with yellow flowers in summer and a prettier leaf than laburnum (see p.109).

Sweet gum ❀

Liquidambar styraciflua
HAMAMELIDACEAE

This medium-sized tree may be easily mistaken for a maple as the leaf is very similar, but it has a more conical shape and a rugged, cork-like bark. Its chief attraction is the brilliant orange-red leaves in autumn. It produces pollen which is known to have caused hay fever, and so should be excluded from the low-allergen garden.

ALTERNATIVE
Crab apple Hardy
Malus
There are several good Malus for autumn colour, including *M. transitoria*, a small tree with excellent yellow autumn colour, and *M. tschonoskii*, a larger,

more upright tree with brilliant shades of red, purple and orange in autumn (see p.110).

Balm of Gilead poplar ❀

Populus x *candicans* 'Aurora'
SALICACEAE

This is a very pretty tree with balsam-scented leaves that are boldly splashed pink and cream, particularly when young. It eventually becomes a large tree and is best kept pruned or pollarded. As with all poplars, masses of allergenic pollen is produced in the spring which is known to cause asthma and hay fever. The balsam scent may also trigger asthma attacks.

ALTERNATIVE
Handerkerchief tree Hardy
Davidia involucrata
When in full bloom this tree looks very similar but will not need pruning or pollarding (see p.109).

Kilmarnock willow ❀ ✪

Salix caprea 'Kilmarnock'
SALICACEAE

Many willows are used as garden plants, and this small tree is one of the most decorative, with long, weeping branches from a small, compact head. The branches will grow down to the ground but are frequently clipped back to form an 'umbrella'. In spring the bare branches are covered with catkins – the familiar 'pussy willows' – which release clouds of allergenic pollen.

ALTERNATIVE
Cotoneaster salicifolius 'Pendulus' Hardy
This is a similar size and shape, with weeping branches of dark green, semi-evergreen leaves and white flowers in spring and bunches of red fruits in autumn.

ABOVE: *The new foliage of* Populus *x* candicans *'Aurora' showing its green, cream and pink colouration.*

ADDITIONAL TREES TO AVOID

Common name	Botanical name	Family name
Maple ❀	*Acer* spp.	ACERACEAE
Horse chestnut ✪	*Aesculus hippocastanum*	HIPPOCASTANACEAE
Tree of heaven ❀ ◧	*Ailanthus altissima*	SIMAROUBACEAE
Alder ❀	*Alnus* spp.	BETULACEAE
Angelica tree ◧	*Aralia elata*	ARALIACEAE
Birch ❀	*Betula* spp.	BETULACEAE
Hornbeam ❀	*Carpinus* spp.	CORYLACEAE
Hickory ❀	*Carya* spp.	JUGLANDACEAE
Hazel ❀	*Corylus* spp.	CORYLACEAE
Quince ◧	*Cydonia oblonga*	ROSACEAE
Beech ❀ ✪	*Fagus* spp.	FAGACEAE
Ash ❀	*Fraxinus* spp.	OLEACEAE
Walnut, Butternut ❀	*Juglans* spp.	JUGLANDACEAE
Laburnum ✪	*Laburnum* spp.	PAPILIONACEAE
Mulberry ◧	*Morus* spp.	MORACEAE
Southern beech ❀	*Nothofagus* spp.	FAGACEAE
Plane tree ❀	*Platanus* spp.	PLATANACEAE
Poplar and aspen ❀	*Populus* spp.	SALICACEAE
Wing nut ❀	*Pterocarya fraxinifolia*	JUGLANDACEAE
Oak ❀	*Quercus* spp.	FAGACEAE
Willow ❀ ✪	*Salix* spp.	SALICACEAE
Elm ❀	*Ulmus* spp.	ULMACEAE

VEGETABLES

ABOVE: *An old variety of tomato 'Gardener's Delight' but still an excellent choice for growing outdoors, with a delicious flavour.*

ABOVE: *The very decorative as well as edible, flowering heads of the globe artichoke. Harvest before blue flowers emerge.*

Spinach, sea kale and beetroot are members of the family Chenopodiaceae; and lettuce, chicory and endive are all members of the family Asteraceae. Both families produce allergenic pollen, but as the vegetables are usually cut before flowering they should be safe to include in the low-allergen garden.

This book has not expanded on food allergies but many of these vegetables may cause a range of allergic reactions when eaten by susceptible people. No alternative plants are listed, because for most growers the visual appearance of these plants is not important.

Celery

Apium graveolens
APIACEAE

Celery is a useful plant to grow as it can be eaten either raw in salads or cooked and served hot as a vegetable. However, traditional white-stemmed celery is hard work to produce, requiring planting in well-prepared trenches and earthing-up at intervals while it is growing. Contact with the plant during bright sunlight can cause photodermatitis, which is another very good reason for putting this vegetable on the black list. Parsnip, being a closely related plant, also causes photodermatitis, and if you are allergic to celery you will almost certainly be allergic to parsnips.

Asparagus

Asparagus officinalis
ASPARAGACEAE

This is one of the very best of all vegetables to grow if you have light, well-drained soil and plenty of room. Unlike most vegetables, it is a perennial crop and needs to be planted in a bed on its own in carefully prepared ground. The fact that the young shoots may cause dermatitis will limit its use only if the person responsible for the care of the asparagus is the gardener or the cook.

Globe artichoke

Cynara cardunculus
ASTERACEAE

It is not surprising that this plant may cause allergic reactions when handled, as it is so prickly. The tall stems are covered in short, prickly hairs and the thistle-like flower has sharp points to its enclosing scaly bracts. The flower is harvested before opening and, after boiling, the swollen base of the bracts is the part of the vegetable that is eaten. If allowed to flower, the plant, being a member of the family Asteraceae, produces allergenic pollen. Also, handling the flower may irritate the skin. It is not a crop suitable for growing in the low-allergen vegetable garden.

Tomato

Lycopersicon esculentum
SOLANACEAE

We can grow tomatoes either in the greenhouse or outdoors in the vegetable garden, depending on the variety. In both cases this is a plant to handle with care if you suffer from skin allergies, as the sticky leaves are known to cause a range of allergic reactions. The scent of tomatoes has also been known to trigger attacks of asthma and hay fever. In addition, tomatoes and tomato products are a frequent cause of food allergies.

Broad bean

Vicia faba
PAPILIONACEAE

There are a wide range of different bean crops which we can grow in our gardens, including broad beans; lablab, *Dolichos lablab*; runner beans, *Phaseolus coccineus*; and French beans, *Phaseolus vulgaris*. All of the beans have been implicated in a variety of allergic reactions. The scented flowers, particularly of runner and broad beans, can trigger attacks of asthma and hay fever and handling the furry pods of broad beans may irritate the skin. Many beans are also a frequent cause of food allergy. If you find the scented flowers a problem, it is probably best to forgo growing your own beans.

Sweet corn

Zea mays
POACEAE

Sweet corn is a one of the largest-growing grasses, and the corncob that we harvest is, in fact, the fruit of a very large grass flower. When the flowers open they produce masses of allergenic pollen that can cause asthma and hay fever. Sweet corn is a cultivar of the crop plant maize, the source of most of the corn products we consume. Unfortunately, these corn products are a major source of food allergies. Therefore sweet corn is not a good plant for the low-allergen garden.

ADDITIONAL VEGETABLES TO AVOID

Common name	Botanical name	Family name
Sweet pepper	*Capsicum annuum*	SOLANACEAE
Courgette	*Cucurbita pepo*	CUCURBITACEAE
Parsnip	*Pastinaca sativa*	APIACEAE
Radish	*Raphanus sativus*	BRASSICACEAE

FRUIT

Many of the varieties of soft fruit grown in our gardens, including blackberries, gooseberries, loganberries and raspberries have prickles or thorns, and these may irritate the skin of susceptible people. However, planting thornless varieties such as 'Oregon Thornless' blackberry, which has very pretty foliage, and handling the plants with care should prevent problems.

Hazel

Corylus avellana
CORYLACEAE

This is usually grown as a hedging plant or as part of a tree screen, but it is also the source of both hazelnuts and filberts. When grown commercially in orchards, cultivars are selected for known fruiting potential and if you plan to grow your own hazelnuts, choose a variety such as 'Pearson's Prolific' or 'Cosford Cob'. However, the hazel produces masses of highly allergenic pollen in spring and is a major cause of asthma and hay fever early in that season. Hazelnuts are also a cause of food allergies, so you may wish to exclude it from your low-allergen garden.

Fig

Ficus carica
MORACEAE

The fig is one of the oldest fruits in cultivation and an attractive plant, with or without its edible fruits, due to its large, shiny beautifully lobed leaves. It cannot be relied on to produce a good crop, but restricting the roots and choosing a suitable variety, such as 'Brown Turkey', should ensure some fruit. Unfortunately, if the plant sap comes into contact with the skin in bright sunshine the skin may develop a severe reaction, with redness, itching and blistering rather like extreme sunburn. Always wear gloves when in contact with this plant and if you or anyone in your family suffers from skin allergies it is prudent to remove the tree.

Walnut

Junglans regia
JUGLANDACEAE

Walnuts are frequently planted in gardens as avenue trees or for shade, rather than just as a source of walnuts. They are handsome medium-size trees with large, glossy, pinnate leaves and grow in deep, fertile, well-drained soil and in either sun or shade. Relatively fast-growing their only horticultural problems are late appearance of their leaves in spring and a dislike of root disturbance. However, walnuts are not welcome in the low-allergen garden being wind-pollinated and having allergenic pollen, so causing problems in spring for asthma and hay fever sufferers. Walnuts are also known to cause food allergies.

Mulberry

Morus nigra
MORACEAE

The mulberry eventually makes a majestic tree and is suitable only for large gardens, but it does produce quantities of dark purplish-red, oval fruit in late summer or early autumn that are delicious eaten raw and which make the most marvellous jam. It is now also available as an espalier for the smaller garden which produce fruit at an earlier age and can be grown in pots. But beware, treading on ripe mulberries and then walking indoors can leave stains on the carpet, which are virtually impossible to remove. The dark green leaves, which are heart-shaped and furry, may irritate the skin when handled. The tree also produces quantities of allergenic pollen which may cause asthma and hay fever. If you already have a mulberry tree you may not wish, or be allowed, to remove it, but avoid planting a new tree in the low-allergen garden.

Rhubarb

Rheum x *hybridum*
POLYGONACEAE

Rhubarb is a perennial plant that needs a large area of its own in the vegetable garden. Grow in a permanent position in rich, well-fed soil, where it will provide fleshy, red stems for cutting in spring and summer. Later in the season the enormous shiny leaves make a dramatic focal point in the vegetable garden and completely cover the soil beneath. However, when the large, creamy flowers open they are full of allergenic pollen which may cause asthma and hay fever. The stems are delicious and perfectly safe to eat when cooked, but the raw leaves contain potent toxins which can cause poisoning. This is probably not a plant for the low-allergen garden, particularly where there are young children.

ABOVE: *The bright red stems of Rhubarb almost ready to harvest in spring with large leaves not yet fully developed.*

ABOVE: *Strawberries, ripe and ready for eating but try to avoid contact with the leaves which can cause skin irritation.*

ADDITIONAL FRUIT TO AVOID

Common name	Botanical name	Family name
Quince	*Cydonia oblonga*	ROSACEAE
Strawberry	*Fragaris* x *ananassa*	ROSACEAE
Olive	*Olea europaea*	OLEACEAE
Gooseberry	*Ribes uva-crispa*	GROSSULARIACEAE

HERBS

ABOVE: *The finely-dissected foliage of lawn chamomile,* Chamaemelum nobile *which makes a scented, but allergic, carpet.*

ABOVE: *The strongly scented spikes of lavender flowers which are frequently dried and used in pot-pourri and lavender bags.*

In most herbs the aromatic fragrance does not act as a trigger for asthma and hay fever and they can be included in the low-allergen garden. However there are a few exceptions, of which lavender is one. Other herbs listed are members of the Asteraceae, the daisy family and most of the others are skin irritants. I have included alternative plants which share the same visual properties as the named herb but do not necessarily share the same herbal qualities or uses.

Wormwood

Artemisia absinthium
ASTERACEAE

Historically, wormwood was grown for use as an insect repellent and as such was an essential element of every herb garden. A tall plant with upright stems of silky, divided, grey leaves, nowadays it is usually seen in the flower border, where it provides a foil for more brightly coloured plants. The tiny flowers have allergenic pollen which may cause asthma and hay fever, and the flowers and leaves may irritate the skin. The pungent fragrance proves unpleasant to some people.

ALTERNATIVE
Russian sage Hardy to –10°C (14°F)
Perovskia atriplicifolia
This has the same shape and grey leaves. Although these are not quite so silky, it offers the compensation of lavender-blue flowers.

Chamomile

Chamaemelum nobile
ASTERACEAE

This plant, with its rosettes of feathery green leaves and white, daisy-like flowers, is used to create a chamomile lawn or seat. All parts are strongly aromatic, which is one of the pleasures of walking over, or sitting on, chamomile. The flowers produce allergenic pollen and any part of the plant may irritate the skin. You can avoid the problem of pollen by using the cultivar *C. n.* 'Treneague', which does not produce flowers, but you may still suffer from sore skin.

ALTERNATIVE
Thyme Hardy
Thymus serpyllum
Use to create a lawn effect. Forms a flat mass of tiny leaves with small, purple flowers in summer.

Lavender

Lavandula angustifolia
LAMIACEAE

Lavender is a lovely garden plant and is an integral part of most herb gardens. There are a number of different species, all forming rounded bushes of upright stems of grey-green leaves and spikes of lavender-coloured flowers. Unfortunately, it is recorded as being implicated in attacks of asthma and hay fever. The other aromatic herbs, such as sage, do not seem to be problematic.

ALTERNATIVES
Rosemary, *Rosmarinus officinalis* – Hardy to –10°C (14°F) – and **Hyssop**, *Hyssopus officinalis* – Hardy – are similar, but the first is taller and the second has greener leaves.

Rue

Ruta graveolens
RUTACEAE

This evergreen shrub with small, blue-green leaves and open, yellow flowers is among the worst plants for skin damage, and must be treated with extreme caution. Handling any part of the plant in hot, sunny weather can result in blistering of the skin that lasts several weeks and may reappear when the skin is exposed to sunlight, in which case permanent damage may follow. This reaction can occur in anyone, not just individuals who suffer from skin allergies. Never handle the plant without gloves and remove every part of it from a garden where there are children, as they might inadvertently touch it.

ALTERNATIVE
Hebe Hardy to –5°C (23°F)
Hebe albicans
This makes a rounded bush with evergreen grey-green leaves, and is a possibile substitute, although it has white rather than yellow flowers.

ADDITIONAL HERBS TO AVOID

Common name	Botanical name	Family name
Angelica	*Angelica archangelica*	APIACEAE
Arnica	*Arnica montana*	ASTERACEAE
Horseradish	*Armoracia rusticana*	BRASSICACEAE
Southernwood	*Artemisia abrotanum*	ASTERACEAE
Tarragon	*Artemisia dracunculus*	ASTERACEAE
Borage	*Borago officinalis*	BORAGINACEAE
Mustard	*Brassica nigra*	BRASSICACEAE
Marigold	*Calendula officinalis*	ASTERACEAE
Hop	*Humulus lupulus*	CANNABACEAE
Sorrel	*Rumex acetosa*	POLYGONACEAE
Cotton lavender	*Santolina chamaecyparissus*	ASTERACEAE

WEEDS

A weed may be defined as 'a plant in the wrong place', and in fact many weeds are perfectly attractive when in the wild or controlled within a specific area. In our gardens we try to eliminate them because they look untidy, take the place of more valued plants and can be a nuisance if they get out of control and become invasive. In the low-allergen garden it is even more important to control weeds, as the effort of removing them by hand can itself cause an attack of asthma in susceptible individuals.

Another consideration is that some of our common weeds are producers of masses of allergenic pollen, a major cause of asthma and hay fever attacks in summer. Among the worst known offenders are docks, mugworts, nettle and plantain. Other weeds that are commonly found in our gardens, such as buttercup, hawkbits and yarrow are also allergenic but not to the same extent as the culprits given individual entries below. The list includes some of the common weeds likely to be found in lawns, beds and borders.

Mugwort ✺

Artemisia vulgaris
ASTERACEAE

Mugwort has upright stems of divided, grey-green leaves terminating in spikes of small, yellow flowers from mid-summer to early autumn. It is fairly easy to control as a garden weed.

Pellitory ✺

Parietaria spp.
URTICACEAE

P. judaica is known as the 'asthma weed' in Australia, where it was introduced from southern Europe in 1900 and has since spread throughout the eastern part of the continent. Pellitories have tiny, wind-pollinated flowers producing allergenic pollen all summer.

Plantains ✺

Plantago spp.
PLANTAGINACEAE

The plantains have upright flower stalks of tiny, brown flowers that produce pollen from late spring to early autumn. Often found as a weed in grass areas and borders, they should be ruthlessly eliminated from the low-allergen garden. If there are only a few to remove, the most effective method is by hand.

Docks ✺

Rumex spp.
POLYGONACEAE

The docks are easily recognized by their large, shiny leaves and extraordinary flowers which appear in summer and ripen into winged fruits. Often found in fields and open spaces alongside stinging nettles, dock leaves are well known as an antidote to the sting when rubbed over the affected area.

Stinging nettle ✺ 🍃

Urtica dioica
URTICACEAE

The stinging nettle seems to occur everywhere. The coarse, toothed leaves are covered with hairs that break when touched, releasing into the skin chemicals that cause soreness and raised white patches that can remain painful for several hours. The tiny flowers are wind-pollinated and produce masses of allergenic pollen in summer.

How to Reduce Weeds and Weeding

• start with clean ground ie get someone to dig the ground thoroughly and/or spray with herbicide before planting

• select plants which will act as ground cover

• ensure all new plants are weed-free, particularly plants lifted from other gardens – if necessary wash off all soil round roots before planting

• feed plants after planting to ensure rapid growth

• plant all parts of beds – use annuals to cover ground in first year if necessary

• mulch with gravel after planting

• water new plants regularly to encourage fast growth

• if necessary use a hoe to remove any small weeds as soon as they appear – little and often is the best method

ADDITIONAL WEEDS TO AVOID

Common name	Botanical name	Family name
Yarrow ✺ 🍃	*Achillea millefolium*	ATERACEAE
Couch grass ✺ 🍃	*Agropyron repens*	POACEAE
Scarlet pimpernel 🍃	*Anagallis arvensis*	PRIMULACEAE
Burdock 🍃	*Arctium lappa*	ASTERACEAE
Cuckoo pint ⊗	*Arum maculatum*	ARACEAE
Daisy ✺ 🍃	*Bellis perennis*	ASTERACEAE
Shepherd's purse 🍃	*Capsella bursa-pastoris*	BRASSICACEAE
Greater celandine 🍃	*Chelidonium majus*	PAPAVERACEAE
Fat hen ✺ 🍃	*Chenopodium album*	CHENOPODIACEAE
Thistle ✺ ✹	*Cirsium* spp.	ASTERACEAE
Spurges 🍃	*Euphorbia* spp.	EUPHORBIACEAE
Giant hogweed 🍃	*Heracleum mantegazzianum*	APAICEAE
Meadow grass ✺ 🍃	*Poa annua*	POACEAE
Buttercup 🍃 ⊗	*Ranunculus repens*	RANUNCULACEAE
Ragwort ✺ 🍃	*Senecio jacobea*	ASTERACEAE
Nightshade ⊗	*Solanum* spp.	SOLANACEAE
Dandelion ✺ 🍃	*Taraxacum officinale*	ASTERACEAE

Plant hardiness

All the plants listed as being hardy in the text can withstand temperatures down to –15°C (5°F). Plants that will only withstand temperatures of either –5°C (23°F) or –10°C (14°F) are marked as such in the text.

The term half-hardy is used for annual plants that will not withstand temperatures below freezing 0°C (32°F); these plants are usually planted out after the danger of late spring frosts has passed.

Finally, the term tender is used for perennial plants that will not withstand temperatures below freezing 0°C (32°F).

Further reading

Healthy Fruit and Vegetables
Pauline Pears and Bob Sherman
(HDRA and Search Press)

Pests
Pauline Pears and Bob Sherman
(HDRA and Search Press)

Weeds
Jo Readman
(HDRA and Search Press)

Useful addresses

British Allergy Foundation
Deep Dene House
30 Belegrove Road
Welling
Kent DA16 3BY
*Information and educational
literature – membership scheme.
Enclose stamped self-addressed envelope.*

British Lung Foundation
6th Floor
New Garden House
78 Hatton Gardens
London EC1N 8JR
Enclose stamped self-addressed envelope.

**British Society for Allergy
and Clinical Immunology**
Secretariat
66 Weaston Park
Thames Ditton
Surrey KT7 0HL
*List of NHS Allergy Clinics available to
GPs and Health Professionals only.
Enclose stamped self-addressed envelope.*

**Capel Manor Horticultural and
Environmental Centre**
Bullsmoor Lane
Enfield
Middlesex EN1 4RQ
*Home of the National Gardening
Centre displaying a permanent
low-allergen garden.*

Heritage Seed Library
(members only)
Henry Doubleday Research Association
Ryton on Dunsmore
Coventry CV8 3LG
*Source of traditional varieties of
seed that are no longer in general
or commercial cultivation.*

Lucy Huntington
Cothelstone
Taunton
Somerset TA4 3DS
Garden design consultants.

National Asthma Campaign
Providence House
Providence Place
London N1 0NT
*The UK Medical Charity offering support for
people with asthma and hay fever, funding
research and campaigning.*
**Asthma Helpline 0345 010203
Monday to Friday, 9am to 7pm**

**Royal Botanic Gardens
Enquiry Unit**
Kew
Richmond
Surrey TW9 3AB
*Source of information on poisonous
plants. Joint originators of the
poisonous plants CD-ROM.*

SMP (Playgrounds) Limited
Pound Road
Chertsey
Surrey KT16 8EJ
Manufacturers of rubberized play surfaces.

**START – Skin Treatment
and Research Trust**
Chelsea and Westminster Hospital
Fulham Road
London SW10 9NH
*Information on skin allergies.
Enclose stamped self-addressed envelope.*

Stationery Office Limited
Publications Centre
51 Nine Elms Lane
London SW8 5DR
Publishers and distributors of Plato-UK,
the poisonous plants CD-ROM.

The Pollen Research Unit
Worcester College of Higher Education
Henwick Grove
Worcester WR2 6AJ
*National centre for collating pollen counts and
producing pollen forecasts. Enclose stamped
self-addressed envelope.*

Index

Page numbers in *italic* refer to picture captions; those in **bold** refer to main entries.

A

abutilon *35*
Acanthus mollis **92**
Acer 80
    A. griseum 118, **118**
    A. platanoides 118
Achillea millefolium **114**
Aconitum 24, **114**
Actinidia kolomikta 100, **100**
Actinomycetes 18
Aesculus 24, 82
Agapanthus campanulatus 67, 78, **92**
Agaricus campestris 18
Agrostemma githago 24
Ajuga reptans 96, **96**
Alcea rosea 26
Alchemilla mollis 31, 55, 67, 70, 74, 96, **96**, **114–15**
alder 29, 80, 81
Alisma plantago-aquatica 59
allergens 11–12, 14–15
allergic responses 11–12
allergy, meaning 11
Allium 34
    A. hollandicum 12
    A. schoenoprasum 102, **102**
alpines *77, 77,* 78
Alstroemeria 24, **115**
Alternaria 18–19
alum root *see Heuchera micrantha*
alveoli 14, *15*
Ambrosia 21
Amelanchier lamarckii 108, **108**
America 11
anaphylaxis 12
Anemone x *hybrida* **92**, **115**
angels trumpet *see Brugmansia*
annuals 78, 79, **90–1**, **113**
Antirrhinum majus 90, **90**
aphids 34–5
Apium graveolens 84, **120**
Aponogeton distachyos 59
apple *see Malus*
Aquilegia vulgaris 24, 27, **92**
Arbutus unedo **108**
archangel, yellow *see Lamium galeobdolon 'Florentinum'*
Arctostaphylos uva-ursi 76
Armeria maritima 26, 112, **114**

aromatic plants *see scented plants*
Artemisia absinthium **122**
    A. vulgaris **123**
artichoke, globe see *Cynara cardunculus*
arum lily *see Zantedeschia aethiopica*
arum, water *see Calla palustris*
Aruncus aethusifolius 69
ash 29, 80, 81
    golden *see Fraxinus excelsior*
Asparagus officinalis 84, **120**
aspergillosis 18
Aspergillus 15, 18
Aster 21
    A. x *frikartii* **114**
Asteraceae 21, *21,* 87
asthma 9, 10, 11, 12, **14–15**, 18, 19, 20, *30*
Astilbe 72, 73
    A. chinensis 72
    A. x *arendsii* **92**
Astrantia major 26, 71, 96, 97
atopy 11
Atropa 24
Aubrieta deltoidea 26
Aucuba japonica 104, **104**
Australia 10
Azalea 62
Azolla filiculoides 59

B

Balm of Gilead poplar *see Populus* x *candicans*
banks **76–7**
barrenwort *see Epimedium perralderianum*
basil *see Ocimum basilicum*
bay *see Laurus nobilis*
beans 84, **120**
    broad *see Vicia faba*
bear's breeches *see Acanthus mollis*
beauty bush *see Kolkwitzia amabilis*
bedding plants 62
beds and borders 62, **64–7, 70–1**
bee balm *see Melissa officinalis*
beech 54, 80, 81
    purple (copper) *see Fagus sylvatica*
bees *16, 26,* **26–7**, 30
beetroot **120**
Begonia x *carrierei 90,* **90**
bellflower *see Campanula*
Bergenia 78
    B. cordifolia **96**

Betula pendula 38, 81, **118**
biennials **90–1**, **113**
birch 29, 80
    silver *see Betula pendula*
blackberry **121**
black spot 34, 74
blue fescue grass *see Festuca glauca*
bog gardens **72–3**
bonfires **32–3**
box 55
breathing 14, *14, 15*
broad bean *see Vicia faba*
bronchi 11, 14, *15*
bronchioles 14, *14, 15*
Brugmansia 24
Brunnera macrophylla 69
buckeye see *Aesculus*
buckthorn *see Rhamnus*
    Buddleja davidii 81
bugle *see Ajuga reptans*
bulbs 22, 23, 25, 79
burning bush *see Dictamnus albus*
busy lizzie *see Impatiens walleriana*
Butomus umbellatus 59
butterfly bush *see Buddleja davidii*

C

Calceolaria integrifolia **113**
Calendula officinalis 21, 23, *113,* **113**
calico bush *see Kalmia*
Calla palustris 59
Caltha 24
Camellia japonica 78, 104, **104**
Campanula 74
    C. carpatica 77
    C. lactiflora 67, **114**
    C. latifolia **114**
    C. latiloba 93
    C. persicifolia **92**, **114**
Canna indica **113**
cardiovascular system 12
carnation *see Dianthus*
Carpinus betulus **118**
castor oil plant *see Ricinus communis*
catalpa 82
catarrh 15
Catharanthus roseus 24
catmint *see Nepeta racemosa*
cats 15, 51, 52
Ceanothus 10, 117
celery *see Apium graveolens*
Centranthus ruber 26
Cercis siliquastrum 108, **108**
Chaenomeles speciosa 104, **104**
Chamaecyparis 83

Chamaemelum nobile 122, **122**
chamomile *see Chamaemelum nobile*
chemicals, garden **34–5**, 123
cherry
    Japanese *see Prunus serrulata*
    ornamental *see Prunus avium*
    shrub *see Prunus tenella*
    winter-flowering *see Prunus* x *subhirtella*
cherry laurel *see Prunus laurocerasus*
cherry plum *see Prunus cerasifera*
chicory **120**
children's play areas 40, 44–5, *51,* **51–2**
Chinese woodbine *see Lonicera tragophylla*
chive *see Allium schoenoprasum*
Christmas rose *see Helleborus*
Chrysanthemum 21, 23
Cistus 71
    C. x *hybridus* **104**
    C. x *pulverulentus* 71
Cladosporium 18–19
Clematis 67, 100, 100, **116**
    C. armandii **116**
    C. cirrhosa 53
    C. flammula **116**
    C. montana 54, 77, **116**
    C. rehderiana **116**
climbers **53–4**, **100–1**, **116**
clothing, protective 25, **28–9**
Colchicum 24
colour schemes **66–7**
columbine *see Aquilegia vulgaris*
comfrey *see Symphytum grandiflorum*
companion planting 34, *34*
compost-making *33, 33,* 38, 85
conifers **83**
conjunctivitis 12
contact dermatitis 11, 12, **22–3**
container gardening 62, **78–9**
Convallaria majalis 24
Convolvulus cneorum 78
copper beech *see Fagus sylvatica*
coral bells *see Heuchera sanguinea*
Cordyline australis 78
corncockle *see Agrostemma githago*
Cornus 65
    C. alba 81

    C. controversa **118**
Cortaderia selloana 112, **112**
Corylus 17, 17, 28, 80
    C. avellana **121**
Cotinus coggygria **104–5**
Cotoneaster 54, **105**
    C. dammeri 76, **96–7**
    C. horizontalis 26
    C. microphyllus 76
    C. salicifolius **119**
    C. simonsii 55
coumarin 32
courgette 84
crab apple *see Malus tschonoskii*
cranesbill *see Geranium* spp.
Crataegus 26
    C. laevigata **108–9**, *109*
Crocosmia 67
crocus 79
Cupressocyparis leylandii 24, 32, 54
Cupressus 83
currant, flowering *see Ribes sanguineum*
cut flowers **35**
Cynara cardunculus **120**
Cytisus 26
    C. x *kewensis* 78

D

Daisies 21, 38
    Michaelmas *see Aster* x *frikartii*
    shasta *see Leucanthemum*
Daphne 24, 81
    D. laureola 24
    D. mezereum 24, **117**
Datura 24
Davidia involucrata 109, **109**, **119**
daylily *see Hemerocallis*
deadly nightshade *see Atropa*
Delphinium elatum 24, 27, *67,* 74, **93**, **114**
Dendranthema 24
dermatitis 32 *see also* contact dermatitis; eczema; photodermatitis
Deutzia scabra **105**
Dianthus 21, **114**
Dicentra spectabilis 69, **93**
Dictamnus albus 24, **114**
Dieffenbachia 24
digging **32**
Digitalis 20, 24
diseases, plant 18, 34–5, *34*
dock *see Rumex*
dogs 52
dogwood *see Cornus*
Dolichos lablab **120**
dust mite 14, 15, 35

E

ears 12
Echinops ritro 26
Echium 24
eczema 11, 12, **22**
elder see Sambucus nigra
elephant's ears see
        Bergenia cordifolia
elm 80, 81
endive **120**
Epimedium
        E. perralderianum 68,
            76, **97**
        E. rubrum 69
Erica
        E. carnea 76, 97, **97**
        E. cinerea 78
Eryngium
        E. amethystinum **93**
        E. giganteum **93**
        E. x tripartitum 71, **93**
Escallonia rubra **105**
Euonymus 24
Euphorbia 24, 25, **114**
evening primrose see
        Oenothera biennis
Exochorda x macrantha **105**
eyes 12, 15

F

Fagus sylvatica **118**
false helleborine see
        Veratrum
farmer's lung 18
feather grass see Stipa
        gigantea
fencing 52–3, *52, 53,* 68
fennel see Foeniculum
        vulgare
ferns *19,* **19–20**
fescue grass see Festuca
        glauca
Festuca glauca **112**
Ficus 85
        F. benjamina 35
        F. carica 24, **121**
fig see Ficus carica
Filipendula 73
        F. ulmaria 26
flax, New Zealand see
        Phormium tenax
foamflower see Tiarella
        cordifolia
Foeniculum vulgare 26, **102**
forget-me-not see Myosotis
        alpestris
formal and informal
        designs 40–1, 48, 53,
        62, *62,* 86
Forsythia
        F. suspensa **105**
        F. x intermedia **105**
fountains 46, 56, **57–8,** *59*
foxglove see Digitalis
Fraxinus excelsior **118**
fremontia see
        Fremontodendron
        californicum

Fremontodendron
        californicum 23, *23,*
            24, **117**
French bean see Phaseolus
        vulgaris
fruit 26, 34, 44, 63, **84–5,**
        121
Fuchsia 79, **113**
        F. magellanica *71,* 78,
            105
fungal spores 12, 14, 16,
        18, **18–19,** 28, 29,
        30–1, 32, 33, 34,
            34, 35, 50–1,
            63, 123
Futureworld Exhibition,
        Milton Keynes, UK 10

G

gardener's garters see
        Phalaris arundinaria
        picta
gastritis 12
Gaultheria 24
Genista lydia 76
Gentiana asclepiadea alba 73
Geranium spp. 26, *31,* 67,
        68, 69, 70, 71, 74,
            75, 76, **97, 115**
geranium see Pelargonium
Geum 67
        G. chiloense **93**
        G. rivale 73
Gleditsia triacanthos **118**
globe artichoke see Cynara
        cardunculus
Gloriosa superba 24
glory lily see Gloriosa
        superba
golden ash see Fraxinus
        excelsior
golden chain tree see
        Laburnum x watereri
golden rain tree see
        Koelreuteria paniculata
gooseberry *84,* 85, **121**
grasses 16, 17, 22, 28, 29,
        30–1, 38, **50–1, 112**
gravel 32, 33, 42, 49, *49*
green manure 33–4
grey foliage 66, 72, 81
ground cover *31,* 50, 63,
        64, 65, 68, 70, **70,**
        96–9, 114–15
gut 11
Gypsophila 65
        G. paniculata **112**

H

hairy plants 22, 66, 81
handkerchief tree see
        Davidia involucrata
hawthorn see Crataegus
        laevigata
hay fever 9, 10, 11, 12,
        15–16, 19, 20
hazel see Corylus
heather *64*

winter-flowering see
        Erica carnea
Hebe 55, 71, 78
        H. albicans **106, 122**
        H. rakaiensis 55
        H. salicifolia **106**
Hedera 24, 53, 79
        H. helix 22, 23, *116,* **116**
hedges 32, **32–3,** 38, 52,
        54–5, 68
Helianthemum 71, **114**
        H. nummularium 76, 77,
            97, **98**
Helleborus 24, **115**
Hemerocallis 21, 67, 73,
            93, 114
        H. fulva **112**
henbane see Hyoscyanus
herbs 20, 41, 44, 62,
        86–7, 102–3, 122
Heuchera 69
        H. cylindrica 69
        H. micrantha *71,* **115**
        H. sanguinea **98**
Hibiscus syriacus 78
hickory 80
histamine 10, *10*
hives see urticaria
holly see Ilex
honey locust see Gleditsia
        triacanthos
honeysuckle see Lonicera
horizontal surfaces **48–51**
hornbeam 54
        upright see Carpinus
        betulus
horse chestnut see Aesculus
Hosta 10, 34, 72, 73, 98, **98**
        H. sieboldiana elegans
            73, 78
Hottonia palustris 59
houseplants 35, **35**
Houttuynia cordata 59, *73*
HTA code of
        recommended retail
        practice 23, **24**
humidity 30
Hyacinthus 22, 24, 79
Hydrangea
        H. anomala petiolaris
            (climbing) 53, *100,*
            116
        H. macrophylla 78, *106,*
            106
Hydrocharis morsus-ranae 59
Hyoscyanus 24
Hypericum **117**
        H. calycinum 76
        H. perforatum 24
hyssop see Hyssopus
        officinalis
Hyssopus officinalis 26, 55,
        122

I

IgE antibodies 10, *10*
Ilex 25, *25,* 54
illicin 25
immune system 10

immune tolerance 10
Impatiens walleriana *90,* **90**
insect bites and stings
        26–7, 30
insect-pollinated plants *16,*
        17, 20–1, *20,* 26, 30
intestines 12
Ipomoea 24
Iris 24, 27
        I. pseudacorus 59
        I. reticulata 79
        I. sibirica 72, *73,* **93**
iris, water 58
ivy see Hedera
        poison see Rhus radicans

J

jacob's ladder see
        Polemonium
        caeruleum
Japanese anemone see
        Anemone x hybrida
Japanese cherry see Prunus
        serrulata
Japanese honeysuckle see
        Lonicera japonica
Japanese laurel see Aucuba
        japonica
Japanese quince see
        Chaenomeles speciosa
Japanese wisteria see
        Wisteria floribunda
jasmine see Jasminum
Jasminum 53
        J. nudiflorum **116**
        J. officinale *116,* **116**
Judas tree see Cercis
        siliquastrum
Juglans regia 80, **121**
Juniperus 83
        J. sabina 24

K

Kalmia 24
Kerria japonica 66
Kilmarnock willow see Salix
        caprea
Kniphofia 67, **114**
Koelreuteria paniculata *109,*
        119
Kolkwitzia amabilis *106,* **106**

L

lablab see Dolichos lablab
Laburnum 24, 27
        L. alpinum **118**
        L. x watereri **119**
lady's mantle see Alchemilla
        mollis
Lamium
        L. galeobdolon
            'Florentinum' 76, **98**
        L. maculatum 70, 76, **98**
Lantana 24
laurel
        cherry see Prunus
        laurocerasus

Japanese see Aucuba
        japonica
Laurus nobilis 78, *79,* **102**
laurustinus see Viburnum
        tinus
Lavandula angustifolia 20,
        122, **122**
lavender see Lavandula
        angustifolia
lawns and lawn-mowing
        22, **31–2,** 38, 48, **50–1**
lemon balm see Melissa
        officinalis
lettuce *84,* **120**
Leucanthemum **115**
        L. x superbum 21
Ligularia **114**
Ligustrum ovalifolium 24,
        32, 54, 80–1,
            117, **117**
lilac see Syringa
lilies 21
        African see Agapanthus
            campanulatus
        arum see Zantedeschia
            aethiopica
        daylily see Hemerocallis
        glory see Gloriosa
            superba
        plantain see Hosta
        torch see Kniphofia
        water see Nymphaea
Lilium regale 21
lily of the valley see
        Convallaria majalis
Limnanthes douglasii 26
Linaria purpurea 26
Liquidambar styraciflua **119**
Liriodendron tulipifera 82,
        109, 118
Lobelia 79
        L. erinus **90**
        L. tupa 24
loganberry **121**
Lonicera 20, 53
        L. japonica **116**
        L. periclymenum 20
        L. sempervirens 53
        L. tragophylla **100**
loosestrife, purple see
        Lythrum salicaria
love-in-a-mist see Nigella
        damascena
lungs 12, 14, *15*
lungwort see Pulmonaria
        saccharata
lupin see Lupinus
Lupinus 10, 24
Lycopersicon esculentum *84,*
        120, **120**
Lythrum salicaria 26, 72,
        115

M

Macleaya 65
Madagascar periwinkle see
        Catharanthus roseus
Magnolia x soulangeana **108**
Malus 26, 85

M. tschonoskii 82, *110*, **110**, **118**, **119**
maple *see Acer*
marigold *see Calendula officinalis*
 marsh *see Caltha*
marjoram *see Origanum vulgare*
marsh marigold *see Caltha*
mast cells 10, *10*
masterwort *see Astrantia major*
meadow saffron *see Colchicum*
medlar *see Mespilus germanica*
Melianthus major 78
Melissa officinalis 26, 78, 86, 87, 102, **102**
Mentha **102**
 M. spicata 102, **102**
 M. suaveolens **102**
 M. x gracilis **102**
 M. x piperita **102**
Mespilus germanica 110, **110**
mezereon *see Daphne mezereum*
Michaelmas daisy *see Aster x frikartii*
mildew 18, 34, 74
Mimulus luteus 59, **113**
mint *see Mentha*
mock orange *see Philadelphus*
monkey musk *see Mimulus luteus*
monkshood *see Aconitum*
monoculture 34
morning glory *see Ipomoea*
Morus nigra 80, **121**
mould spores *see* fungal spores
mountain ash *see Sorbus aucuparia*
mucosa 14
mucus 14
mugwort *see Artemisia vulgaris*
mulberry *see Morus nigra*
mulches 33–4, 42, 123
mushroom, *see Agaricus campestris*
mycelium 18
Myosotis 26
 M. alpestris **90–1**
 M. scorpioides 59

N

Narcissus 24, 79
nasal pasages 11, *15*
National Asthma Campaign low-allergen gardens 9–11, *9*, 42–7
National Garden Centre, Capel Manor 11, 65
neighbouring gardens 38, 83

Nepeta 79
 N. racemosa 70, 74, **98**
 N. x faassenii 26, *71*
Nerium oleander 24
nettle *see Urtica dioica*
nettle rash *see* urticaria
New Zealand 11
New Zealand flax *see Phormium tenax*
Nigella damascena **91**
night-scented stock 20
nightshade
 deadly *see Atropa*
 woody *see Solanum dulcamara*
Norway maple *see Acer platanoides*
nose 11, 12, 15, *15*
Nymphaea 58–9
Nymphoides peltata 59

O

oak 29, 80, 81
Ocimum basilicum 102–3
Oenothera 67
 O. biennis 20, *113*
oleander *see Nerium oleander*
olive 80
Omphalodes verna 69
oriental poppy *see Papaver orientale*
Origanum
 O. laevigatum 71
 O. vulgare 26, 67, 93, 103, **103**
Ornithogalum 24
otitis 12

P

Paeonia officinalis 65, 74, 94, **94**
pampas grass *see Cortaderia selloana*
pansy *see Viola*
Papaver orientale 26, 94, **94**
paperbark maple *see Acer griseum*
Parietaria **123**
Parrotia persica 111
parsley *see Petroselinum crispum*
parsnip 84
Parthenocissus quinquefolia 53, **100–1**
Passiflora caerulea **101**, *101*
passion flower *see Passiflora caerulea*
paulownia 82
paving 32, 42, 48, 49, **49–50**, *50*
pear *see Pyrus*
Pelargonium **113**
pellitory *see Parietaria*
Penicillium 15
 P. chrysogenum 18
Penstemon 63, **94**

peony *see Paeonia officinalis*
perennials 78, **92–5**, **114–15**
periwinkle *see Vinca minor* Madagascar *see Catharanthus roseus*
Perovskia atriplicifolia 26, *71*, **122**
pests 34–5
Petroselinum crispum 86, **103**
Petunia 79, *79*, **91**
Phalaris arundinaria picta **112**, *112*
pharynx 15
Phaseolus
 P. coccineus **120**
 P. vulgaris **120**
Philadelphus 81
Phlox 65
 P. drummondii **91**
 P. paniculata 94, **94**
Phormium 78, 79
 P. tenax **106**, **112**
photinia 79
photodermatitis 12, **22**, **23**, 30, 81, 84
Phytolacca 24
Pieris 80
Pileostegia viburnoides 53
pink *see Dianthus*
Pinus 83, *83*
plane 29
 London *see Platanus x hispanica*
Plantago 29, 38, 70, **123**
plantain *see Plantago*
plantain lily *see Hosta*
Platanus x hispanica 82
Platycodon mariesii 67
plum, purple-leaved (cherry) *see Prunus cerasifera*
poison ivy *see Rhus radicans*
poisonous plants *see* toxic plants and substances
pokeweed *see Phytolacca*
Polemonium
 P. caeruleum 26, **94**
 P. foliosissimum 67, 95
pollen 12, 14, *16*, **16–18**, *17*, 28, *28*, 29, 30, 35
pollen count 21, 63
Polygonatum 24
Polypodium vulgare 19
Pontederia cordata 59
poplar *see Populus*
poppy, oriental *see Papaver orientale*
Populus 28, 80, 81
 P. x candicans **119**, *119*
potato 84
Potentilla
 P. fruticosa 55
 P. recta 67
prickles **25**, 81
pride of India *see*

Koelreuteria paniculata
primrose *see Primula*
Primula 23, **115**
 P. obconica 23, 24
privet *see Ligustrum ovalifolium*
Probus, Cornwall, UK 11
Prunus 82, **118**
 P. avium 26, 80, *110*
 P. cerasifera **110**, **118**
 P. x cistena 55, *71*
 P. laurocerasus 24
 P. serrulata **110**, **118**
 P. x subhirtella **111**, **118**
 P. tenella **117**
Pulmonaria
 P. angustifolia 69
 P. saccharata 69, **98–9**
Pyracantha 54
 P. rogersiana 55
Pyrus 82, 85, **111**
 P. calleryana **111**
 P. salicifolia *111*, **111**

Q

Queen Anne's lace 72
quince, Japanese *see Chaenomeles speciosa*

R

radish 84
ragweed *see Ambrosia*
raised beds 85
rashes *see* skin allergies
raspberry **121**
red-hot poker *see Kniphofia*
red spider mite 27
respiration 14, *15*
Rhamnus 24
Rheum x hybridum 84, **121**
rhinitis 12, 17
Rhododendron 62
 R. yakushimanum 78
rhubarb *see Rheum x hybridum*
Rhus 81
 R. radicans 24, 81
 R. succedanea 24
 R. verniciflua 24
Ribes sanguineum 81
Ricinus communis 24, **113**
rock gardens **76–7**, *77*
rock rose *see Cistus x hybridus*; *Helianthemum nummularium*
Rodgersia 10, **94–5**
 R. pinnata 73
Rosa 20, 34, *34*, 40, 46, 53, *53*, 62, 63, 65, 67, 74, **74–5**, 76, 78
 climbing roses *101*, **101**
 R. 'Chanelle' 75
 R. 'Free as Air' 75
 R. glauca 55
 R. 'L'Oréal Trophy' 75
 R. moyesii 74

R. 'Peace' 75
R. 'Wandering Minstrel' 75
R. 'Warm Welcome' 75
rose *see Rosa*
Rosmarinus officinalis 26, 55, 86, **103**, **12a**
rosemary *see Rosmarinus officinalis*
rose rust 18
rowan 82
rubber, sensitivity to 35, 44, 51
Rubus tricolor 76
rue *see Ruta graveolens*
Rumex 29, 70, **123**
runner bean *see Phaseolus coccineus*
Russian sage *see Perovskia atriplicifolia*
rust disease 18
Ruta 24
 R. graveolens 23, 62, 81, **122**
rye grass 31

S

sage *see Salvia officinalis*
 Russian *see Perovskia atriplicifolia*
Sagittaria sagittifolia 59
Salix 80, 81
 S. caprea **119**
Salvia
 S. farinacea **91**
 S. officinalis 26, 78, 86, 93, **103**, **103**
 S. sylvestris 71
Sambucus nigra **117**
sap 22
Satureja montana 26
Scabiosa 67
 S. caucasica 71
scented plants 20, **20–1**, 38
Schefflera 24
Scilla 24
Scrophularia aquatica 73
 S. auriculata 26
sea holly *see Eryngium x tripartitum*
sea kale **120**
seasonal variations 12, 29–30
sedge *35*
shade **68–9**, *70*
shrubs 62, 79, **80–1**, **104–7**, **117**
Siberian iris *see Iris sibirica*
silver birch *see Betula pendula*
Sisyrinchium striatum **95**
skin allergies 10, 11–12, **22–3**, **25**
slugs 34
smoke bush *see Cotinus coggygria*
snapdragon *see Antirrhinum majus*
snowy mespilus *see Amelanchier lamarckii*

Solanum 53
S. dulcamara 24
solomon's seal see
Polygonatum
Sorbaria sorbifolia 117
Sorbus
S. aria 82, 111, 118
S. aucuparia 111
S. sargentiana 81
S. vilmorinii 111
sori 19, 19
spiked speedwell see
Veronica spicata
spinach 84, 120
Spiraea japonica 106–7,
107
spores see ferns; fungal
spores
spurge see Euphorbia
Stachys
S. byzantina 31
S. macrantha 76
star of Bethlehem see
Ornithogalum
Stephanandra incisa 76
steps 77, 77
stinging nettle see
Urtica dioica
Stipa gigantea 112
stomach 12
Stratiotes aloides 59
strawberry 85
strawberry tree see Arbutus
unedo
strimming 32

sunlight 22, 23, 30
sweet bay see Laurus
nobilis
sweet chestnut 80
sweetcorn see Zea mays
sweet gum see
Liquidambar
styraciflua
sweet William see Dianthus
sycamore 29, 81
Sydney Royal Botanic
Gardens, Australia 10
Symphoricarpos x
doorenbosii 55
Symphytum 69
S. grandiflorum 99, 99
S. uplandicum 69
Syringa 32, 81

T
Taxus 24, 38, 54
Tellima grandiflora 69
Teucrium chamaedrys 55
Thalictrum aquilegiifolium 12
thorn apple see Datura
thorns 25
thrift see Armeria maritima
Thuja 24, 83
thunder storms 30, 31
thyme see Thymus
Thymus 26, 86
T. serpyllum 76, 122
T. vulgaris 55, 102
Tiarella cordifolia 69, 99

time of day, effect 31
tomato see Lycopersicon
esculentum
torch lily see Kniphofia
toxic plants and substances
22, 24, 27, 53
trachea 15
Trapa natans 59
tree preservation orders
55, 81–2
trees 16, 29, 38, 52, 68,
80, 81–3, 108–11,
118–19
Tricyrtis formosana 73
Tulipa 22, 23, 24
tulip finger 23
tulip tree see Liriodendron
tulipifera

U
Ulex europaeus 26
upright hornbeam see
Carpinus betulus
Urtica dioica 29, 38, 70,
123
urticaria 11, 12, 22, 27

V
varnish tree see Rhus
verniciflua
vegetables 10, 34, 44,
84–5, 120
Veratrum 24

Verbascum chaixii 67
Veronica
shrubby see Hebe
albicans
V. austriaca 95
V. beccabunga 59
V. gentianoides 67
V. peduncularis 71
V. spicata 26, 71, 95
V. teucrium 75
vertical features 52–5
Viburnum
V. davidii 69
V. sargentii 69
V. tinus 107, 107, 117
Vinca faba 84, 120
Vinca 70
V. major 76
V. minor 76, 99, 99
vine see Vitis
Viola 79, 91
Virginia creeper see
Parthenocissus
quinquefolia
Vitis
V. coignetiae 101
V. vinifera 101, 101

W
Waldsteinia ternata 76, 115
wall germander see
Teucrium chamaedrys
walnut see Juglans regia
water 42, 46, 48, 56–9

waterfalls 56, 57–8, 76
water hawthorn see
Aponogeton distachyos
watering 123
water lily see Nymphaea
wax tree see Rhus
succedanea
weather conditions 30–1
weeds 16, 32, 33, 38, 65,
70, 123
Weigela florida 71, 78, 107,
117
wheezing 14
whitebeam see Sorbus aria
willow see Salix
windflower see Anemone x
hybrida
wind-pollinated plants 17,
17–18, 29, 30–1, 38
Wisteria floribunda 10, 24,
53, 116
woody nightshade see
Solanum dulcamara
wormwood see Artemisia
absinthium

Y, Z
yarrow see Achillea
millefolium
yew see Taxus
Yucca flaccida 78, 79
Zantedeschia aethiopica 59
Zea mays 84, 120
zinnia 21

Photographic acknowledgements

Eric Crichton 66 top, 68 bottom, 72 bottom, 97 top right, 102 bottom left, 104 centre, 104 top, 105 bottom, 106 bottom left, 108 bottom left, 109 top left, 110 bottom left, 116 bottom.

Garden Picture Library David Askham 74 top, 84 top; John Baker 53 top; Philippe Bonduel 23; Rex Butcher 110 bottom right; Brian Carter 94 top left, 112 bottom, 113 bottom; Dennis Davis 76; Robert Estall 32; Christopher Fairweather 97 top left; John Glover 25, 31, 33, 80 bottom (Savill Gardens, Windsor) 86 bottom, 90 bottom right, 98 bottom left, 109 top right, 111 bottom, 113 top, 114 top, 117 top; Neil Holmes 5, 94 bottom, 108 top; Lamontagne 52; Howard Rice 20, 68 top, 78, 114 bottom, 116 top; Gary Rogers 12, 13; Jerry Pavia 107 top left; JS Sira 79; Ron Sutherland 56, 96 left; Ron Sutherland (des: Lucy Huntington) 44; Brigitte Thomas 83; Juliette Wade 72 top, 97 bottom; Steven Wooster 34.

John Glover 1, 21, (Barnsley House) 27, (des: Lucy Huntington) 7, 46, 87, (des: Peter Tinsley) 77 bottom, (des: Julie Toll – RHS Garden, Wisley, Surrey) 57.

Reed International Books Ltd 35, 118 top, 120 bottom, 121 top, 122 top; Neil Holmes 122 bottom; Steven Wooster 85, 106 bottom right, 117 bottom; George Wright 88/89.

Jerry Harpur 3, 103 bottom, 110 bottom centre, 111 top, 119, (des: Sheila McQueen) 9, 60 /61, (des: Lucy Huntington) 42, (grower: Bob Flowerdew) 121 bottom.

Lucy Huntington 8, 51, 55.

Andrew Lawson Photography 4, 22, 38, 48, 53 bottom, 59, 63, 77 top, 90 bottom centre, 93 top left, 96 right, 98 right, 99 bottom left, 99 top, 112 top, 119, (des: Anthony Noel) 36/37.

Clive Nichols Photography 2, 54, 70, 80 top, 81, 94 top right, 99 bottom right, 102 top , 102 bottom right, 107 top right; (Hexham Herbs, Northumberland) 86 top, (Le Manoir aux Quat' Saisons, Oxon) 84 bottom, (Old Coach House, Turn End, Bucks) 49 top, (Saling Hall, Essex) 81 bottom, (des: Lucy Huntington) 11, 66 bottom, (des: Lucy Huntington – Mrs Dymock's Garden) 49 bottom.

Photos Horticultural 50, 64, 74 bottom, 82, 90 bottom left, 95, 100, 101, 103 top, 104 bottom, 105 top, 106 bottom centre, 108 bottom right, 115, 118 bottom, 120 top.

Science Photo Library; Dr Vic Bradbury 30; Dr Jeremy Burgess 17, 18, 19 bottom left, 26; Darwin Dale 19 bottom right; Claude Nuridsany 16; Alfred Pasieka 28.